VENTURE SMITH

"My freedom is a privilege which nothing else can equal."

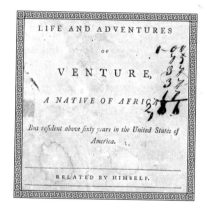

LIFE AND ADVENTURES

OF

VENTURE,

A NATIVE OF AFRICA

But resident above sixty years in the United States of
America.

RELATED BY HIMSELF.

Chandler B. Saint

with Robert Pierce Forbes

foreword David Richardson

Beecher House Center for the Study of Equal Rights
TORRINGTON, Connecticut

This book is related to *VENTURE SMITH - Making Freedom* published in 2015 by the *Documenting VENTURE SMITH Project* which was a revised and expanded edition of *Making Freedom-The Extraordinary Life of Venture Smith*, published by Wesleyan University Press in 2009. This new work reflects the continuing, intensive research by the *Documenting VENTURE SMITH Project*, and provides information not available in Venture Smith's *Narrative*, which was first published in 1798,

or by historians since then.

For more information or to order a copy, please contact: info@venturesmith.org

This paperback edition published in 2018 by Documenting VENTURE SMITH Project

&

Beecher House Center for the Study of Equal Rights

Torrington, CT 06790

Printed in U.S.A.

ISBN 978-0-692-05218-1 (paperback: alk, paper)

9 8 7 6 5 4 3 2 1

For

Rachel Freeman Saint

(1906-2007)

Peter "Pete" Seeger

(1919-2014)

George A. Krimsky

(1942-2017)

— *admirers of* VENTURE SMITH
and fighters for freedom and equality

On January 20, 2017 my colleague George A. Krimsky died.

George and I were born just a year apart and came of age in the 1950s during the Cold War and then the Civil Rights Movement. As expats, we learned our history and came to understand the country we loved by seeing it from afar.

We brought this world perspective to our work on VENTURE and the story of American Slavery. As a result we were able to see the Middle Passage in its totality – Africa, Europe, and the Western Hemisphere.

Over the last twenty odd years, we went from my being a story he wrote about in newspapers to our researching and writing together. George was my complete and true friend.

We both were committed to solving the problem my other late friend, Pete Seeger, tasked us with – *"this extraordinary problem which sooner or later the entire world has to face up to, how people of very different ethnic backgrounds can learn to live together on this earth; doesn't mean they have to live right on top of each other, but they have to treat each other decently"*.

This paperback will fulfill what we wanted from the start - to make VENTURE's story known in every household and school in America. George and I realized, there needed to be a readable but very accurate book available at a minimum cost, to students throughout the country. Hopefully, *"VENTURE SMITH"*, and the *Project's* companion traveling exhibit *"Making Freedom:* The Life of VENTURE SMITH ~ *In His Own Voice"* will provide this.

Chandler B. Saint

Contents

✦ ⋅◄⋅ ◄⋅ ‹◈◆◈›⋅►⋅► ✦

"One of the joys of history is to uncover and make accessible compelling stories that inform us about the past and illuminate the important issues of our times. Venture Smith is just such a story – one that we hope will inspire people to see the world around them in new ways."

–LONNIE G. BUNCH, Smithsonian Institution
National Museum of African American History & Culture, February 2014

✥◂◂◂◈❖◉▸▸▸✥

PREFACE

The *Documenting VENTURE SMITH Project* is now in its 13th year. It has turned into the largest interdisciplinary effort ever to document a survivor of the Middle Passage from birth in Africa, capture, enslavement, the Passage, slavery, and finally regained freedom in the Western Hemisphere. The *Project* is a collaborative effort of the *Beecher House Center for the Study of Equal Rights* in Connecticut, the *Wilberforce Institute for the study of Slavery and Emancipation* at the University of Hull in the UK, and the *University of Cape Coast* in Ghana. Its mission is not only to document a remarkable man's life and times, but to use his story of courage and perseverance as a tool to help abolish slavery in all its forms today.

For the public, its work will be widely seen in the travelling exhibit "*Making Freedom*: The Life of Venture Smith ~ *In His Own Voice*"; the CD reading of VENTURE's autobiography, *The Narrative of an African American 1798*; the reprint of the *Narrative*; and in this book. The exhibit lets the viewer follow VENTURE from his birth in Africa to his final resting place in East Haddam, Connecticut. It links his words with images and facts on 22 panels to tell his story.

This new book, VENTURE SMITH, answers many of the questions that have puzzled historians and descendants of the young African prince who was forced into slavery in 1739 and then taken to Colonial New England, where he labored for a quarter-century before purchasing his freedom and becoming a prominent citizen and businessman in Connecticut.

This book basically is an annotated edition of VENTURE SMITH's *A Narrative of the Life and Adventures of Venture*, published in 1798. The *Narrative* is the original autobiographical work by one of the great intellects of the early Republic. All I needed to do was add in between his words the details of his life that research by myself and the *Project* have uncovered.

Perhaps, most importantly, this book demonstrates my, and the *Project's*, firm conclusion, based on 17 years of research, that VENTURE SMITH's *Narrative*, an autobiography published in 1798, is the earliest known completely African American literary voice. When judged against the whole of early American literature – not just African American – it will soon be recognized as an American literary masterpiece, and we hope will become required reading in all schools.

As a sign of respect and appreciation, I have taken the style and format of the 1798 work and used it for this book. The typeface is the same VENTURE chose and the page size, type size, and spacing are similar. In his *Narrative*, VENTURE and the printer Charles Holt chose the unusual format of setting VENTURE and VENTURE SMITH in large/small caps throughout. As an act of respect for VENTURE, I have used this same format for his name in my book.

I chose to publish this book as a deluxe paperback edition rather than as a classic academic cloth edition. Some people will not take the book as seriously as they would a hardbound university press book. This format will allow us to sell the book to schools and educational programs at a substantially reduced price.

For students of history, the *Documenting VENTURE SMITH Project* shows how much can be learned about one individual if uncovering that history is lead by an interdisciplinary team and that evaluates the data using all the systems, criteria, and frames of reference of the different cultures of the subjects. Hopefully, this will lead to oral, and other forms of documentation being accepted on equal footings.

In many retellings of VENTURE's story, if a statement of fact is not documented and recorded in the town records, deed books, or diaries of the colonial leaders, it has been treated as hearsay or as if it did not occur. VENTURE prided himself for being a man of "truth and integrity". These were the highest standards of the society he came from in Africa. Much of his peoples' history had been carefully recorded and preserved in oral form and passed from generation to generation. Every bit of research by the *Project* has shown that VENTURE lived his life and wrote his memoir to these standards - he gave us the facts and left it up to us to interpret their meaning. Therefore, we have concluded that his 1798 *Narrative* is a true autobiography, his own personal work. Therefore it is the primary source document to be used in interpreting his life, who he was, what he did, and how his life experience shines a light on the bigger story of slavery, freedom, and how African Americans helped to build America.

We believe, most likely VENTURE's son wrote the *Preface*, and was right to compare VENTURE to Washington and Franklin and to argue that his father was their equal. It is our conclusion that VENTURE's *Narrative* is as important as Franklin's autobiography in recording the history of the Early Republic.

CHANDLER B. SAINT
Connecticut, January 2018

Foreword

✢ ⊰ ⊰ ⊰ ⊜ ◈ ⊜ ⊱ ⊱ ⊱ ✢

I first met Chandler Saint and Robert Forbes in January 2004 when I was visiting research fellow at Yale's *Gilder Lehrman Center for the Study of Slavery, Abolition, and Resistance.* They introduced me to the *Narrative* of VENTURE SMITH, an autobiography of an African stolen from his homeland as a youth, and who after more than a quarter of a century of enslavement, recovered his freedom and established a family dynasty in Connecticut. It was a narrative of which, as an historian of slavery, I was aware but had barely studied. The meeting launched a research co-operation that has endured to this day, as Chandler, Rob and myself, with others, have sought to bring knowledge and understanding of the life of VENTURE, his family, and descendants to the widest possible audience. As an increasingly multidisciplinary project, it anticipated research on other African-Americans such as Henry Louis Gates Jr's recent study of Oprah Winfrey.

The task of developing the *Documenting VENTURE SMITH Project* that arose from the initial meeting of Chandler, Rob, and me has not been evenly shared. As a British based academic and founder-director in 2004-2012 of the *Wilberforce Institute for the study of Slavery and Emancipation* at the University of Hull, I have never been more than a junior partner in driving forward the *Project.* Chandler has been throughout, its heartbeat and most fervent and consistent advocate in both private and public spheres; Rob its research advisor and critical interpreter. My primary task was to raise the *Project's* international profile and recognition. As a partnership, it has proved mutually satisfying and productive, building international networks, delivering conferences and exhibits in North America, Britain and Ghana, constantly engaging with VENTURE's descendants and with political and other leaders in their delivery, and producing a series of publications by a number of authors from different academic backgrounds. The *Project*'s engagement with the general public, a goal consistent with that of the *Wilberforce Institute*, has always been one of its primary objectives. VENTURE's appearance as one of the key figures in the *National Museum of African American History & Culture* in Washington DC's Smithsonian Institution is testament to the *Project*'s success in that regard.

We know that there remains more to discover about VENTURE SMITH's life, but even as things stand, his life story is surely now among the best researched of all African-Americans before Frederick Douglass. As the *Project* has developed, it has provided another model of sustained international co-operation in research typical of much recent academic scholarship on transatlantic slavery. But it adds to that research by reminding us that behind the well-documented transatlantic story of slavery, with its statistics, databases and other essential research resources, there were human stories of personal and collective tragedy and thwarted ambition and yet, as in VENTURE's case, stories, too, of hope, redemption, and recovery of dignity and freedom. As with stories of others who fought against and escaped slavery, VENTURE SMITH's life reminds us of humanity's capacity to contest and overcome the most brutal forms of oppression and adversity. It is a life whose meaning transcends time and place. It is one that deserves to be universally recognized. Embodying the latest research findings, this modestly priced book by Chandler Saint and Robert Forbes is another vital step towards that goal. I am delighted and privileged to be associated through this *Foreword* with it.

David Richardson
Hull, January 2018

A

NARRATIVE

OF THE

LIFE AND ADVENTURES

OF

VENTURE,

A NATIVE OF AFRICA:

But resident above sixty years in the United States of America.

RELATED BY HIMSELF.

New-London:
PRINTED BY C. HOLT, AT THE BEE-OFFICE,
1798.

"It's important his story be told and spread throughout all the United States, because it's such a positive African-American story."

– David P. Warmsley, 8th-generation descendant of Venture Smith

INTRODUCTION

If only Venture Smith had written more.

Perhaps one should not begin the tale of a remarkable man with regret. But because he was such a remarkable man, we want to know more. The core of what we know about him comes from a published autobiography, and a tombstone erected more than 200 years ago.

The rest has been painstakingly stitched together by recollection, research, and scholarship.

Did a school teacher, who folklore claimed was the recording scribe,[1] or the newspaper publisher Charles Holt, who printed it, or both of them, assume the role of editing his narrative in the interest of saving space? Did Venture himself avoid telling everything in order to spare his audience "the bulk?"

Posterity can at least be grateful for the professed efforts of those who helped Venture produce his *Narrative*, which leaves an accurate account of his life "in which nothing is added in substance to what he related himself," as the *Preface* to the published account stated in 1798.[2] It is not what may have been added, however, but what may have been left out that gives pause.

The main gift to the historical record is the compression of a full and unique life of 76 years into a narrative of fewer than 10,000 words, barely the length of a class thesis today. One cannot help but compare this with the extensive autobiography written by Smith's contemporary, the highly literate former slave Gustavus Vassa (Olaudah Equiano), which is much richer in detail, observation, and context.[3]

What seems apparent from reading Venture's life narrative, however, is that the paucity of information can be traced in part to the man's character as much as to the mechanics of storytelling. This was

Gustavus Vassa (Olaudah Equiano)
frontispiece of his narrative

a man of action, not of words. Unlike Vassa, who garbed himself in the trappings of British society and was not above gilding his credentials, VENTURE most valued simplicity, privacy, frugality, and prudence. He was the kind of man who took pride in saying *"Expensive gatherings of my mates I commonly shunned, and all kinds of luxuries I was perfectly a stranger to."*

Although frustrating to historians and archaeologists, who hunger for the small details that fill in the puzzle of the past, such people do tend to tell the truth. Historians could hardly ask for more.

Another anomaly about VENTURE SMITH's *Narrative* is that nearly one-third of the story is given to the first decade of his life in Africa, before he evolved into the man who became a legend. We see more detail about the African environment of his boyhood than about the land where he made his mark.

Over the years of telling his story of Africa, VENTURE would have added details in response to the questions of his listeners, where as the recounting of events in America would have been dictated and recorded without questions or the resulting contextualization. The family members writing down VENTURE's words would have been around when most of the events in New England occurred, and knew them in detail.

There was a growing interest in things African among the English-reading public at the end of the 18th century, largely as a result of widely published slave's narratives.[4] Charles Holt, the *Narrative's* printer, a savvy and ambitious 26-year-old printer, newspaper publisher, and book seller from New London, Connecticut, believed there was a market for VENTURE's *Narrative*. His advertisement promoting the *Narrative* describes VENTURE: "On Afric's *savage plains* a PRINCE in this *free land* a SLAVE." VENTURE was likely charged a fixed price for the printing, including the ads. They ran in *The Bee* of New London for six weeks starting on December 28, 1798. Next VENTURE ran a simpler ad for almost 4 months in the *Journal of the Times,* a new newspaper in Stonington, Connecticut. It first ran in issue #20 on February 20, 1799, and continued for a total of eleven times.[5]

Just published, and for sale at this office,
PRICE 1*s*.
A NARRATIVE
OF THE
LIFE AND ADVENTURES
OF
VENTURE,
A native of Africa, but above sixty years an inhabitant of the United States of America.

Related by himself, and attested by respectable witnesses.

[Venture is a negro remarkable for size, strength, industry, fidelity, and frugality, and well known in the state of Rhode Island, on Long Island, and in Stonington, East Haddam, and several other parts of this state.
　　Descended from a royal race,
　　Benevolent and brave;
　　On Afric's *savage plains* a PRINCE,
　　In this *free land* a SLAVE.]

FOR SALE AT THIS OFFICE,
A Narrative of the Life and Adventures of
VENTURE,
a native of Africa :—but resident above sixty years in the United States of America.

Journal of the Times of Stonington

Promotional ad for VENTURE's 1798
Narrative in *The Bee* of New London

Speculation about what may have been stressed or omitted in the first-person story invariably raises the specter of a "black message in a white envelope," as a scholar of slavery John Sekora, described the genre of as-told-to narratives. An American slave, even a freed one, had limited access to printing facilities in those days and generally needed white patrons to fund the publication of his writings. The Countess of Huntingdon in England, paid for the printing of Albert Gronniosaw's narrative (illust. p. 7) and Phillis Wheatley's poems. In addition, a published narrative was often "certified" for its veracity by established members of the white community, who knew the author and the facts. In VENTURE's case, five prominent residents of Stonington, Connecticut, including two relatives of his former owners, signed a certificate at the end of the *Narrative*, endorsing its substance.[6]

The recorder and his influence over VENTURE's story constitute another facet of this puzzle.

In the end, we are persuaded for many reasons that the account is rendered by the subject himself, and, although there are some gaps in his life story, it is a treasured document. Historian Robert P. Forbes, speaking at the American Historical Association in 2011, "Rather than a 'black message in a white envelope,' we have been looking at a purloined letter: an accomplished literary masterwork has been before our eyes, unrecognized, all along."[7]

VENTURE's *Narrative* opens a rare personal window on the faceless institution of slavery and offers compelling testimony to its lesser-known practice in the northern states. Add to this the extraordinary nature of the man himself, who was present at the very birth of the American nation as a self-emancipated free man, and it is no wonder that VENTURE SMITH's life has fostered an extensive body of scholarship and inquiry.

The most focused and thorough investigation to date is the *Documenting VENTURE SMITH Project*, which mobilized in 2005 a remarkable coalition of historians, archivists, anthropologists, geneticists, poets, philosophers, and civil rights activists to pursue and share research under the leadership of the Connecticut based *Beecher House Center for the Study of Equal Rights*, the *Wilberforce Institute for the study of Slavery and Emancipation*, in Hull, UK, and now the *University of Cape Coast* in Ghana. This collaboration coincided with the 200th anniversary of VENTURE's death.

The continuing research has been bolstered by several factors. To begin with, a great deal of scholarship has been conducted about the institution and chronology of the Atlantic slave trade, which spanned more than three centuries. Because slaves were treated as commodities and the British were meticulous in keeping track of their business transactions, the record of slavery to their American colonies was voluminous, and, at least in dry financial terms, quite precise. Thanks to the historical preservation communities in Britain, the United States, and the West Indies, these records have been retained and made available for study.

Also adding immeasurably to the documentation project is a clear genealogical line from VENTURE to the present day. His descendants not only live, but care. Some of them, who reside in his adopted State of Connecticut, have given their approval, time, memories, and correspondence to this effort.

Annual wreath-laying by VENTURE SMITH descendants at East Haddam gravesite september, 2006

Advances in DNA technology have also been utilized to determine VENTURE's origins and the environment in which northern slavery existed in the 18th century.

Because of such allies, much can be added to one man's brief narrative.

Before reviewing VENTURE's life journey, much of which we owe to his own voice, we should note that there are details of time and place in his *Narrative* that are open to interpretation.

VENTURE's account is not questioned, at least by legitimate scholars, for any lack of truthfulness. No one could read his story without being persuaded that he was a man lacking in both guile and self-aggrandizement. But the written account varies in precision in several respects for what we believe are understandable reasons. First, VENTURE related his life story more than half a century after leaving Africa. Not only can memory be skewed by time, but the aged narrator revealed himself to be almost blind and wracked with pain during the telling.

Second, neither VENTURE nor his family had access to the shipping records, custom house data, or other references that we do today.

Moreover, there is the transcription problem. When the narrator said VENTURE was born in *"Dukandarra,"* a place found on no contemporary map, can one be sure that it was written down correctly, or the typesetter did not change it? There is no proof that VENTURE could write, he never says whether he could or could not write, and even if he could, by 1798 his vision was gone – *"My eye-sight has gradually failed, till I am almost blind"*, so he could hardly have helped with spelling. Between a member of his family writing a name and then a typesetter possibly "correcting" it, errors crept in. On the cover of the family copy of the *Narrative*, there are hand-written corrections to *"Dukandarra"* and several other names[8] (see cover illustration pages 151 & B-i). In general in the 18th century, spelling of names was notoriously inconsistent.

But the biggest conundrum has to do with dates. VENTURE said he *"had then completed my eighth year"* when first arriving in America. Recent investigation, based on ships' logs, custom house records, verifiable names, and details, supplied by VENTURE himself, strongly suggests he was 10 or 11 at the time. It is important to keep in mind that the culture from which he came may have operated with different measurements of time. Furthermore, during the first 50 years of his time in America, in his day to day life, he had no need to know the exact date of his birth. Not until around 1790 when he was designing his tombstone, and in 1798 when writing his memoir did he need a birth date. But for the purposes of this modern-day interpretation, knowing his age is vital to matching the progression of his life against known historical events and dates. But, like the various currencies of the time, the confusion is understandable. Interestingly, the reconciliation of the dates in Venture's *Narrative* and those in the historical record ironed itself out with time.[9]

Last, the *Narrative* said Venture was born with the name "*Broteer Furro*." Like everything else about this man, his name has been put under a scholar's microscope, and interpretations will be discussed for years to come.

For the most part, we have spared the general reader the details of these sometimes conflicting ruminations in order to tell, without undue interruption, the story of an extraordinary man who lived in extraordinary times.

In the fall of 1798 Venture and his family were raising money. They could expect to make money with the story of Venture's life.[10] In 1792 the New York publisher of Equiano's autobiography had shipped nearly 100 copies to the greater Middletown, Connecticut area. In the summer of 1798 *The Bee* had printed and sold over 100 copies of Benjamin Franklin's autobiography, a book that would have inspired Venture – Franklin being another self-made man, and an extremely important Freemason (in the *Preface* Venture is compared to Franklin).

In 1793, the first American edition of *Letters from an American Farmer*, by Hector Saint John de Crèvecoeur, was published in Philadelphia. De Crèvecoeur helped found botanical gardens in New Haven and in 1788 he received the key to the city. Like Franklin's autobiography, de Crèvecoeur's book, by another literate farmer, would likely have inspired Venture.

In 1765, the same year Venture regained his freedom and became a British subject, de Crèvecoeur, a French immigrant, also became a subject of the Crown and was naturalized in New York as J. Hector St. John. His definition of America as the place where "individuals of all nations are melted into a new race of men", is certainly a fitting

Introduction

description of VENTURE, his family, and others he helped free.

The 1772 autobiography by Albert Gronniosaw, a freed slave living in England, was published in more than ten editions in England, Ireland, Wales (translated into Welsh), and Scotland before 1798. James Albert Ukawsaw Gronniosaw came from a country in West Africa near to VENTURE's, made a similar march to the Gold Coast, left Africa from almost the same location, and was the first black author to be published in Britain. Since it was re-printed in Newport RI in 1774[11], it seems likely that VENTURE saw Gronniosaw's pamphlet or acquired a copy, since at that time he was active in the wood trade to Newport.

James Albert Ukawsaw Gronniosaw
Cover of 1774 reprint by
S. Southwick, Newport, RI

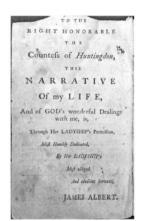

Gronniosaw, inside cover dedication to
his patron, Countess of Huntingdon

This does not imply that VENTURE was inspired by either Equiano or Gronniosaw, one too highly polished and the other a failure with money. It was their narratives' successes, reflected by multiple printings in both England and the Colonies, that would have inspired him.

In the summer and fall of 1798 VENTURE was in poor health and, like many prominent and successful men facing death, he would have wanted to secure his legacy. VENTURE knew where he was born, what he had done, and what he had achieved. All he needed to do was, like Franklin, write down his history for posterity. He appears to have designed his tombstone and arranged for a burial befitting his status as a Connecticut gentleman.[12]

Scholars generally agree that making the pamphlet was fairly simple. Since VENTURE was nearly blind he would have needed logistical help from his family, likely led by his son Solomon. The part about Africa and the Middle Passage already existed as an oral story VENTURE had been reciting for years; it just needed to be written down. Then VENTURE only had to record the accounts of his life after arriving in America. The recorder – or recorders – logically, would have come from his own household. A frugal man, VENTURE would never have paid a professional scribe to do something he could get done for free at home. Solomon probably served as the "editor" with his father, first taking the story of Africa and then selecting enough other stories to fill a 32-page booklet.[13]

What was left out in this process, we can only imagine and surmise. We would have very much liked, for example, to know what VENTURE thought of the War of Independence, through which he lived and toiled but failed to mention in his *Narrative*.

In 18th century Connecticut, especially in business and the military, it was hard to get ahead if you were not a Freemason. VENTURE never tells us what his relationship with the Masons was – did he belong?

Were these the people he looked to for advice, and to form business partnerships? If he did not formally join a lodge, he certainly aligned himself with Freemasons in choosing where to live and with whom to do business.

We believe that to finish the *Narrative*, Solomon wrote the *Preface*, an act of respecting and honoring his father.[14] He likely then had Edward Smith (VENTURE's last owner's son) organize the *Certificate*.[15]

The text would then be taken to *The Bee* in New London for contract printing. Holt printed the *Narrative* using the same type, style, and layout he used a month earlier for his own pamphlet on the *Yellow Fever*. Except he set VENTURE and VENTURE SMITH in large small caps though out the document. This is one of less than twenty known 17th and 18th century American published autobiographical works.[16]

The *Narrative* is the earliest known entirely African American literary voice, a treasured document: written, recorded, edited, and printing paid for by African Americans in the 18th century.[17]

Charles Holt started *The Bee* in New London in 1787. He published a weekly paper, printed books for sale, and printed stationery and other works for the citizens of the greater New London area. Most newspapers lost money, especially one that had a Republican tone in a predominantly Federalist area, so he was struggling to survive by promoting book sales and other work. VENTURE, the consummate business man, would have been able to negotiate a good deal for the printing work and the advertising. When the SMITH family brought

Charles Holt's advertisement for his printing business

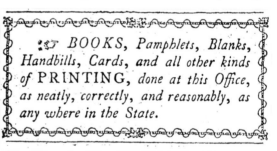

☞ *BOOKS, Pamphlets, Blanks, Handbills, Cards, and all other kinds of* PRINTING, *done at this Office, as neatly, correctly, and reasonably, as any where in the State.*

him the manuscript of the *Narrative*, it was a finished autobiography. One can say Holt edited it, in that he would have advised VENTURE on print size, style, and format, but not editing of the actual text. Neither Holt's literary style nor his political agenda appear in VENTURE's *Narrative*. His largest contribution might have been the suggestion that VENTURE's name be set in large/small caps.

Introductory remarks.

THE year 1798 seemed to have been marked by Providence as pregnant with uncommon fatality to the people of the United States. Philadelphia, New-York, Boston, Portsmouth, and several places of inferior note, were doomed to see their streets depopu-

Formatting and typeface are the same as in VENTURE's *Narrative*, including an early version of the decorative device

Cover for Holt's *Yellow Fever*, printed in the summer before and which was likely shown to VENTURE as a model

This clearly made VENTURE the principal character in the story, and treated him with great respect.

"SEVERAL editions of the *Life of Venture* have been published successively by his family, and by them circulated throughout the county,"

H. M. Selden, Haddam, Conn., 1896

INTRODUCTION

French map of West Africa in use during the time VENTURE took the Middle Passage[1]

❖·❄·❄·❀❖❀·❀·❀·❖

THE EARLY YEARS

VENTURE SMITH's *Narrative* opens with his birth, which he estimated was "about the year 1729,"[2] the first son of a wealthy prince in
West Africa.

Although he did not mention his specific ethnicity, it is known he
came from a cattle-herding people from the interior of West Africa.

*"I descended from a very large, tall and stout race of beings, much
larger than the generality of people in other parts of the globe,"* VENTURE
said, a description that fit his own adult dimensions.

He said the place of his birth was *"Dukandarra, in Guinea."* At the
time, Guinea was a geographic term that served to include a broad
area of West Africa. Guinea in the early 18th century was almost four
times the size of America's 13 colonies and had not yet been divided
into the dozen or so European colonies that would eventually emerge
as independent nations in the 20th century.

Three modern-day countries have since adopted the name –
Guinea, Guinea-Bissau, and Equatorial Guinea – but together they
constitute only about ten percent of the former territory.

After considerable investigation into the whereabouts of a place
called *"Dukandarra,"* the author discovered and purchased a French
map, based on Guillaume Delisle's 1772 edition, which was printed in
Paris by his son-in-law Philippe Buache in 1742, that listed a region
called royaume d'Ouangara. Further research supported the conclusion that this was probably where young Broteer Furro was born.
French maps were the most accurate for the interior of West Africa
at the time, and the designated region conforms to VENTURE's descrip-

tions in the *Narrative*.[3]

Guillaume Delisle was the first map maker to place the continent of Africa on the right meridian. His maps were the first to accurately show the Great Lakes and Florida; as a result they were used in British Colonial North America. This accuracy was the result of his scientific skills combined with his working extensively with the explorers of these areas.

This area is located today near Lake Chad where the Far North

ROYAUME D'OUANGARA
—
KINGDOM OF OUANGARA
"from where one extracts gold of the Sene and slaves"

Region of Cameroon borders Nigeria, Niger, and Chad, and was in the 18th century on one of the major Sub-Saharan trade routes across West Africa and up to Timbuktu and the Mediterranean.

VENTURE came from this hinterland area rich in wildlife, gold, vegetation, and with plentiful savanna grasslands for raising cattle

Cattle herder in the savannah of Far North Region of Cameroon

and sheep, both of which his father owned in vast numbers.

The earliest event *"worthy of notice"* in the young man's life was a disagreement between his mother and father, Saungm Furro, over the father taking a third wife without her consent, which was against custom. His mother was so upset, she took her three children and left. As VENTURE recalled:

She took not the least sustenance along with her, to support either herself or children. I was able to travel along by her side; the other two of her offspring she carried one on her back, and the other being a sucking child, in her arms. When we became hungry, my mother used to set us down on the ground, and gather some of the fruits which grew spontaneously in that climate. These served us for food on the way. At night we all lay down together in the most secure place we could find, and reposed ourselves until morning. Though there were many noxious animals there; yet so kind was our Almighty protector, that none of them were ever permitted to hurt or molest us.

They traveled eastward for a week, taking five days to cross a *"great desert,"* (probably the desert of Seth) until they reached an area of fertile plains. There, his mother left him in the care of a rich farmer and set out *"for her own country,"* which was not defined, presumably with her two youngest children. It was common practice for a noble son to be apprenticed with a trusted elder to prepare him for future leadership. This is likely what the youth's mother had in mind when she left him in the man's care.

The youth was put to work tending sheep. Unbeknownst to him, this would prove to be valuable training later in his life. Every day, he would, *"with the assistance of a boy,"* herd a flock of about 40 sheep to pasture two or three miles away and return at night.

VENTURE remembered a searing event during this early period of his life:

One incident which befel me when I was driving my flock from pas-

ture, was so dreadful to me in that age, and is to this time so fresh in my memory, that I cannot help noticing it in this place. Two large dogs sallied out of a certain house and set upon me. One of them took me by the arm, and the other by the thigh, and before their master could come and relieve me, they lacerated my flesh to such a degree, that the scars are very visible to the present day.

The guardian was sent for and carried the youth back to his place, where Broteer recuperated. The young apprentice resumed his chores until his father sent a man on a horse for him, and he returned home. VENTURE guessed that he had spent about a year away.

Back in his parents' home, he discovered that his mother had already come back and had reconciled with her husband. *"On my return, I was received both by my father and mother with great joy and affection, and was once more restored to my paternal dwelling in peace and happiness."*

By returning and making up with her husband, VENTURE's mother would have ben protecting VENTURE's future, especially his right to succeed his father as ruler. To assure this, she needed to retain her position as the "number one wife".

This was an important time for VENTURE, as the heir apparent he would have been receiving education and training from a very early age and now after finishing his year of apprenticeship, he was ready for the rites of passage to adulthood. VENTURE's father sent a man to collect the youth, settle the charges for his apprenticeship, and bring him home for the ceremony. This must have occurred shortly after VENTURE returned home, since in just over six weeks the country was invaded. That the ritual happened is confirmed by the scarification on his face.[4]

It would be a long time before that youth had reason to smile again.

VENTURE variously described his father as both a prince and a king. While his lineage may well have been long and distinguished, Saungm Furro was probably more akin to a village chieftain presiding over a generous amount of territory where his herding people could roam. His wealth was in cattle, sheep, horses, and it was common for a man in his position to own slaves. Wealthy men also tended to amass gold, various currencies used at the time, and cowry shells, a popular form of money imported by Arab traders from Indian Ocean beaches.

Chief Furro was clearly not prepared for what was to come.

Much of West Africa in the first half of the 1700s was contested territory. The colonial powers of Europe were already active on the coast, building forts and castles to trade in rum, tobacco, onions, guns, and other commodities for gold, indigo, ivory, and slaves, while the interior was being fought over by warring African nations seeking to expand their empires.

Shortly after young Broteer returned home, his father received word that a large army "*from a nation not far distant, furnished with musical instruments, and all kinds of arms then in use*" had invaded that same area from where the youth had come, less than 150 miles away.

The peaceful agrarian people under siege sought sanctuary in Chief Furro's dominion. Being "*a kind and merciful prince*," he readily agreed. But almost before his messenger could relay the acceptance, the people had already fled into his territory. His father gave them "*every privilege and all the protection his government could afford.*" But when they heard the enemy army was headed in their direction, the refugees fled south.

Then, VENTURE recalled:

> *Two days after their retreat, the report turned out to be but too true. A detachment from the enemy came to my father and informed him, that the whole army was encamped not far out of his dominions, and would invade the territory and deprive his people of their liberties and rights, if he did not comply with the following terms. These were to pay them a large sum of money, three hundred fat cattle, and a*

great number of goats, sheep, asses, &c.

My father told the messenger he would comply rather than that his subjects should be deprived of their rights and privileges, which he was not then in circumstances to defend from so sudden an invasion. Upon turning out those articles, the enemy pledged their faith and honor that they would not attack him. On these he relied and therefore thought it unnecessary to be on his guard against the enemy. But their pledges of faith and honor proved no better than those of other unprincipled hostile nations.

The chief had gotten word from a reliable informant that the enemy army, while expressing satisfaction with the tribute he had paid, was in fact secretly planning to attack. He was advised to flee.

Around daybreak, the chief spirited his family out of their village and headed for a shrub plain *"some distance off."* While they rested there, smoke from a cooking fire gave away their position to an enemy scouting party. Chief Furro fired arrows at them.

This was what I first saw, and it alarmed both me and the women, who being unable to make any resistance, immediately betook our- selves to the tall thick reeds not far off, and left the old king to fight alone. For some time I beheld him from the reeds defending himself with great courage and firmness, till at last he was obliged to surren- der himself into their hands.

The warriors found the family hiding. They hit Broteer on the head with a gun and put a rope around his neck. He and the women were led to the nearby army camp where his father was being held *"pinioned and haltered."* It is not known what happened to Broteer's younger brothers, Cundazo and Soozaduka.

When telling this story some 60 years later, VENTURE said the events that followed remained vivid in his mind throughout his life, *"and I have often been overcome while thinking on it"*:

The women and myself being pretty submissive, had tolerable treatment from the enemy, while my father was closely interrogated respecting his money which they knew he must have. But as he gave them no account of it, he was instantly cut and pounded on his body with great inhumanity, that he might be induced by the torture he suffered to make the discovery. All this availed not in the least to make him give up his money, but he despised all the tortures which they inflicted, until the continued exercise and increase of torment, obliged him to sink and expire. He thus died without informing his enemies of the place where his money lay. I saw him while he was thus tortured to death.

In retrospect, one might wonder why the chief would surrender his life so painfully to save his wealth. Perhaps he knew that he would not be spared, even if he revealed the hiding place. But, more importantly, his honor and even his very identity as a leader were at stake in keeping his fortune from the hands of the enemy.

The effect of his father's resistance and death, and his being witness to both, cannot be overestimated when examining VENTURE SMITH's later life and the shaping of his character.

The youth and women were taken prisoner by an army he estimated to be about 6,000 strong. *"Their leader was called Baukurre"* (probably King Boukar, a convert to Islam, who was known to be raiding in the area at that time). Claiming he and his men where on a religious crusade, in fact Baukurre was a terrorist who killed off the men and took the women and children to sell as slaves to finance his army. Sadly, 275 years later in this very same spot, Boco Haram today is doing exactly the same thing – wiping out entire villages, killing the men, and trafficking the women and children into the sex trade to finance their army in the name of God.

This was what I first saw, and it alarmed both me and the women, "After destroying the old prince, they decamped and immediately marched toward the sea, lying to the west, taking the with them myself and the women prisoners."

They marched west on a sub-Sahara trade route, laying waste to the countryside and capturing everyone and everything they could along the way.

An 18ᵗʰ-century French explorer, the Chevalier des Marchais, wrote that some armies in the West African interior announced their attacks "with overpowering noise, including shouting, drumming, the beating of gongs, and gunfire,"[5] a description similar to VENTURE's account. Like the drums and bagpipes used by colonial armies, such loud announcements served to inspire one's fighters and intimidate an enemy.

During the march, covering a distance the young Broteer estimated to be about 400 miles to Malagasco, the first village they raided, he was forced to serve his captors and act as bearer. *"I was obliged to carry on my head a large flat stone used for grinding our corn, weighing as I should suppose, as much as 25 pounds; besides victuals, mat and cooking utensils."*

VENTURE described himself as *"pretty large and stout of my age."* Given the level of detail he observed on the march, the weight of his load, and records of later events, VENTURE was probably at the time at

Late 18th-century illustration of African slavers with captives

least ten or eleven.[6] Historians estimate he was captured in early 1739.

After more victorious skirmishes where the army collected more captives, they finally reached the sea near the port of "Annamaboe"

Slave fort still standing today on the Anomabo Coast

in the middle of the Gold Coast, the preferred trading and supply point for New England slave ships in what is present-day Ghana. Of all the slaves carried on North American vessels between 1730 and 1759, almost two thirds were obtained on the Gold Coast, with more than half from Cape Coast or Annamaboe.[8]

Here, the inhabitants took advantage of the arriving army's depleted strength and provisions and counterattacked, seizing its prisoners. It

The Early Years

is not mentioned who the youth's new captors were, but they were not inclined to let a valuable commodity go free.

"*I was then taken a second time*," VENTURE said, and thrown into the castle where he was "*kept for market*." The *Narrative* does not name the castle, but the Annamaboe district was infamous for its string of coastal fortresses that were used as human vaults, holding slaves for transport to Europe and the colonies. Broteer was probably held in one of the remaining parts of Fort Annamaboe.[9]

Phillip Atta-Yawson (curator) in one of the women's and children's dungeons of Fort Annamaboe 16 September 2014 with VENTURE'S descendants

"For 100 years (1707-1807), Annamaboe served as the epic center on the Gold Coast of West Africa for the British Atlantic slave trade. It was the point **where every day from Dawn to Dusk – every hour, for 100 years, an African was stripped of his or her freedom to become a commodity** and then shipped by the Middle Passage to become the labor force of the West Indies and Colonial North America." [10]

The town of Anomabo also, was a major source of foodstuffs, notably corn, as well as water for visiting slave ships. At Annamaboe, it is estimated that nearly 450,000 left Africa in this hundred year period to a life of slavery in the Americas. It was one of the six largest slave ports in Africa during the age of the Atlantic slave trade, and thus a site of a major crime against humanity.

Given the distance and terrain covered from the point of capture to the coast, the forced march took approximately two to three

months. Albert Gronniosaw, who had taken a similar route ten years earlier, estimated the total march at over 1,000 miles. Broteer could have possibly spent another month or two locked up in the portside castle. The sound of unseen waves breaking on the rocks outside the castle must have seemed strange, if not frightening, to the youth.

Laser-mapped image of Fort Annamaboe today

Records of the period indicate that from 1736 to 1743 captives

The Early Years

were often first taken by canoe from Annamaboe to an intermediary British trading ship, the *Argyle* – commonly called the "Floating Factory" – anchored permanently off the coast.[11] There, slave ship captains would often make their final purchase of human cargo, completing their rosters of men, women, boys, and girls. Some New England ship owners discouraged their captains from buying young children on their account because the buying price and transport cost often exceeded their sale price in Boston. A child would take almost the same space and food as a profitable male adult.[12] Lastly, they would load up on foodstuffs and water for the Atlantic crossing.[13]

2014 photo of an Anomabo fisherman by his canoe, identical to the 18th century canoes

Broteer was taken out to a ship called the *Charming Susanna* from Rhode Island,[14] and there sold to the steward. This was clearly a personal purchase outside normal slave transactions.

> *I was bought on board by one Robertson Mumford, steward of said vessel, for four gallons of rum, and a piece of calico, and called* Venture, *on account of his having purchased me with his own private venture. Thus I came by my name.*

Mumford, whose actual given name was Robinson, evidently thought it clever to label his new acquisition for what he thought it was – a smart commercial transaction.[15]

"*. . . four gallons of rum, and a piece of calico.*" The price was indeed a good one by the standards of the time. The smaller Albert Gronniosaw was bought for just two yards of check by his ship's captain.[16] An adult male in his prime could go for 100 or more gallons of rum, which was the favored currency of Rhode Island slavers.[17]

Young males were particularly prized as apprentices in Rhode Island, and ship's officers often paid for them out of their own pockets as personal investments, "their privilege."[18] Robinson Mumford was buying his future manservant.

And so began the saga of an American slave.

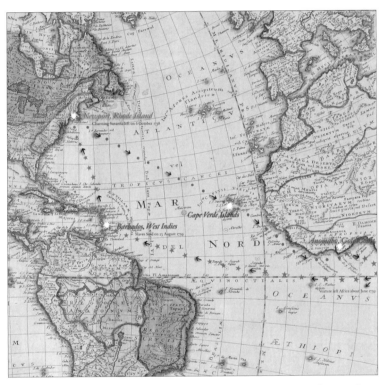

Route for the *Charming Susanna* from Newport, RI to Annamaboe on the Gold Coast to Barbados and back to Newport, RI

The Early Years

The *Charming Susanna* embarked from the Gold Coast in late May or early June 1739, destined for Barbados.[19] This was a typical route at the time in what came to be known as the "Triangular Trade."[20]

Boston lighthouse and an armed sloop in 1729

Colonial ships, mainly sloops,[21] sailed from American ports loaded with rum and other goods[22] to West Africa. They traded rum for other commodities with foreign ships off shore and then purchased captive Africans with the rum, tobacco, onions, textiles, and guns.[23] They returned home by way of the West Indies. There they sold their human cargo and used the proceeds to load up with molasses and raw sugar to resupply New England's abundant distilleries.

Meanwhile, New England exported livestock, lumber, and food-stuffs (to feed the slaves working the plantations) to the West Indies, supporting what was by far Britain's most lucrative plantation economy at the time. New England had been shipping livestock to run the sugar plantations for years. In the first half of the 18th century, horses to the West Indies, were a principal export commodity for New London. On one day, June 26, 1724, 6 vessels loaded with horses sailed for the West Indies.[24]

The whole circuit was a very symbiotic arrangement.

VENTURE unknowingly was near the crest of a historic surge in African slave traffic. Until 1741, 70 percent of slaves exported to the New England colonies came from the Caribbean and only 30 percent were shipped directly from Africa. After that time the percentages were reversed.[25] There were many reasons for this, most having to do with the increased demand for labor and the high profit margins slavers could get from buying directly at the source. But there was also a perception among mainland slave owners that blacks raised in the West had picked up some dangerous notions of independence. Better to get them fresh from their homeland.

Captives were usually brought out to the ship from the African shore in small numbers under guard to reduce their chances of escape, but sometimes the canoes capsized in rough water or during a skirmish with the crew.

Slaves being taken out to a slave ship on the coast near Anomabo

Once aboard ship, the slaves were often stripped and branded with a hot iron, if they had not already been branded onshore, so that owners would later be able to identify their property.

When the ship got underway, panic often broke out as the captives realized they were being taken from their homeland, and bringing them to heel resulted in more casualties among both slaves and sailors.

When it became clear to the captives that resistance was futile, a "fixed melancholy," the loss of desire to live, overcame many of them.[26] Some resisted by refusing to eat, but were force-fed by the crew. Slaving captains knew that their cargo was valuable only if delivered alive and in good health, and they had to balance that reality against the temptation to pack their ships as fully as possible.

The women and children (about 15 years old or younger) were locked away in a separate bulkhead from the men. Men were kept in the hold of the ship, which was dark and so fetid from body heat and waste that it was difficult to breathe. On the large British ships like the *Brookes* the men were chained together on double-decked wooden pallets, they had less than two feet of headroom and could hardly move, except when thrown against each other in rough weather. Historian William Weeden said that on the smaller, New England sloops, brigantines, schooners, and snows, generally of 35 to 50 tons, "the headroom was 3' 10" with 20" waist. Early the rule was 2 ½ slaves per ton, and later by law decreased to 1 ½ slaves per ton."[27] For the early period of the Rhode Island trade (1730-1759), 50% of the voyages carried 80 or less slaves, unlike the hundreds carried on the large British ships like the Brookes.[28]

In VENTURE's case, Robinson would have kept him nearby[29] and begun teaching him a few words of English and how to behave as his manservant. This closeness to his captive would have resulted in a bonding (commonly referred today as "Stockholm Syndrome")[30] between Robinson and a frightened youth.

Slaves were also kept in the dark as to their fate. When the British slave Olaudah Equiano claims he remembered being taken aboard ship as a boy, "I asked if we were not to be eaten by those white men with horrible looks, red faces and long hair?"[31]

In order to reduce the threat of disease and atrophy, the slaves were periodically brought on deck for exercise, fresh air, and to be bathed with vinegar and water.

It has been calculated from departure and arrival records spanning more than three centuries, that on average, an estimated 12 percent of slaves died during the "Middle Passage" as a result of storms, disease, infection, suicide, or at the hands of the crew. It is estimated that 12.5 million captive Africans entered the Atlantic Slave Trade, 10.7 million of whom reached the Americas alive.[32] Losses among crewmen were considerable, although seldom as high. They called the West African voyage "The White Man's Grave."[33] It is known that at least two of the *Charming Susanna* officers died at sea, both of them Mumfords.[34]

The round trip from New England to Africa to the West Indies and home again usually took from 8 to 14 months, depending on weather and the length of time spent in ports trading for slaves. In the early period of the Rhode Island trade, the average voyage was 308 days,[35] with 60 days the average duration of a slaver's voyage from the Gold Cost of West Africa to Barbados.[36]

Bridgetown harbor, Barbados by John Waller

The *Charming Susanna* arrived in Barbados, the easternmost Caribbean island, and on August 23, 1739, all but four of the captives were sold. Records show that agent David Minvielle paid a total of 18 pounds 10 shillings in taxes on the sale of 74 slaves.[37]

The Early Years

It would seem there could hardly be a more cynical and inappropriate name for a slave ship than the *"Charming Susanna,"* although naming ships of all kinds after favored women was quite common at the time. It turns out that David Minvielle's wife was named Susanna and was a recognized slaver in her own right.[38]

A sidelight: By remarkable coincidence, August 23, the day VENTURE began 26 years of bondage in the Western Hemisphere, is recognized today by the United Nations as the "International Day for the Remembrance of the Slave Trade and Its Abolition." That date commemorates the start of the 1791 slave revolt in the Caribbean colony of St. Domingue, now known as Haiti.

But all that took place 52 years after the West African youth peered over the ship's railing in the harbor at Bridgetown, the Barbadian capital.

Loading sugar hogsheads in the West Indies in the 18th-century

In his *Narrative*, VENTURE says little about the transatlantic voyage, except to estimate that about one-quarter of the captives died of smallpox before arriving in Barbados. Perhaps he blocked out the horror of it. Many eyewitness accounts of the infamous "Middle Passage," as the transatlantic slave voyages were called, evoked a veritable hell at sea. VENTURE describes the voyage as *"an ordinary passage, except great mortality by the small pox."* The term "ordinary" sounds mild for a voyage of hell but what VENTURE must have learned from other survivors he met over the 50 plus years in New England, was that his passage was no different than theirs.[39]

VENTURE was one of the majority on his ship to survive the experience. According to British customs' records, 78 of the estimated 91 slaves aboard the *Charming Susanna* actually made it to Barbados.[40] All but four were sold on the island by the agents Minvielle and Company. Because VENTURE belonged to the Rhode Island ship's steward, the youth stayed aboard.

As the Caribbean island closest to Africa, Barbados was the first stop – a throbbing economic powerhouse, studded with plantations that produced the "white gold" so coveted by Britain and its minions. The economy in Barbados and throughout the West Indies was totally dependent on enslaved Africans, who worked from morning to night to harvest and process sugar cane under the most oppressive heat and working conditions.

As an African, the ship-bound youth might have gazed wistfully at the tropical port, with its swaying palms, stately buildings, and the distant sugar plantations, which may have looked idyllic from afar.

What he could not have known was that Barbados, Jamaica, Hispaniola, and other such Caribbean islands were unsurpassed as slave killing fields.

A telling fact: To replace their rapidly dying workers, the West Indies imported more slaves from Africa during the 17th and 18th centuries than did the entire North American continent. Barbados alone imported an estimated 493,000 slaves from Africa,[41] compared with an estimated 455,000 brought to the North American mainland over the lifetime of the Atlantic slave trade.[42]

VENTURE may have been headed for an unfamiliar environment in the north, but his chances of surviving and shaping his own destiny there would be far greater than ever possible in Barbados.

The *Charming Susanna* arrived in Rhode Island sometime in September 1739, after what VENTURE's *Narrative* described as a "*comfortable passage.*"

Newport in 1740

In contrast to the Atlantic voyage, during which most were confined, the remaining slaves may have had the run of the ship on that final leg and were probably well fed on the newly provisioned vessel by a greatly relaxed crew relieved to be going home.

On arrival in Rhode Island, Robinson placed VENTURE with one of his sisters before bringing him later to the family's main residence on Fishers Island in Long Island Sound.

The Mumfords were a comparatively prosperous family that first settled in Rhode Island in the 1630s. Within half a century, Mumford men were heavily engaged in the international slave trade and in managing farms and plantations with slave labor. There is even a city called Mumford on Africa's Gold Coast, east of where Broteer was held for transport.

One can only imagine the depth of bewilderment felt by this young African. He presumably spoke no English, was likely experiencing an unwelcome chill from the New England autumn, and had not the slightest idea how to comport himself in a bustling, foreign culture.

Slaves just off the ship often arrived weakened and disoriented, and some did not survive the transition. But VENTURE was young, robust, and resourceful, and his *Narrative* makes no mention of any particular difficulties.

He arrived at a time when it was no longer a novelty to see a black African on a New England street, although it was not nearly as commonplace as it would become in another decade. Between 1720 and 1750, the slave population of Rhode Island multiplied more than six fold.[43]

New England, however, never achieved the status of a "slave society," as did the South. Enslaved African labor became the primary engine of the southern economy, while in the mid-18th century the North depended on a labor force comprised of Africans, Native Americans, indentured servants from Britain and Europe, and its own sons and daughters to get the job done. African slaves were one of the lowest in this hierarchy and often suffered at the hands of resentful white laborers.

Although VENTURE was probably unaware of it, the year after he arrived in America, Virginia passed a law that defined its slaves as "chattel personal in the hands of their owners and possessors for all intents, construction, and purpose whatsoever."[44] By virtue of their greater diversity, the northern states may not have defined the institution of slavery quite so strictly, but in the mid-1700s, New England was far from a place of refuge.

The institution of slavery was widely accepted in the North as a means of filling a growing demand for manual labor. Although some in the New England establishment opposed slavery on moral grounds, abolition would not enter mainstream social thought in the North for nearly another century.

VENTURE stayed for "*some time*" with one of Robinson Mumford's married sisters – most likely his eldest, Mercy, who lived in Newport. Her husband William Dyer was a ship's captain and made at least one Atlantic voyage. It is presumed that Robinson wanted VENTURE to spend his early days with his sister because she could teach the youth how to speak rudimentary English, how to perform household chores, and, in general, how to behave in "proper" colonial society. In Newport, VENTURE would be exposed to an urban life and culture, better preparing him to be Robinson's personal man-servant.

Sometime in late 1740 or early 1741, the young slave was retrieved and taken to his owner's home on Fishers Island. Immediately south of the Connecticut mainland, Fishers Island had become the base for the

Connecticut and Rhode Island coast, including Fishers Island

Mumford family branch headed at the time by Capt. George Mumford, Robinson's father. But they did not own it. They leased it from relatives, the Winthrops, who constituted one of the most prominent New England families, producing governors in both Connecticut and Massachusetts. The recently discovered leases show they were not just renting a home but a complete business - land, house, barns, orchards, crops, and the livestock for wool and meat. (see color plates C vi and C vii after page 200)

This explains the large number of slaves; in Mumford's case we know of at least 16 slaves, who worked what was clearly a complete "provisioning plantation" for the triangular trade.

Indeed, the Mumford clan pointedly did not amass its own property in the 18th century, but rather acted as itinerant agents, brokers, and managers for others. In effect, the array of Mumford enterprises, ranging from New England to Africa to the West Indies, served as an 18th-century version of "one-stop shopping" for those who needed ships, slaves, financing, and provisions for the various

The Early Years

trades.

As VENTURE would soon learn, the nearly 3,000 acre Fishers Island played a significant role in the slave economy as part of the crucial breadbasket for the Caribbean sugar plantations. But first the young slave had some adjustment issues. Shortly after arriving on the island VENTURE faced his first real test as a captive servant.

As VENTURE described the incident in his *Narrative*, Robinson sent him ahead to the island while his owner took care of business on the mainland, and had turned over the keys of his ship's trunks to the youth, with instructions *"not to deliver them up to any body, not even to his father without his orders."*

Evidently Robinson suspected that members of his family would pry. Indeed, his father tried.

He insisted that I should deliver to him the keys, threatening to punish me if I did not. But I let him know that he should not have them let him say what he would. He then laid aside trying to get them. But notwithstanding he appeared to give up trying to obtain them from me, yet I mistrusted that he would take some time when I was off my guard, either in the day time or at night to get them, therefore I slung them round my neck, and in the day time concealed them in my bosom, and at night I always lay with them under me, that no person might take them from me without being apprized of it. Thus I kept the keys from every body until my master came home. When he returned he asked where VENTURE was. As I was then within hearing, I came, and said, here sir, at your service. He asked me for his keys, and I immediately took them off my neck and reached them out to him. He took them, stroked my hair, and commended me, saying in presence of his father that his young VENTURE was so faithful that he never would have been able to have taken the keys from him but by violence; that he should not fear to trust him with his whole fortune, for that he had been in his native place so habituated to keeping his word, that he would sacrifice even his life to maintain it.

VENTURE had bonded with Robinson on the voyage and was loyal and protective of his master.

Robinson Mumford realized that he had found a gem forged by African traditions of honor. What he likely did not know was that the youth's searing memory of his father's death reinforced such tenaciousness and would become the adult's hallmark.

Fishers Island was primarily used for grazing when the Mumfords leased it. At any given time, they raised from 1,000 to 2,000 sheep and up to 300 beef and dairy cattle (from the lease to Mumford 1741/42- 1350 Sheep with their fleaces and their lambs, 20 Swine, 8 Mares, 81 Neat cattle, 12 yearlings, 7-2 year Heifers, 7-2 year Stears, 1-3 year Heifer, 1-3 year Bull, 1-3 year Stear, 4-4 year Stears, 2- 5 year Stears, 42 Cows, 4 oxen).[45] The island was a major meat supplier, and the Mumfords paid their cousins the Winthrops 950 pounds a year in Connecticut Colony bills (in new tenor about 135 pounds), a staggering amount at the time, for the privilege of using it.[45 (lease illustration, color plates C vi and C vii after page 200, transcription in endnote 46-Early Years)]

The Mumfords also had a long-standing history of slaveholding. George's nephew, of Salem Valley, Connecticut, "John Mumford maintained a gang of 350 slaves that he rented out to area farmers to clear land."[47]

George's mother was murdered on the Rhode Island mainland by a slave in 1707. The incident served as an example of how slave crimes were dealt with. Abigail Mumford had ordered her slave whipped. He turned on her and beat her to death. When he realized he could not escape capture, he drowned himself in Narragansett Bay. The citizens were so outraged at being deprived of their retribution, the Rhode Island Assembly ordered the dead slave's head, arms, and legs be cut from his body and hung in public view, and his torso burned to ashes "that it may, if it pleased God, be something of a terror to others from perpetrating of the like barbarity for the future."[48]

Since it was an ingrained family legend, the new youth called VENTURE must have heard the story as he adjusted to life as a slave in the Mumford household.

Islands like Fishers were ideal for raising livestock, because they were protected from one of the great scourges of the time – wolves. Packs of them had roamed the Northeast with impunity and cut heavily into livestock herds on the mainland before they were hunted out by the mid-18th century. As testimony to their importance as refuges for sheep, no fewer than six "Ram" islands could be found along the

Connecticut and Long Island coasts.

All the islands in the Long Island basin, whose owners had been given special status by the crown as "Lords of the Manor," were similarly mobilized. Between them, they served as a major provisioning source for the Caribbean sugar plantations, and later, for the soldiers fighting in the War of Independence. By 1750, the area had become the North's major livestock exporter, the equivalent of the Iowa beef empire in later times. VENTURE was already well suited for herding work, having come from such a culture in Africa, with an apprenticeship already served. Whether his owner was aware of this when he purchased VENTURE is not known, but it certainly added to the boy's value.

Their relationship was to be short lived. Within two years after VENTURE's arrival, Robinson died, apparently at sea. His father, George, became the slave's owner and the one VENTURE now called "*master.*"

Initially, young VENTURE was put to work in the Mumford household carding wool and performing other domestic chores. Eventually, because he was big and strong for his age, VENTURE was assigned to work outdoors. With Robertson's death he was no longer a man servant but just another slave owned by George Mumford to work the plantation.

Initially, the old man, himself a former sea captain, was wary of his new charge, remembering the incident over the ship's trunks and perhaps the fate of his mother. But VENTURE's formidable work ethic eventually won him over. VENTURE said Mumford began to put more confidence in him "*After many proofs of my faithfulness.*" VENTURE described his demeanor in those days as obedient and submissive, but it would soon be shaken. The old man started imposing harder and harder tasks on the youth, such as forcing him to pound bushels of corn for the chickens late into the night "*or be rigorously punished.*"

He then faced a new problem that was not uncommon in the slave culture — serving two masters. In this case, Mumford's eldest son, James, the late Robinson's brother, evidently took pleasure in flexing his authority. When the old man was away, James would order VENTURE to do chores that were different from those the father assigned. The young slave quietly complied, until one day:

> ... *his son came up to me in the course of the day, big with authority, and commanded me very arrogantly to quit my present business and go directly about what he should order me. I replied to him that my master had given me so much to perform that day, and that I must therefore faithfully complete it in that time. He then broke out into a great rage, snatched a pitchfork and went to lay me over the head therewith; but I as soon got another and defended myself with it, or otherwise he might have murdered me in his outrage. He immediately called some people who were within hearing at work for him, and ordered them to take his hair rope and come and bind me with it. They all tried to bind me but in vain, tho' there were three assistants in number. My upstart master then desisted, put his pocket handkerchief before his eyes and went home with a design to tell his mother of the struggle with young VENTURE. He told her that their young VENTURE had become so stubborn that he could not control him, and asked her what he should do with him. In the mean time I recovered my temper, voluntarily caused myself to be bound by the same men who tried in vain before, and carried before my young master, that he might do what he pleased with me. He took me to a gallows made for the purpose of hanging cattle on, and suspended me on it. Afterwards he ordered one of his hands to go to the peach orchard and cut him three dozen of whips to punish me with. These were brought to him, and that was all that was done with them, as I was released and went to work after hanging on the gallows about an hour.*

This incident showed VENTURE what bondage was all about, and he took from it some lessons. First he behaved submissively, but found he could be jolted into rage by unwarranted abuse. He also learned that he could physically handle himself well, even with three grown men. But when his rage cooled, he surrendered himself back into submission.

In retrospect, one wonders what else an intelligent young man with an urge to live could have done on an island in an unfamiliar land. He took his punishment.

But this early affair in his slave life may well have been the spark that ignited VENTURE SMITH's determination to become his own man. From then on, he bided his time and learned the ways of the owner class.

Daily life for a slave in a New England household was quite different in texture from that of a southern plantation slave; the environment and the type of work were so different in the two regions. While much of the southern and mid-Atlantic colonies was flat and fertile, ideal for the growing of large crops, rocky and hilly New England could mostly sustain small farms with a small number of slaves.

The two economies had not yet been joined by the collaboration of raw cotton and the textile mills powered by New England's fast-moving rivers. Eli Whitney, native of Massachusetts, did not invent the cotton gin until the late 18th century.

As testimony, however, to the North's growing role as a major supplier for the Caribbean sugar-growing slave population, a number of spacious farms emerged in the Narragansett area flatlands of Rhode Island, in the Manor Islands of Long Island Sound, in eastern Connecticut, and the Dutch plantations of the Hudson Valley. All of them used slave labor in the 18th century to raise sheep, beef cattle, dairy cows, and horses as well to as grow the foodstuffs that were shipped to the West Indies.[49]

Northern supplies weren't just for the sustenance of overworked slaves in the West Indies, of course, but for the white owners and managers who pampered themselves in typical British colonial style. Among the items that Connecticut plantations were known to have shipped south were trotting horses and massive quantities of ice.

Timber, especially the white oak prized by New England shipyards, was also a precious northern commodity shipped south to make the barrels that carried sugar and molasses on the return trip north.

1771 price list for goods sold in the West Indies (see endnote 48 p. 224 for transcription)

VENTURE spoke little of his surroundings on Fishers Island, where he probably shared quarters with nearly 20 other slaves needed to operate a vast livestock enterprise.[50] Because most northern farms were smaller, slaves were usually not housed in outside barracks-like quarters, as in the South. They would usually live in the attic or basement of the main house, in cramped and spartan conditions, or in a nearby barn. In the winter, some of the men would sleep in the kitchen and hallways inside a bedroll, with the task of keeping the fires burning through the night.

Such proximity to owners did not necessarily foster racial cohesion in the North. A family's slaves may have lived in the main house but were not allowed to use the front entrance, for example. They entered and left through the "slave door," which usually adjoined the kitchen. They also had a separate outhouse, far removed from the one used by the whites.

Instead of the southern field hand's monotonous routine of tending and picking crops like tobacco in Virginia or rice in Georgia from dawn to dusk, a northern slave usually had a variety of chores. Depending on the need of the moment, he might work in the field in the morning and the shop in the afternoon. The standard tasks for male slaves included chopping wood, repair work of all kinds, shoeing horses, making bricks, mucking out stalls, feeding livestock, or plowing and sowing. In the evening, slaves might polish boots, crush grain for the poultry, and keep the fireplace stoked.

In the provisioning trades, a black man could work alone – minding and herding stock, loading and driving wagons, or running a fishing boat. He was judged by the results at the end of the day and could well face a whipping if the job was not done to his owner's satisfaction.

Female slaves in a middle-class household usually worked indoors – mostly cooking, laundering, and cleaning – and as dairy maids in the barn. In the evening, they would work in the kitchen, cleaning up after dinner and preparing the next day's meals or sewing and darning their owner's clothes.

On small subsistence farms, slaves often worked side by side with their owners to get the daily job done. They might normally work in comfort together, but there was a social line, one seldom crossed. Not learning it carried a price.

One might think that the proximity of master and slave in the North encouraged more tolerance and kindness than in the South, where the demands of massive crop production for a hungry world more greatly pressed its slaves. But as the respected slavery scholar Ira Berlin noted in his seminal work on the first two centuries of slavery in North America, *Many Thousands Gone*, just the opposite often proved true: "Slaveholders in such societies could act with extraordinary brutality precisely because their slaves were extraneous to their main business. They could limit their slaves' access to freedom expressly because they desired to set themselves apart from their slaves."[51]

Berlin and other historians have also noted that the system of mixed living in the North had a profound impact on slave family life and connectedness to their heritage. The absence of separate slave quarters not only broke up family units but hastened the dissolution of the African communal structure. As a result, northern slaves were less able than their southern counterparts to practice their African religions or preserve ancient traditions and adapt them in any cohesive way to their new conditions and environment.

On the other hand, because their work ran the full gamut of maintaining hearth to building the economy in the North, slaves there tended to develop skills that could serve them well in independence. Few got the opportunity to prove that.

VENTURE spent the first 14 years of his slave life in the keep of the Mumfords on Fishers Island.

Fishers Island in 1762 by Ezra Stiles

The seven-mile-long island, tucked away between the eastern tip of Long Island and the Connecticut mainland, bears a passing resemblance to a fish swimming westward, with a small harbor cut behind its head. A map hand-drawn by Ezra Stiles and dated 1762 shows only one dwelling near the harbor and a few patches of forest. Interestingly, the map's legend mentions 50 deer in residence but makes no mention of livestock or slaves.

New London auction sale 1772, signed by Winthrop Saltonstall

This was not uncommon. Property bills of sale at the time often lumped together household goods, animals, and slaves.[52]

The privileged Winthrops behaved like the English landed gentry from the Old Country. Solely for their pleasure, they even kept a herd of albino deer on Naushon, one of the Elizabeth Islands, off the southern coast of Massachusetts.[53]

VENTURE's skills as a woodsman, herder, builder, and fisherman were honed here. It is not known if he hunted. Slaves were normally not allowed to use guns.

He grew to be a man of enormous size, by his own account *"measuring… six feet one inch and an half, and every way well proportioned."*

There was no job he could not do, and he seemed to take pride in doing it in shorter time and in greater quantity than anyone else. Once, to test his strength, *"I took up on my knees a tierce of salt containing seven bushels, and carried it two or three rods. Of this fact there are several eye witnesses now living,"* he recounted a half century later. Translated into modern measurements, the young man had carried a weight of over 400 pounds a distance of approximately 40 feet.

Occasionally he took trips to the Connecticut and Rhode Island mainland, less than an hour north by small boat, in the company of George or James, to deliver wood

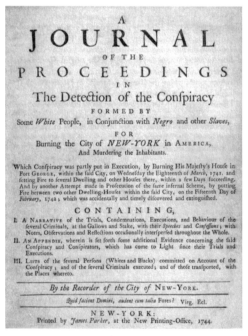

1744 report on the New York riots

or produce. He also made deliveries to the eastern end of Long Island. Port towns like Groton, New London, and Stonington in Connecticut, Westerly in Rhode Island, and Southold on Long Island were the only populated places he would experience in those formative years. It is not known how much he learned of the wider world at the time.

For example, he might have heard something through the slave network about an insurrection in New York City in 1741 that newspapers of the time labeled a "Negro Conspiracy." Although it was not a slave revolt, the incident served as a horrendous example of explosive race relations in the growing cities. A series of building fires had set off mass hysteria, and scores of blacks were rounded up as suspects. A total of 31 were executed. Some were burned at the stake and others were hanged. Interestingly, whites were also implicated in this so-called plot, and five of them were hanged.[54] These were mostly Irish immigrants, whom the English colonists labeled a separate "race" in those days.

Of an even wider world, VENTURE might have overheard something about "King George's War," as the third French and Indian war was called. Mostly centered in upper New York and Canada, the war was physically distant, but it nevertheless wielded an indirect impact. Blacks became more essential to the northern economy as able-bodied whites went off to join the British war effort, which would last off and on until 1763.

VENTURE and his people worked harder as a result, comforted by the dubious solace of knowing that their value as slaves had increased.

Coming from a culture that measured time by nature's clock, VENTURE must have also found it a particular curiosity that England and her colonies, after much calculation and debate, reverted in 1752 from the Julian to the Gregorian calendar. It was an edict that prompted riots among white citizens who felt cheated out of 11 days.

While VENTURE labored in the fields and tidewaters of an off-shore island, preoccupied with his daily chores and orders, revolutionary notions about the rightness of scientific reasoning, the limitations of the divine right of kings, the equality of men, and a people's right to self-determination, were swirling through the parlors and assembly halls on the colonial mainland.

What he would soon come to learn was that such notions did not apply to him.

"Meg, the wife of my youth,

whom I married for love,

and bought with my money, is still alive."

VENTURE 1798

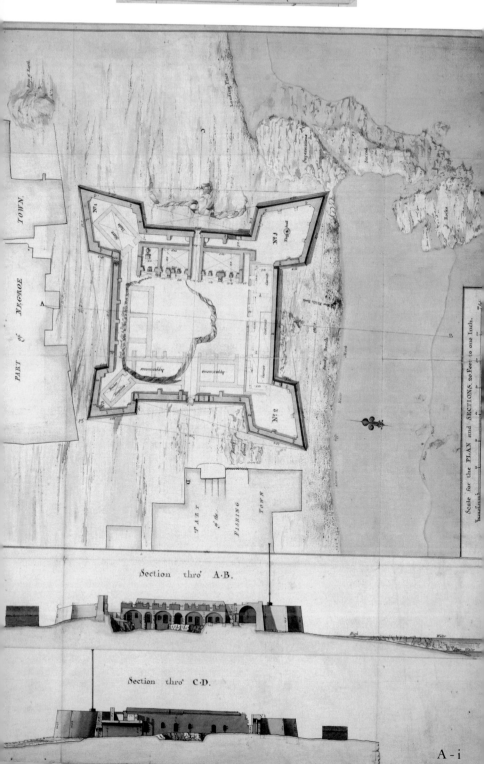

PLAN and SECTIONS
of
ANNAMABOE FORT. *AFRICA*

Surveyed in February & March 1756 by Justly Watson Director of Engineers

Nº 1. Flag Bastion	*The Yellow Colour shews what*	Nº 3. N.W. Bastion
Nº 2. S.W. Bastion	*Work remains to be done.*	Nº 4. N.E. Bastion
	✳	

Section thro' A·B.

Section thro' C·D.

A-i

"I was bought on board...
for four gallons of rum, and a piece of calico
and called VENTURE. Thus I came by my name."

The display platform in the slave sale building
almost exactly as it was in 1807 when the last
African was sold on it.

right - top: Annamaboe Fort
middle: Slave sale building
bottom left: Passage to "Door of No Return"
bottom right: Walkway to the canoes out to ships

Venture's Descendants and Friends visited Anomabo, Ghana for the 275th Anniversary of his leaving Africa September 13th to 19th, 2014

Chiefs welcoming the Descendants outside the Royal Palace
Anomabo, Ghana

Clockwise - Chief Amonu XI receiving the Descendants

Author spreading soil from VENTURE's grave
(in East Haddam, Connecticut) into the Atlantic Ocean by the Fort

Canoe ride out into the Atlantic Ocean similar to VENTURE's

Chief Nana Okodom VI, Corrine Henry-Brady 9th, Angi Perron 9th,
Gina Ryan 10th, Jaser Ryan 11th, Floyd Henry, Nana Baffoe IV

A - v

Far North of Cameroon, we believe within 100 miles of where VENTURE was born.

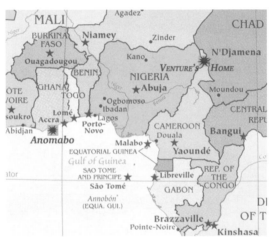

Modern West African map - showing where we believe Broteer Furro
was born and Anomabo where he left Africa in the spring of 1739

Ram Island in Bullhead Bay,

On March 27, 1754 VENTURE is looking for a place to live, work, and raise his family in freedom. In a Native American village, where he and his family would blend in. He headed for the village of Matsepe where the Massepe River enters South Oyster Bay. *1. Fishers Island to Montauk Point* sailing in a schooner - 25 miles - 5 hours. *2. Montauk Point to Southampton* on land about 32 miles. *3. Montauk Point to Massepe River* by boat 93 miles – about 15 hours.

1770-1774 VENTURE is living on Long Island and *going back and forth* to Stonington-point.

Southampton, New York

Anomabo fisherman paddling a canoe out into the Atlantic with
Annamaboe Fort in the background. The dark spot center bottom of the fort is
the "*door of no return*". The last view of Africa for
those taking the Middle Passage to slavery in the Americas.

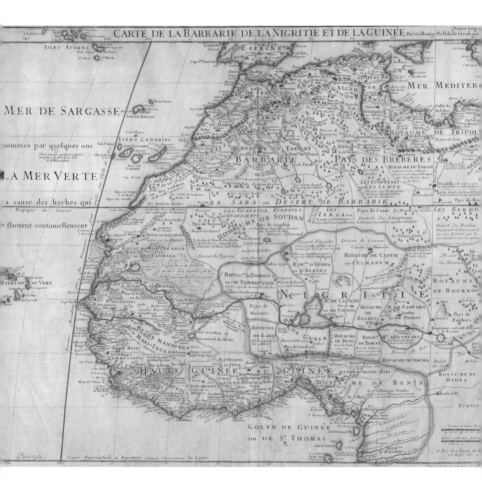

Delisle's 1722 map of West Africa, issued by Phillippe Bauche, Paris 1742

"People might not get all they work for in this world,
but they must certainly work for all they get."

–Frederick Douglass, August 3, 1857

THE CRUCIBLE YEARS

The year 1754 marked a turning point in VENTURE's life.
He was now about 25 and in the prime of his life. He had been
confined to the Mumford household for a decade and a half and was
bursting to expand his horizons.

VENTURE had clearly been planning something, for he had put
aside quite a bit of money by doing odd jobs at night like polishing
boots, trapping muskrats and minks, fishing, and selling vegetables he
was evidently allowed to raise by himself.

This was not unusual in the right circumstances. A northern
slaveowner with any understanding of how to motivate servants realized that he would get good work from a man during the day if that
man had the opportunity to work for himself in off-hours. And
VENTURE was clearly a good worker. What also distinguished him
was how he dealt with his money. He saved nearly everything as an
investment for the future. VENTURE had almost an obsessive aversion
to spending money on items that were not absolutely essential.

One event he was saving for was matrimony. VENTURE took a wife
in late 1753 or early 1754. His bride, Marget, whom he called *"Meg,"*
was a slave in the Mumford home. Not enough is known about her, to
the great frustration of her descendants and to scholars who at the
very least want to know if she was born in Africa or America or if she
was Native American. All VENTURE says is *"I married for love."*
University of Connecticut geneticists, who retrieved a bone from her
grave for DNA testing in the summer of 2006, have not yet been able
to solve the puzzle. One fact learned from that excavation was that

Meg was quite small in size. Her coffin was made for someone under five feet in height. With her husband standing more than a foot taller and weighing three times as much, the couple must have made a striking sight.

Scholars say she carried a Dutch name and was probably from Long Island, in an area settled by the Dutch. For a variety of reasons, it is believed she was part or full Native American, possibly from the Massapeag people who lived there. In the 17th and the first part of the 18th century New England Native Americans were enslaved and sold, and for them freedom was just as unlikely as for someone from Africa.[1]

Not long after VENTURE started his family, something inexplicable happened. In his own words:

My master owned a certain Irishman, named Heddy, who about that time formed a plan of secretly leaving his master. After he had long had this plan in meditation he suggested it to me. At first I cast a deaf ear to it, and rebuked Heddy for harboring in his mind such a rash undertaking. But after he had persuaded and much enchanted me with the prospect of gaining my freedom by such a method, I at length agreed to accompany him. Heddy next inveigled two of his fellow servants to accompany us. The place to which we designed to go was the Mississippi.

The recently married VENTURE wanted a home for himself and his expecting wife. On March 27, 1754 VENTURE sought a place to live, work, and raise his family in freedom. An escaping New England slave had few practical choices. New York City had a large free black population for a runaway to blend in, but because of his unusual size, VENTURE would stand out and risk capture. In a Native American village, a slave and his family could assimilate. By 1754 intermarriage of Indians and blacks was common, and if one's family were part Indian they would be welcome and protected.[2] Native Americans were known to hide escaping slaves, and especially one whose wife was one of their people. VENTURE planned to establish a home elsewhere and then come back and get Meg. VENTURE's reference to the *"Mississippi river"* was probably a misinterpretation in the transcription or an error in the typesetting of his story, because even an isolated Northern slave would know that the famous river that cut through America's midsection would be unattainable. However, on the south shore of Long Island there was a Native American village where the Massepe River enters South Oyster Bay.[3] Heddy assured him he knew where the "Massepe River" (and the village of Matsepe) was, so VENTURE agreed to join him.

1. Fishers Island to Montauk by boat 2. Montauk to Southampton by road
3. Montauk to Massepe River by boat

To prepare for the escape they stole provisions – *"privately collected"* is the way the *Narrative* phrases it – from the Mumford larder, gathered extra clothes, sneaked out to the shore at about midnight, stole their owner's boat, and *"directed our course for the Mississippi river"* (Massepe River).

We mutually confederated not to betray or desert one another on pain of death. We first steered our course for Montauk point, the east end of Long-Island. After our arrival there we landed, and Heddy and I made an incursion into the island after fresh water, while our two comrades were left at a little distance from the boat, employed at cooking.

While no one was looking, Heddy the ringleader quietly abandoned his companions and stole off on his own by foot. When they discovered his absence, VENTURE asked the help of local towns people, who sent two men after Heddy. They caught up with him in Southampton, about 30 miles away and brought him back. VENTURE continued the story:

I then thought it might afford some chance for my freedom, or at least a palliation for my running away, to return Heddy immediately to his master, and inform him that I was induced to go away by Heddy's address. Accordingly I set off with him and the rest of my companions for our master's, and arrived there without any difficulty. I informed my master that Heddy was the ringleader of our revolt, and that he had used us ill. He immediately put Heddy into custody, and myself and companions were well received and went to work as usual.

Although the story cries for explanations, we learn no more, except that Heddy ended up in jail.

. Venture had a Ker-
fey dark colour'd Great Coat, three Kerfey Jackets, two Pair of Breeches of the same, a new Cloth colour'd Fly-Coat, with red Shalloon Lining, a green Ratteen Jacket almost new, a trimson birded Stuff ditto, a Pair of large Oznabrigs Trowfers, a new Felt Hat, two Pair of Shoes, one Pair new, feveral Pair of Stockings; he is a very tall Fellow, 6 Feet 2 Inches high, thick fquare Shoulders, large bon'd, mark'd in the Face, or fcar'd with a Knife in his own Country.

Detail from runaway ad for VENTURE in 1754

It is not known how much time elapsed between escape and

return, but they were gone long enough for Mumford to place an advertisement in a New York newspaper, offering a reward for their return. It was one of hundreds of fugitive slave notices to be found in northern newspapers in any given year. The ad appeared in *The New-*

The Crucible Years

York Gazette on April 1, 1754,[4] and began: "Run away from George Mumford, of Fisher's Island, the 27th Instant, four Men Servants, a white Man and three Negroes, who hath taken a large two-Mast Boat, with a square Stern, and a large white Pine Canoe; . . ."

The man VENTURE called Heddy was identified as "Joseph Heday, (who) says he is a Native of Newark, in the Jerseys."

Offering a reward for their return of 20 pounds in "New-York Currency"[5], which would be equal to about $1,000 today, the notice describes in detail the clothes that the fugitives were wearing or carrying and then offers the first known description of VENTURE – "he is a very tall Fellow, 6 Feet 2 Inches high, thick square Shoulders, Large bon'd, mark'd in the Face, or scar'd with a Knife in his own Country."

It is not clear if George Mumford knew the meaning of the facial scarring VENTURE received as a youth, likely just before he was captured. Ritual scarring was commonplace in Africa to mark the formal passage from childhood to adulthood. Mumford knew putting it in the ad would help identify VENTURE.

The newspaper advertisement offered a reward for the three runaway slaves and the stolen boat. For George Mumford, they were all just property with a value, to be owned, bought, and sold, with the boat being the most valuable.

How could VENTURE so readily have abandoned his new wife within a few months of marrying her? "Cold feet" seems an unlikely explanation for someone who believed so fervently in keeping his word and who, according to his own accounts, was devoted to this woman.

A more likely explanation is that marriage unlocked in him even a greater yearning to take charge of his life. One can imagine him telling Meg that as soon as he could establish himself as a free man he would find a way to get her so they could live together as a family, beholden only to themselves.

When contemplating this episode, or at least the *Narrative's* limited version of it, we come across the first recorded instance of VENTURE's vaunted code of honor being violated. Given their mutual pledge of not betraying one another "*on pain of death*," Heddy got off easily.

On the other hand, we also see a shrewdly practical, even opportunistic side to VENTURE. By turning over his betrayer to Mumford, VENTURE figured that he and his cohorts would be treated leniently. Amazingly, they were.

There are many recorded examples of slaves being severely punished for much less. And yet these three were just put back to work. In the examination of VENTURE's motives, historians point to a tactic that slaves developed in the 18th century called "laying out." Knowing that an owner lived in fear of losing his investment, a slave would run away and go into hiding in order to extract concessions for better treatment in exchange for his return. A third party, usually a freed slave, would act as a go-between, taking the slave's demands back to the owner and the response back to the slave. Sometimes this worked, and sometimes it backfired, if the owner did not keep his word

Although it is not known if this tactic was part of VENTURE's plan (he also faced the problem of, without Heddy, he would not know how to find the Massepe River), his account of the escape and return suggests some kind of deal was struck, because it seems clear he avoided punishment.

However, the master's forgiveness or reward, if that is what it was, did not last long.

At the close of that year I was sold to a Thomas Stanton, and had to be separated from my wife and one daughter, who was about one month old. He resided at Stonington-point.[6]

Just like that. We learn he was sold in late 1754 and separated from his family, which by then included his first child. Why?

Apparently, VENTURE's attempted escape undermined the Mumfords' faith in him as a trustworthy investment and they didn't want to risk losing it again. It is known that George first transferred ownership of the slave couple to his remaining son, James. The son then sold VENTURE and, later, Meg and their newborn daughter Hannah to a farmer in Stonington, Connecticut.

This dramatic change in their lives came about eight months after VENTURE's failed escape.

SOUTH VIEW OF NEW-LONDON & FORT TRUMBULL.

Looking north on the Thames River with New London in background
by J. W. Barber

All this transpired as the Mumfords were getting ready to relocate to the Connecticut mainland. Records show that George purchased a house in 1755 in New London, where he moved his family and retinue of slaves the following year. That port town on the Connecticut mainland was the home base for the extended and interrelated family of Winthrops, Saltonstalls, and Mumfords.

The lease for Fishers Island was transferred to Benjamin Brown, who came from one of the slave-trading Brown families of Rhode Island (a relative of the one who financed what would later become Brown University).[7]

George Mumford died unexpectedly in New London in 1756 at the age of 67. The probated list of his property included 14 slaves, but

THOMAS STANTON'S HOMESTEAD.

Thomas Stanton house in Stonington, CT, built circa 1710, lost to fire in 1967

not Meg, VENTURE, or Hannah, because James had already taken over their ownership.[8] James sold VENTURE earlier and then Meg and Hannah about the time of his father's death. The Hannah listed could be the person VENTURE and Meg's daughter was named after.

The Crucible Years

By then, VENTURE was residing with the Stantons in the nearby town of Stonington, then a young seaport and farming community that would later become one of New England's busiest sailing ports and whaling centers. In those days, it had a slave population almost equal to that of New Haven, which was much larger.

Fishers Island stayed in Winthrop hands for another 108 years. First granted to future colonial Connecticut Governor John Winthrop "the Younger" in 1645 and made a Manor by the Crown in 1668,[9] the island was the subject of a long-standing border dispute between New York and Connecticut. In 1880 a two-state commission determined that the island was, in fact, part of New York. Today, Fishers Island is home to a full-time population of nearly 300 and a summer resort for the very wealthy.

After 14 years, VENTURE had become someone else's property and moved to the mainland for the first time.

To this place I brought with me from my late master's, two johannes, three old Spanish dollars, and two thousand of coppers, besides five pounds of my wife's money . . . All this money amounting to near twenty-one pounds York currency, my master's brother, Robert Stanton, hired of me, for which he gave me his note.

In other words, VENTURE put his hard-earned savings in a white man's safekeeping and got a promissory note in return. VENTURE, the consummate businessman, had *"hired"* – loaned – his capital to Robert Stanton, expecting to earn interest on his money. One can wonder about the wisdom of that, but what else could a slave do when pressured by an owner? He could have hidden it, but the Stantons would have easily found out from the former owners that VENTURE had amassed his own money. Lying about it probably would have earned him punishment.

The amount was equal to more than a year's wages for a laborer. Coincidentally, it is almost the same amount as the reward money Mumford had put up to get his four slaves and boat back.

The two leases show that what was being rented was a complete business — land, house, barns, crops, orchards, sheep for wool, and breeding livestock for meat. The only thing the lessee provided was the labor to produce the goods and to ship the products to market. In George Mumford's case, we can document at least 16 slaves he owned to work the plantation. Fishers Island was a complete "provisioning plantation" for the triangular trade.

At this point, VENTURE's *Narrative* jumps ahead 18 months to report that his owner purchased Meg and their daughter Hannah *"for seven hundred pounds old tenor,"* equal to about 100 pounds of new currency, which was issued in 1755.[10]

After satisfying themselves that VENTURE was of good value, the Stantons evidently thought it would be in everyone's best interests to reunite his family.[11] To refuse him that could cause problems. There are many stories about how slaves resisted their owners without actually escaping or refusing to work. They could slow down, get sloppy and break things, pretend not to understand, or find any variety of ways to express their unhappiness without overtly rebelling to the point of inviting the lash or re-sale.

However, from what is known about VENTURE's personality, it is unlikely he would have played such games. It is more likely that he simply asked his master to buy his wife and daughter, persuading Stanton it would make him more productive as a slave and provide new assets to the household. VENTURE was developing a good head for business.

So, he got his family, and the Stantons got two new slaves. A slave woman's child was, of course, born into slavery.

At this point in the *Narrative*, it would be perfectly understandable if the reader starts to get a little cranky. There is much information missing. The scribe clearly served as little more than a secretary taking dictation. Words, like *"inveigled,"* in the *Narrative* were not commonly used by a slave. The education Broteer would have received as a privileged child raised to be the leader in his father's village in Africa, would not have included English. On the other hand, articulation and eloquence in speaking a language do not require literacy. Many words attributed to Venture in this first-person narrative could easily have come from his own lips, especially precise business terms like "*procure*" and "*solicit*." The language one speaks is based on the teacher; in Venture's case, the Mumfords and, later, a prominent citizen of Hartford who were educated and spoke the finest colonial English.

We do not know, for example, how much Stanton paid for Venture, who by this time was garnering a reputation as a human dynamo and who had to have been regarded as a highly valuable commodity. Stanton clearly enjoyed showing off his new investment.

One time my master sent me two miles after a barrel of molasses, and ordered me to carry it on my shoulders. I made out to carry it all the way to my master's house.

Such a load would have weighed nearly 300 pounds.

Venture and Meg had two more children, both sons, while Meg was still owned by Stanton. Solomon was born in 1756 and Cuff in 1761. Interestingly, Cuff's name was derived from the West African word "Kofi," meaning Friday. It was the tradition there to name children for the day of the week they were born.[12] Solomon, while of Old Testament origins, was a name also frequently used in Africa, due to the influence of European Christians and North African Muslims.

Much has been debated about why Venture chose to live with his given slave name and to later adopt the surname of his final owner. Time and again we see a man who was determined to be a fully vested American who nevertheless took pride in being born an African of royal birth.

One point is certain: He would never have chosen Stanton for his surname. The reason is found in the *Narrative*.

Sometime around late 1758 or early 1759, four years after Venture arrived at the Stanton household, Stanton's wife, Elizabeth, had a serious quarrel with Meg while the head of the house was off hunting.

VENTURE had been working in the barn when he heard a *"racket"* in the house, and came running to find out what it was all about. In his words:

When I entered the house, I found my mistress in a violent passion with my wife, for what she informed me was a mere trifle; such a small affair that I forbear to put my mistress to the shame of having it known. I earnestly requested my wife to beg pardon of her mistress for the sake of peace, even if she had given no just occasion for offence. But whilst I was thus saying my mistress turned the blows which she was repeating on my wife to me. She took down her horse-whip, and while she was glutting her fury with it, I reached out my great black hand, raised it up and received the blows of the whip on it which were designed for my head. Then I immediately committed the whip to the devouring fire.

It is not known what set off Elizabeth Stanton. Whatever the cause, it apparently was not Meg's doing or at least not intentionally so. It seemed more to do with VENTURE's defense of Meg that unleashed their mistress' fury. The slave culture exacerbated such outbursts. The slightest word or gesture that could be inferred as rebellion from an "inferior" could not be tolerated. This overwhelming sense of owner entitlement could not be more clearly demonstrated than when a supposedly well-bred woman undertakes for a *"mere trifle"* to punish with a horsewhip two grown adults, one of them a man more than twice her size.

VENTURE was seeking conciliation, not retribution. Although he may have feared the consequences of striking back, his words and demeanor suggested he simply wanted to cool the situation down. He knew by now what it took to function in a world that was not always rational, and was certainly not fair.

After Elizabeth's husband, Thomas, returned home, she told him about the incident – or at least her version of it. VENTURE said his master *"seemed to take no notice of it, and mentioned not a word about it to me.*" So, Venture and Meg went back to work, thinking the matter closed. His *narrative* went on:

Some days after his return, in the morning as I was putting on a log in the fire-place, not suspecting harm from any one, I received a most violent stroke on the crown of my head with a club two feet long and as large round as a chair-post. This blow very badly wounded my head, and the scar of it remains to this day. The first blow made me have my wits about me you may suppose, for as soon as he went to renew it, I snatched the club out of his hands and dragged him out of the door.

To end the fight, Venture turned to the law.

While Thomas Stanton called his brother Robert for help, the assaulted slave took off, carrying the bloody club to a neighboring justice of the peace. If he had lived in the South at the time, such a recourse would not have been possible, but Connecticut had enacted laws against unjustifiable abuse of slaves, and Venture knew it.

The justice of the peace seemed to be a reasonable man but chose not to take immediate action. He listened to Venture's complaint and advised him to return to the Stanton farm and then to reissue a complaint if it happened again. Venture agreed to do this, but as they were talking, the Stanton brothers rode up and angrily demanded the slave's return. The justice turned on Thomas rebuking him for treating his slave "*thus hastily and unjustly, and told him what would be the consequence if he continued the same treatment towards me,*" Venture recalled.

Thus chastised, the Stantons left for home with Venture in tow. He described what happened next:

When they had come to a bye place, they both dismounted their respective horses, and fell to beating me with great violence. I became enraged at this and immediately turned them both under me, laid one of them across the other, and stamped both with my feet what I would.

VENTURE's strength was formidable and he could have easily killed both brothers, but he just wanted to overpower them. He did not have the advantage for long, however, because after they all returned home Stanton had a local constable and two others haul VENTURE off to a blacksmith's shop and handcuff him.

He was then brought to the house, where VENTURE said his mistress asked if he was secured. When assured that he was, Elizabeth smiled with satisfaction. *"In the midst of this content and joy, I presented myself before my mistress, shewed her my hand-cuffs, and gave her thanks for my gold rings."*

Not only had VENTURE shed the submissive and obedient garb that he had worn in his early slave days, but he gave as good as he got. Enraged at such insolence, Stanton had his slave padlocked with a large ox chain.

I continued to wear the chain peaceably for two or three days, when my master asked me with contemptuous hard names whether I had not better be freed from my chains and go to work. I answered him, No. Well then, said (he), I will send you to the West-Indies or banish you, for I am resolved not to keep you. I answered him I crossed the waters to come here, and I am willing to cross them to return.

Those words would set into motion another change in VENTURE's life, but it would be a road that took many turns before straightening out.

While he and the Stantons coexisted in cold silence, a Stonington resident by the name of Hempstead Miner came to VENTURE and asked if he wanted to join his household. When VENTURE said yes, Miner quietly advised him to act as unrepentant and discontented as possible in Stanton's presence in order to bring the sale price down. VENTURE did so, and it worked.

Stanton sold VENTURE to Miner for the remarkably low price of 56 pounds at a time when strong and healthy male slaves in their prime usually commanded much higher prices.[13]

It was the winter of 1758-59 and VENTURE was about 30 years old. He certainly must have been relieved to be free of Thomas Stanton, but he was leaving his wife and two children with Stanton and his embittered family.

Making the break all the more troubling was Robert Stanton's refusal to return the considerable money in savings that VENTURE had turned over to him five years earlier. Thomas had broken into VENTURE's trunk during their dispute and destroyed the promissory note, so VENTURE had no proof of the 21 pounds owed him. Prior to the Revolution in America, an unskilled laborer earned about 12 to 15 pounds per year.[14] VENTURE had lost more than a year's wages. The legal complications this loss could later cause, however, may have been another reason why the Stantons decided to sell their most valuable slave.

VENTURE then got another jolt. He learned that his new owner, Hempstead Miner, had no intention of keeping him, or letting him redeem himself, and had not fully paid Stanton his price.

But VENTURE had his own secret, too. He had amassed more money of his own, evidently from doing odd jobs for people in Stonington, and this time he was not going to trust anyone else to keep it. So before leaving with Miner he buried the money, just over 30 pounds, alongside a familiar road.

Miner took his new acquisition to Hartford, which at the time was a growing city but not yet the single Connecticut capital. There he tried to sell VENTURE to one William Hooker. When Hooker asked the big slave whether he would accompany him to *"the German Flats,"* VENTURE said no.

The area in question was in upper New York and would have taken VENTURE at least a three-day ride away from his family. For a man in perpetual bondage, that might as well have been California. German Flats had been the site of a massacre just two years earlier during the French and Indian wars, the news of which might also have given VENTURE pause.

Hooker threatened to take him anyway by bodily strapping him to his sleigh, to which VENTURE replied with the kind of quickness that served him well throughout his adult life.

I replied to him, that if he carried me in that manner, no person would purchase me, for it would be thought that he had a murderer for sale. After this he tried no more, and said he would not have me as a gift.

Miner then offered VENTURE to another Hartford man, Daniel Edwards, whose wife Sarah was William Hooker's cousin. He did not buy the slave but paid Miner 10 pounds in a pawn arrangement to obtain VENTURE's services for one year. Edwards was a lawyer with two degrees from Yale College where he had roomed and then been a tutor with his cousin Jonathan Edwards (the great philosophical theologian). Now he was a Supreme Court Judge, Hartford Probate Judge, Member of the Upper House of the Colonial Legislature, and advisor on financial affairs to the Governor.

Edwards, a well-to-do urban gentleman, used VENTURE as a manservant – *"his cup-bearer and waiter"* – and came to place a great deal of trust in him. This included sending VENTURE to the cellar to fetch wine for guests, a new level of responsibility that VENTURE regarded as a privilege. In colonial households, in this period, even the sugar was locked up, so giving the keys to the wine cellar to VENTURE showed complete trust by Daniel Edwards.

While in Hartford, VENTURE also experienced a level of urban elegance and sophistication he could not have imagined previously. The erudite conversation around the dinner table, the aura of educational and intellectual stimulation, the fine manners and the beautiful home décor were all new to him and made a lasting impression.

Although VENTURE only spent about a year in Judge Edwards' household, new research indicates it was a transformative period in the two men's lives. Not only is it clear now that the jurist, who owned, for the time and place, an impressive collection of books (see probate inventory on pages C vii and 201-205), likely taught VENTURE the basics of reading, but also seems to have influenced him in an even more fundamental way. VENTURE's whole attitude changed during this period from one of conflict with his oppressors to one of conciliation and negotiation.

In 1759, at the time VENTURE was in Hartford, the Edwards family was going through a religious revival. Their daughter Sarah and son in-law George Lord were admitted to the covenant in November of 1759.[15] Then on 12 Oct. 1760 Daniel Edwards had "Dick, Jethro, and Mima," Negro children he owned baptized, and "publicly engaged to bring up in the knowledge of the Christian religion."[16]

Drawn by J.W. Barber. Engraved by A.Willard.

VIEW OF HARTFORD FROM THE EASTERN BANK OF CONNECTICUT RIVER.

Lithograph of Hartford by J. W. Barber

In the *Narrative*, VENTURE added the term "Esq." to Edwards' name as an expression of respect. Edwards, in turn, clearly respected and trusted VENTURE. This was shown when he challenged the slave to return to Stonington and build a family and a future. Having been a tutor at Yale, who studied and practised the ministry before turning to law at age 33, Edwards certainly would have done everything he could to expand VENTURE's mind and teach him to read. After being together for "*some time*," Edwards asked VENTURE "*why my master wished to part with such an honest negro*" and did not keep him for himself, referring to Hempstead Miner. "*I replied that I could not give him the reason, unless it was to convert me into cash, and speculate with me as with other commodities.*"

From Edwards' probate will, we know the house in the center of Hartford contained the finest furnishings, and it had a major library for the time, filled with books which VENTURE must have encountered daily. How many did he take down, look at, or read? Less than 20% of the entire population of the Connecticut Colony had access to a library like Daniel Edwards'. [17 - see inventory page C-8, pages 201-203]

VENTURE added that he hoped it was not "*on account of my ill conduct*" that Miner did not keep him. Edwards replied that he would happily become VENTURE's owner himself "*if it was not unreasonable and inconvenient for me to be parted from my wife and children.*"

This was one of the rare moments in the *Narrative* when VENTURE held a respectful and rational conversation with a member of the owning class (the first time since Robinson Mumford had complimented him some 20 years previously). But there was something else about this exchange: Here was a slave who had no compunction about saying no to a white man like Stanton or Hooker, but took pride in the way he could serve another.

One senses from their relationship that VENTURE was testing his ability to negotiate with this highly educated white man, by drawing upon his intrinsic business acumen and the need to trust the other party. He was likely encouraged by the exchange with Edwards, who was a leading citizen of the Colony and likely an important Freemason. VENTURE became convinced that he could successfully live and work

The Crucible Years

with these people once he was free and in charge of his life.

VENTURE was not an ideologue who chose to resist the enslaving class at all times and at all costs, but a pragmatist who believed a bond could be struck with all human beings. He lived by the Golden Rule — "Do unto others as you would have them do unto you".

To this he added one conviction that had been ingrained in him by the chaos of the past year: He would not serve at the pleasure of others forever. VENTURE was determined to become his own man. He also knew it would not be easy, for the process of achieving one's freedom was not yet common.

There were four ways that a slave could gain his freedom in 18th-century New England: by escaping, then disappearing into a large city like New York or a Native American village;[18] through manumission, that is, being released by the owner; by legislative act for "meritorious service"; or by "redeeming oneself," as buying one's own freedom was called.

As he had learned six years earlier, escape was out of the question for a man who valued his family. Manumission occasionally occurred, if one was fortunate enough to be bought by someone who became disenchanted with the institution of slavery or decided to release his slaves upon his death. Legislative action was almost unheard of. But freeing a slave by self-redemption was not as simple as it might seem.

Colonial authorities did not want to be burdened with the prospect of supporting freed slaves who were no longer regarded as productive, a social trend that was creating a welfare problem.[19] The Connecticut legislature had passed in 1711 a law that required former owners and their heirs to take financial responsibility for freed blacks if they became itinerant beggars or burdens on society.[20]

Other states had similar laws. Until 1782 Virginia, for example, would allow a slave to be manumitted only if the owner took "responsibility for support of the sick or crippled, all females under 18 and over 45, and all males under 21 and over 45."[21]

In 1723 the Rhode Island General Assembly passed a law that appeared to encourage manumission, but required the freed slave to pay one hundred pounds, in case he was unable to support himself. This financial burden made manumission extremely difficult to attain.

The consequences of this difficulty could be seen throughout the North. The ratio of slaves to free blacks rose sharply in the pre-Revolutionary years with the growth of industry, food production, and a professional class in search of servants. In the period leading up to the War of Independence, Connecticut had the highest number of slaves in New England. Its black population in 1774 was close to 8,000, and about 6,400 were still enslaved.[22]

Good as his word, VENTURE's Hartford patron furnished him with a horse so the slave could return to Stonington to visit his family. When he reached the Stanton farm, a good day's ride south, VENTURE reunited with Meg, whom he had probably not seen for more than a year. Before long, Thomas Stanton appeared. *"As my old master appeared much ruffled at my being there,"* VENTURE departed. It behooved him not to reopen old wounds while his family remained at the mercy of the Stantons.

More than ever now, VENTURE yearned to be near his family and wanted his status resolved. He turned his horse in the direction of Long Point in Stonington where merchant and trader Oliver Smith Jr.

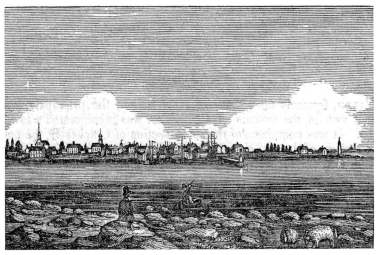

Stonington Long Point by J. W. Barber

Col. Oliver Smith Jr. House built in 1761, Stonington, Connecticut

was taking up residence.

VENTURE had learned that Hempstead Miner, who had still not settled with Stanton, had already given Smith a bill of sale for him. At VENTURE's behest, the two men met to determine which one would finally own him. VENTURE made no secret of his preference for Smith. It was finally agreed that Smith would settle accounts with Stanton and that VENTURE would move in with him. The year was 1760. *"This was the third time of my being sold, and I was then thirty-one years old."*

VENTURE's instincts were good. Miner had used him as a financial pawn – a commodity speculation – and was evidently desperate to liquidate. He eventually ended up in debtor's prison.[23]

Oliver Smith Jr. was a physically big man like VENTURE and wore his authority and means without arrogance. A Groton native and a coastal and West Indies trader, he had married Mary Denison, also from a good shoreline family, in April 1759. The following year, they made plans to build a grand home, shop, and boat works on the Stonington Long Point waterfront.[24] A strong, intelligent slave would clearly be an asset. First they built the house and then the business. They moved into their new home in the spring of 1761.[25]

Although he owned slaves, Smith was not imbued with a rigid sense of entitlement or racial superiority. Local records suggest that he probably had firsthand knowledge of the emerging practice of manumission and questioned the morality of slavery. Richard Smith, another resident of Groton in 1757, who may or may not have been related, had freed a slave girl inherited by his wife. A Quaker, Richard spoke eloquently at the annual South Kingston Quaker Meeting, words that have been preserved in the Rhode Island Quaker records, about the evils of slavery and why he felt morally compelled to free the girl on her 18th birthday, the earliest that law allowed manumission: "the Lord by his free Goodness hath given me a clear sight of the cruelty of making a slave of one that was by nature as free as my own children."[26] This is one of the earliest examples of inspired emancipation in New England, an act that most likely did not escape the attention of Oliver Smith.

These events do not suggest that VENTURE's owner was especially compelled by Christian dogma in his attitude toward slavery. If anything, he was more likely inspired by membership in the Freemasons, as was his mentor, George Washington. The Masonic Order followed a belief in a supreme being but primarily anchored itself to earthly concerns. Many Masons were leading businessmen and military officers in the community, and the Connecticut coast had become a center of the fraternal order in those days.

To succeed in Connecticut, people like Oliver Smith usually belonged to both the Freemasons and the Congregational Church. The Church was also the town Meeting House, where annual Town Meetings were held.

General Washington, a devout Christian, who usually attended the Episcopal Church, was also a senior mason. President Washington, presiding as "Acting Master" of the ceremony, wore a masonic apron when helping lay the cornerstone of the US Capital in 1793.

The average slave owner in the mid-18th century discouraged his slaves from converting to Christianity because it forced him to directly confront a moral problem: If a slave could be baptized, that meant he or she was truly a child of God and thus equal to any person in God's eyes. Enslaving a child of God was a sin against God. Church-going was not encouraged for practical reasons, as well. For slaves, Sunday was the one day that belonged to them. It was their chance not only to be with family but also to work for themselves. Work on Sunday began before dawn and continued well into the night. VENTURE took full advantage of "his own day" during 26 years of enslavement, building the capital he would need to buy freedom for himself and his family. VENTURE's new owner had consented to letting him purchase his freedom some day.

I asked my master one time if he would consent to have me purchase my freedom. He replied that he would. I was was then very happy, knowing that I was at that time able to pay part of the purchase money, by means of the money which I some time since had buried. This I took out of the earth and tendered to my master. . . What was wanting in redeeming myself, my master agreed to wait on me for, until I could procure it for him.

The price was £85. To get a sense of the cost that VENTURE agreed to pay to redeem himself - using the average pay rate for a laborer in the mid-18th century, and comparing it with a laborer earning $10 or $15 per hour today, the redemption price would be equal to $85,000 to $95,000 and take at least four years to amass.[27]

This was a case of mutual benefit. To that end, VENTURE unearthed what was left of his savings and turned it over to Smith as a first installment, £30 16s.

VENTURE had endured the crucible of chattel bondage in obscurity for two decades. Whether he knew it or not, he was about to pursue a course that would make him a legend in his own lifetime.

A

NARRATIVE

OF THE

LIFE AND ADVENTURES

OF

VENTURE,

A NATIVE OF AFRICA:

But resident above sixty years in the United States of
America.

RELATED BY HIMSELF.

New-London:

PRINTED BY C. HOLT, AT THE BEE-OFFICE.

1798.

Top -
Hull History Center
23 August 2011

Middle -
Ted Murphy at the
opening in Hull, U

Bottom -
London Exhibition
16 November 2012
David Richardson,
Robert P. Forbes,
Chandler B. Saint

Top-
CT State Capitol 25 February 2013
Congressman Joe Courtney-CT- 02
Congresswoman Rosa L. DeLauro -CT-03
Chandler B. Saint
Senator Richard Blumenthal, CT
Congressman Jim Himes-CT-04
Congresswoman Elizabeth Esty- CT-05

Middle -
Congresswoman Esty and Peter Tillou

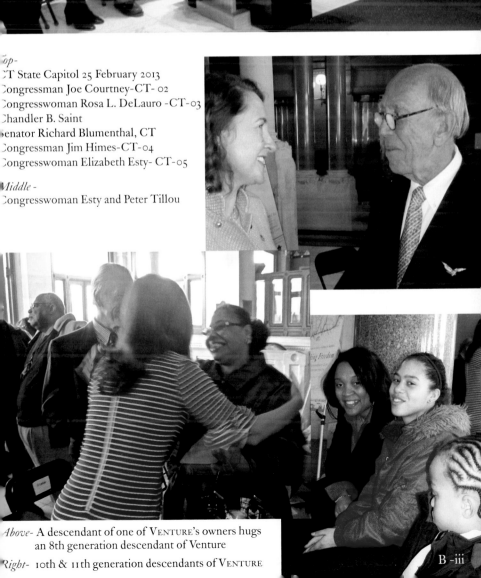

Above- A descendant of one of VENTURE's owners hugs an 8th generation descendant of Venture

Right- 10th & 11th generation descendants of VENTURE

B -iii

Senate

REMEMBERING VENTURE SMITH

MR. DODD. Madam President, today I wish to commemorate the life of Venture Smith, who passed away nearly 205 years ago on September 19, 1805. A Connecticut man who lived not far from where my home in East Haddam currently stands, Venture Smith's life is one of the best documented of the millions of Africans who were kidnapped from their homes and brought to the Americas as part of the transatlantic slave trade. A remarkable individual of uncommon strength and valor, Venture Smith's compelling story of perseverance in the face of seemingly insurmountable odds still serves as a potent source of inspiration and hope more than two centuries after it happened.

Originally born Broteer Furro in 1728—the first son of a West African king—Venture's childhood was cruelly interrupted at the tender age of ten, when he was captured by slave traders, forced to board a crowded slave ship destined for the New World, and sold to Robinson Mumford of Long Island for four barrels of rum and a piece of calico. After more than a decade in the Mumford household, Venture was sold twice more, finally ending up with Colonel Oliver Smith of Stonington, CT, in 1760.

In 1798, by that time an elderly man, Venture dictated his life story to Elisha Niles, a Connecticut schoolteacher, who had it published that same year in New London. One of perhaps only a dozen firsthand accounts of that period in our Nation's history by enslaved Africans, Venture Smith's narrative is a seminal work of early American literature that traces many of the defining moments of his life, beginning with his childhood in Africa.

And while many of the experiences related in Venture's autobiography would be heartbreakingly familiar to anyone who has studied this dark chapter in our Nation's history, Venture's life breaks the mold in one crucial respect. In spite of the tremendous challenges that he faced at nearly every turn Venture was able to win back his freedom through hard work, courage, and an unbreakable spirit.

By the time he was sold to his third and final owner, Colonel Smith, Venture had already spent the vast majority of his formative years in slavery. Having struck a deal with this new owner that would allow him to work for his freedom, Venture labored with incredible determination—fishing and growing food for sale, cutting and cording wood, and hiring himself out during seasonal hiatuses from his duties as Colonel Smith's slave—to acquire the 85 pounds and ten shillings needed to purchase his freedom. Such a sum was considered quite steep by the standards of 18th century colonial America, and even more so for an individual of Venture's means. But in spite of the tremendous hurdles that stood in his path, Venture successfully earned that money and bought his freedom in just over 5 years.

But Venture's story of hard work and dogged persistence in the face of unending challenges did not end there. During the four decades that followed, Venture fought tirelessly to free his wife Meg and three children, who were also enslaved in Connecticut, as well as to build a new life for himself as a free man. Harnessing those same unshakeable qualities of dedication, resourcefulness, and frugality that allowed him to secure his own freedom, Venture not only earned enough money to liberate his entire family from bondage, but also three men he barely even knew.

And if that wasn't remarkable enough, Venture Smith accomplished yet another feat that—in light of the serious financial and legal constraints that existed at the time—was exceedingly rare for a freed slave in colonial Connecticut: become a landowner. In 1775, just 1 year before the Thirteen American colonies declared independence from Great Britain, Venture purchased the first of what would become a nearly 130-acre farm on Haddam Neck, right at the mouth of the Salmon River. And it was there, in 1805, that Venture Smith ultimately died at the ripe old age of 77, having amassed a considerable fortune from his involvement in an array of commercial activities, from fishing and farming to the commodities trade.

Madam President, there are a significant number of historical lessons that can be gained from the life of this remarkable man—from firsthand insights into the evils perpetrated by the institution of slavery in this country, to a more complete understanding of the unique challenges faced by slaves who were able to gain their own freedom. But perhaps just as important are those lessons that transcend the period in which Venture Smith himself lived.

For, after losing almost everything—including that most fundamental of human rights, his freedom—Venture Smith set about tearing down the seemingly impenetrable barriers erected by slavery and racism that kept him from enjoying the same privileges as his White neighbors. And while his journey from slave to wealthy Connecticut landowner was long and arduous, filled with its share of disappointments and setbacks, Venture Smith never lost sight of his goals, ultimately achieving them through nothing more than grit, intelligence, and determination.

In this way, Venture Smith is much more than a mere historical figure. Rather, Venture's life is a testament to the sheer strength of the human spirit. It is a symbol of how a single individual can challenge societal norms and impact history. Perhaps most importantly, it is the embodiment of the principle that, even in the most dire and seemingly hopeless of circumstances, human beings are still capable of truly extraordinary achievements.

As we approach the 205th anniversary of his death, I would like to thank the Documenting Venture Smith Project for all of the wonderful work they have done over the past 5 years to help improve our understanding of this incredible individual. It is my hope that with continuing academic interest in Venture's life, new generations of Americans will be inspired by this timeless story of triumph in the face of adversity for years to come.

In Kingston upon Hull the Black History Partnership has sponsored youth sports programs inspired by VENTURE & Meg Smith.

Top left - Karen Okra and Laura Seddon hold *Meg Smith Football Challenge Cup* - girls under 12.

Center left - The *Venture Smith Trophy* - Rugby tournament - boys under 14

Top right -Dorothea DiCecco and Robert Forbes in front of William Wilberforce's home in Hull.

Bottom - Reception on 25 April 2015, celebrating the 250th of VENTURE's regained freedom at the Mayor's Chambers, City Hall, Kingston upon Hull, UK

May 3, 2015 Sign Dedication
Robert P. Forbes - Congressman Joseph Courtney, CT-1
Congresswoman Rosa L. DeLauro, CT-3
Susan P Whalen, DEEP - Chandler B. Saint

1760
I asked my master one time if
he would consent to have me
purchase my freedom.

SPRING 1765

paid an enormous sum
for my freedom

seventy-one pounds two shillings

Venture Smith

My freedom is a privilege which
nothing else can equal.

VENTURE SMITH'S Freedom Day

We celebrate the 250th anniversary of one of the great human triumphs over adversity
– Venture Smith's regaining his freedom after 26 years of slavery in April 1765 –

Between 1761 and 1765 Venture owned and farmed this land to help earn enough money
to redeem himself.

*"By cultivating this land with the greatest diligence and economy, . . .
in two years I laid up ten pounds."* Venture from his 1798 Narrative

Venture was the slave name for an African prince who was taken into bondage as a youth in the 18th century. He labored as a slave for years in New England before buying his own freedom, then that of his two sons, his wife, and daughter. Adopting the surname Smith, he went on to become a prominent businessman in Connecticut.

Born Broteer Furro, he was seized in the Kingdom of Ouangara in West Africa after his father died defending his people's freedom against an invading army. In 1739, when about 11 years old, he was sold to an officer on the Rhode Island slave ship, Charming Susanna, for "four gallons of rum and a piece of calico." He remained a slave under British colonial rule until 1765 when, through dint of extraordinary intelligence, strength, and perseverance, he earned his freedom and the respect of his community.

By the time Venture Smith died on September 19, 1805, at age 76, he had become a fully vested and respected American. It was an earned status, not a conferred one. Venture succeeded in a world in which he was not meant to succeed. How he accomplished that, is what makes his story so exceptional. He left behind an autobiographical narrative that put a rare human face on the ordeal of some 12.5 million Africans who were forcibly taken from their homeland to the Americas, of whom around 500,000 landed in what would become the United States.

State of Connecticut

By His Excellency Dannel P. Malloy, Governor: an

Official Statement

*W*HEREAS, Venture Smith was born Broteer Furro in the Kingdom of Ouangara in West Africa, and was seized from his home in 1739 and subsequently sold to an officer on the Rhode Island slave ship, the *Charming Susanna*; and

*W*HEREAS, Venture Smith labored as a slave in New England for twenty-six years before saving up enough money to buy his own freedom and that of his family; and

*W*HEREAS, Venture Smith went on to become a successful businessman in the State of Connecticut; and

*W*HEREAS, Venture Smith succeeded in a world in which he was not meant to succeed, overcoming the bondage of slavery to build a life of freedom and prosperity for his family; and

*W*HEREAS, On April 10, 2015, we celebrate the 250th anniversary of Venture Smith buying his freedom; now

*T*HEREFORE, I, Dannel P. Malloy, Governor of the State of Connecticut, do hereby proclaim April 10, 2015 as

VENTURE SMITH'S FREEDOM DAY
in the State of Connecticut.

_____
GOVERNOR

Venture Smith's tombstone, East Haddam, Connecticut

"Freedom's a matter of making history,
of venturing forth toward a time when freedom is free."

– MARILYN NELSON, *The Freedom Business*, 2005

THE TRANSITIONAL YEARS

VENTURE was determined to buy himself and regain the freedom he lost in Africa.

The 1760s were a time of growing political unrest in the American colonies. The French and Indian wars, which were really a struggle between European powers for expanded territory, finally ended after 13 years in 1763. Although Britain would acquire Canada from the French and most of the North American colonies east of the Mississippi, the wars had taken a heavy toll on the British treasury, as well as blood. The colonies were starting to bear the financial brunt and they did not like it.

Taxes would become a major source of anger, but the British were also levying taxes on West Indian sugar and molasses.[1] Northern ship captains and merchants resisted, declaring those products essential for the slave trade, a "vital commerce" for New England.[2] Many were already scofflaws. One study showed that Rhode Island ship captains had paid less than 40 percent of the duties they owed the Crown.

VENTURE had his own money problems. Through the calumny of others, he lost a small fortune, more than a quarter of the amount he needed to buy his freedom. He had turned over his savings, from working odd jobs for 14 years while on Fishers Island, to his second owner's brother, who stole it. He would have to start over and work hard for a year to replace this money to redeem himself.

When a slave and owner agreed on a course of "redemption," it was necessary to enlist a middleman to administer the arrangement.

Usually this was a professional person, like a judge, justice of the peace, or elected official. This person would hold the contract and the money that the slave paid toward his freedom. The agent kept the interest earned on the money as compensation. Only a free man could own property and therefore make a legal and binding contract. As VENTURE explained, "*I was the property of my master, and therefore could not safely take his obligation myself.*" Property cannot own property. VENTURE turned to a friend, whom he only identified as a "*free negro man.*" This person was probably Primas Sikes,[3] a longtime companion whose name crops up in several business transactions with VENTURE.[4] Although free, Sikes lived in the Thomas Stanton household at the time. As a go-between, his job would have been to take the owner's note of security and make the payments with money VENTURE gave him.

A view today of the foundation of VENTURE's farmhouse on Stonington-point, Connecticut.

To make those payments, VENTURE needed to earn money on the side. Oliver Smith had bought a slave and thus required his services. But when VENTURE was not needed in the Smith business, he worked on his own, primarily by fishing off Long Point and selling his catch in the Stonington market. He also sold vegetables he grew on his farm outside of town adjoining the Thomas Stanton property. It appears that around 1761, Oliver Smith's in-laws sold VENTURE this Stonington-point farm. VENTURE would have used a surrogate to hold the title, most likely his friend Primus Sikes.

"By cultivating this land with the greatest diligence and economy, at times when my master did not require my labor, in two years I laid up ten pounds." That was the equivalent of about half a year's full time labor. He turned over these precious proceeds, equal to about one-eighth of the agreed purchase price, to his friend to give to Smith.

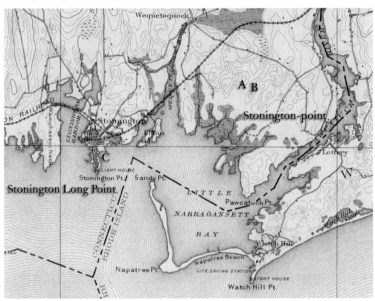

A. VENTURE's first farm   *B.* Thomas Stanton house (where Meg, Hannah, Solomon, and Cuff were slaves)   *C.* Oliver Smith's house and store.

Flush with success, VENTURE then prevailed on Smith to let him work for a full winter on his own to earn more money. Smith agreed on the condition that VENTURE turn over a quarter of his earnings. In effect, VENTURE would pay for the *"privilege"* of working for himself.

New England slave owners regarded this as perfectly logical and fair. After all, a slave, by definition, was meant to serve at the pleasure and profit of his master. For Smith it was good business to contract out VENTURE in the winter when he did not need his labor. What VENTURE's owner may have not known was that such an arrangement had its roots in Africa, specifically from the slave society in that part of Africa VENTURE came from. The process was called *murgu*, payment by slaves to their masters for the right to work on their own account.[5]

Smith, who counted George Washington among his friends and would later earn colonel's rank in the Continental Army, had built with VENTURE's help a small empire that included merchant ships, a store, and a new home. He could afford now to give his trusted slave, who was 10 years his senior, more latitude.

While helping Oliver build his business, both the actual buildings and the trading, VENTURE would have learned how to run a New England Coastal trading operation, but most important, he was forming relationships with the leaders of southeastern CT and the nearby ports. For the next 35 years, VENTURE would work with these people after regaining his freedom; and some, like Elijah and Capt. Amos Palmer, and Acors Sheffield, would sign the certificate in his *Narrative*.

From his first winter of chopping wood and fishing on the islands, VENTURE earned four pounds 16 shillings; 25 percent went to his owner in *"privilege"* and the remainder went toward paying off his purchase price.

And so it went, season-by-season, pound by pound, shilling by shilling.

VENTURE hired himself out to other men, once on Fishers Island and once for an autumn and winter on Long Island. During that later six-month period, he *"cut and corded four hundred cords of wood, besides threshing out seventy-five bushels of grain,"* (in Connecticut today 400 cords of wood cost $80,000.)

It was a lean and Spartan existence. He allowed himself only one pair of new shoes, and the rest of his wages he tucked away. *"At night I lay on the hearth, with one coverlet over and another under me,"* he said.

In the early spring of 1765, when VENTURE returned to Stonington he still owed Smith £33 18s. on his debt. Smith, clearly awed by the man's determination, asked for £20 more and he would call it even. *"My master liberated me, saying I might pay what was behind if I could ever make it convenient, other wise it would be well."*

It might also be that Oliver Smith was happy to consider the money paid as privilege, as principal. When combining the principal and privilege, VENTURE had paid £85 12s in total, 12s more than the original contract price of £85. ^{See the payments chart on page 213.}

VENTURE had turned over £71 2s in principal and £14 pounds 10s *in privilege* to his owner from 1760 to March or April 1765. That was an enormous sum in those days, enough to buy hundreds of acres of land. When VENTURE had asked Smith why he required such an *"unreasonable price,"* his owner said it was for future security in case VENTURE should become unable to work in his old age and should need to be supported. As mentioned previously, this was the law of the land to protect the local towns from having to support abandoned or infirm former slaves. In Connecticut it also included the heirs of the owner, but often a town would assume responsibility for a fee of £100. But, after five years with his slave, Smith must have realized that VENTURE was unlikely to ever become a burden. This realization probably influenced his decision to waive the final payment.

Despite his complaint about the price, the transaction bought something that VENTURE would later call *"a privilege which nothing else can equal"* – his regained freedom.

Now in his mid 30s, after 26 years enslaved, VENTURE breathed the air of liberty for the first time since he was a youth in Africa. He recalled the moment not as one of triumph, but as one of adversity surmounted:

I had already been sold three different times, made considerable money with seemingly nothing to derive it from, been cheated out of a large sum of money, lost much by misfortunes, and paid an enormous sum for my freedom.

For one who had dreamed so long and worked so hard for his independence, this would seem to be an occasion for great celebration. There is no evidence of it. There are several possibilities for why that was. For one thing, VENTURE was not really the celebrating type. He was a very serious man. For another, he had good reason for some bitterness. He might have become a free man much earlier if fate and circumstance had been kinder. Ironically, the same year that VENTURE gained his freedom, Robert Stanton lost his farm after defaulting on his mortgage.

Not least of all, the reasons for somberness was the environment VENTURE was entering as a free man. At this time, Connecticut, and specifically New London County, had the largest concentration of slaves in New England and one of the largest populations of free blacks.

Discrimination against them was rampant. Nearby New London, for example, had a law on its books that forbade free blacks from living in the town, owning land, or going into business without the consent of town government.[6]

Technically free he may have been, but VENTURE knew that there were lesser degrees of freedom for a black man, even one of royal lineage.

The irony of the political struggle underway in the American colonies could not have escaped him. Whites were chafing at the bit of tyranny in 1765, but they treated it as an affront to them alone.

When he purchased himself, Venture became a fully vested British citizen, a subject of the Crown – not "owned" by the King but subject to him.

The Sugar act of 1664 threatened the Rhode Island and Eastern Connecticut economy by taxing the import of sugar from non-British colonies – but worse, it called for vastly increased custom agents and enforcement.

In March of 1765, the British Parliament passed the Stamp Act, which imposed a tax on all newspapers, legal documents, playing cards, dice, almanacs, and pamphlets in the colonies – all precious commodities. The public was outraged, accusing Britain of imposing taxation without representation. It was designed to pay for the British troops stationed in its vast empire.

When Patrick Henry was accused of treason for opposing the tax, he replied: "If this be treason, make the most of it." Such boldness elevated him to the highest rank of patriotism. If a black had uttered such words, the reward would have been 40 lashes or worse.

If a black man were to make it in such a world, it would have to be on the white man's terms. VENTURE would succeed in this world. He would play the game better than those that made the rules and had owned him.

First, he would have to attend to certain practicalities. As a free man who would be entering into contractual agreements, VENTURE would need a full, legal name. He took the surname of SMITH, his last owner.

By taking a surname, VENTURE reclaimed his birthright as free and independent. Slavers had stripped him of his identity as Broteer Furro, the son of the king Saungm Furro. Slaves bore the names their masters gave them. Most had one name, while most free men had two. Adopting the surname SMITH, VENTURE forged a new identity: one that made his given name his own and recognized his connection to Oliver's family.[7]

The decision seemed in keeping with VENTURE's character and sense of priorities. He was a practical man, and Smith was not only a practical name, but a highly influential one in the region. Oliver Smith was related by blood or marriage to the elite business class of Stonington and Groton. Unlike a later generation caught up in revolutionary fervor, VENTURE was uninterested in reinventing his identity or making any political statement. Slaves who earned their freedom fighting in the Continental Army after 1775 often took names that obliterated both their slave and African pasts.[8]

VENTURE was building on his past, not erasing it.

Dubious distinction though it may have been, VENTURE was owned by the right people. The Mumfords, Stantons, Miners, Edwards, and Smiths constituted some of the leading families in southern New England. For example, a Mumford served as no less than Benjamin Franklin's personal secretary in Paris, circa 1783–1785. Stantons are listed on the monument to the Battle of Groton Heights, the 135-foot-tall obelisk that is the first Revolutionary War monument of its kind in the country erected to fallen patriots. The list goes on.

Memorial to the 1781 battle of Groton Heights. Drawing by J. W. Barber

Perhaps most importantly, the name Smith belonged to VENTURE's only owner who kept his word. Over the past five years, VENTURE and Oliver had developed unusual trust between one another. These men could do business together, and VENTURE needed an "extended family" if he were to succeed in southern New England. The New England farm, or sea trading business, required access to other family members for the harvest, constructing buildings, and looking after financial affairs. The best deals in buying and selling, from land to commodities, were between family members and fellow masons. VENTURE had no family connections of his own but the trust he had built with the Smiths would allow him to be an extended part of their family, and through them, Oliver's business associates. The Smith/Denisons had already sold him the small farm in the early 1760s and arranged for VENTURE's redemption on workable terms.

Thus, taking the family name of SMITH was not only a sign of respect and gratitude, it was a shrewd business move.

Then there was the question of where to best earn a living. He wanted to be near his wife and three children, who were still in bondage to the Stantons. VENTURE had learned 5 years earlier that Thomas Stanton did not like seeing him at his farm, and now that VENTURE was a freeman, it would be even worse. Stanton was likely to take out his hatred of VENTURE on Meg and the children. A slave owner could make life a living hell for his slaves without violating the law.

As my old master appeared much ruffled at my being there, I left my wife before I had spent any considerable time with her,

Until he could free his family, VENTURE would need to stay away from the Stanton farm.

Now he needed to earn a great deal of money to buy their freedom, far more money than he earned to buy his own. But work opportunities were limited in southeastern Connecticut, where most of the forestland had long ago been cleared and where an inordinately large population of blacks and Indians, both free and slave, were already toiling.

Now free from slavery, VENTURE was taking control of his life. He finally was in charge of where he lived and worked. As he did in 1760, he looked to the offshore islands and Eastern Long Island for opportunities.

Fate helped make the decision for him. A fire broke out at his house farm on Stonington-point. Evidently an accident, it burned up a chest containing his clothes and 38 pounds in paper currency. VENTURE sold what remaining possessions he had and he moved to less-populated Long Island where landowners were in need of good workers.

VENTURE would be separated from Meg and the children, but

hopefully without him around, Stanton would treat the family better.

More than 10 percent of the population of eastern Long Island was now black, and a large community of freed slaves had settled on Shelter Island in the fork of the larger land mass.[9] If VENTURE had joined up with them at any point, it is not mentioned in the *Narrative*, but given his strong independent streak, it is not likely he would have stayed for long.

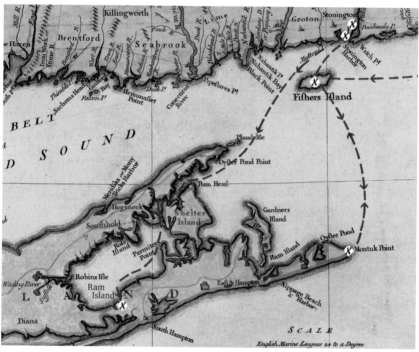

Map detail of eastern Long Island showing Ram Island, Southampton, and Montauk Point

No, this time he headed south, a place where his failed escape a decade before was seared in his memory. But now he was a free man, and he was attracted to an area peopled by Native Americans who conducted their transactions on word of honor, not on paper. In Southampton the Shinnecocks still had 4,000 acres of land.[10]

VENTURE says he spent time on Ram Island, but does not say which one - there are four off Eastern Long Island. The *Project* historians now believe it was the Southampton Ram Island. VENTURE says he *"acquired"* a farm on Long Island in the early 1770s, but no deed can be found for one anywhere on eastern Long Island. However, a deal between VENTURE and the Shinnecocks would not be a sale recorded by a deed; it would be an agreement between honorable people. He *"disposed"* of the farm in 1774 (again no recorded document). *"Acquired"* and *"disposed"* are not the same as "bought" and "sold," and VENTURE understood the words of commerce.

Looking across Bullhead Bay to Ram Island

VENTURE describes his time working on Ram Island.

> *Various other methods I pursued in order to enable me to re-deem my family. In the night time I fished with set-nets and pots for eels and lobsters, ...*

These are all activities that Bullhead Bay, which surrounds Ram Island, would be perfect for. The location was a short boat ride up to North Sea and Sagg Harbors where he would have traded with the sailors and the shippers to the Atlantic world. The island, approximately 32 acres, depending on the tides, even has a small pond with fresh water for his crops.

Ram Island, reachable only by boat, was ideal for VENTURE, who realized early on that he could best operate in an environment that was isolated enough for privacy, yet close enough for access to his markets.

He was an intrinsic loner, most confident in his own abilities to earn a living and express his independence. We see this same proclivity throughout his life in freedom. In rural New England, the "locals" know what everyone else is up to, but VENTURE chose to live where he would not be bothered. It is important to note here that the toll of slavery at that time usually meant that a black man reached the end of his most productive life by his mid-30s, the age at which VENTURE was just setting out on his own.

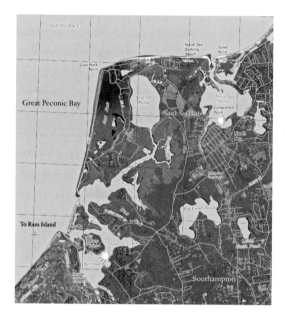

Ram Island
Great Peconic Bay
North Sea Harbor
and Village of
Southampton

Certainly his enormous size and stamina were central to his destiny. In the mid-1700s, the average man was about five feet six inches tall.[11] One who stood a head taller and carried a nine-pound ax like it was a fly swatter had no trouble finding work.

VENTURE spent his first four years on Long Island doing different kinds of work. This most notably included cutting *"several thousand"* cords of wood, which earned him the considerable sum of *"207 pounds 10 shillings"*. According to economic historians, this sum was equal at the time to 14–17 years of wages for an average unskilled laborer.

He was getting rich – very rich for a former slave.

Even the casual reader of SMITH's *Narrative* might wonder how someone could recall with such precision, some three decades after the fact, how much his labors earned and how much he paid out through his lifetime. The short explanation for this is that money was the way VENTURE kept score. People all assume he had a system foreign to America – like an abacus, knots on rope, or using xs and ys. A simple explanation could be, that VENTURE was one of those people who could do precise calculations in his head and accurately remember exact numbers.

Although he berated himself for not having the education that allowed him to manage money well, he had a good head for figures. Perhaps it was inherited.

On the whole question of VENTURE's self-deprecating comment that he could not properly calculate figures, the evidence suggests that he knew how to handle a complex contract, as well as to add and subtract. Given his proclivity for recalling in excruciating detail every transaction he ever made, his remark in the *Narrative* about people *"taking advantage of my ignorance of numbers"* smacks of disingenuousness – perhaps a practiced ruse to gain advantage in negotiations. Over 40 land deeds and contracts that he negotiated are on file in Connecticut town halls. As any businessman knows, understating one's abilities can be a useful strategy.

VENTURE came from a culture of commerce. Like his father, who gave up his life to not surrender his wealth, VENTURE placed ultimate importance on amassing assets. But, as events would later demonstrate, he was not a miser who worshipped money for its own sake. He would spend freely to get what he wanted. For himself, however, he had few wants. As he noted in his *Narrative*:

Perhaps some may enquire what maintained me all the time I was laying up money. I would inform them that I bought nothing which I did not absolutely want. All fine clothes I despised in comparison with my interest, and never kept but just what clothes were comfort

-able for common days, and perhaps I would have a garment or two which I did not have on at all times, but as for superfluous finery I never thought it to be compared with a decent homespun dress, a good supply of money and   prudence. Expensive gatherings of my mates I commonly shunned, and all kinds of luxuries I was perfectly a stranger to . . .

And, he hastened to add, *"I never was at the expence of six-pence worth of spirits."* By not imbibing alcohol, he set himself far apart from most of his contemporaries. Hard cider, beer, and liquor, especially rum, were not only plentiful and cheap but a great source of solace for both the oppressed and profligate (and a reliable source of potable liquid at a time when clean water was in short supply). In short, alcoholism was a major problem in 18th-century America, and a sober businessman had a decided edge over the competition.[12]

VENTURE's first big expense as a free man would be freeing his family. While working on Ram Island, and earning very good money, his family was still owned by the Stantons. It was time to redeem them.

VENTURE had earned and saved "*near three hundred pounds*," more than enough to free his whole family, even at what he expected to be an exorbitant price. In 1770 Stanton agreed to sell the boys to VENTURE for the equivalent of $200 each, a steep price for Solomon, who was productive, but an extremely high price for Cuff, who was 8 or 9 years old. The price was about double their value, but VENTURE paid it to redeem the boys from slavery. The total amounted to half of his savings. Probably out of revenge or just to spite VENTURE, Stanton refused to sell Meg and Hannah. There was nothing VENTURE could do but to try and make Meg's life a little better. A slave owner could not be forced to sell his slaves – they were his property. So in 1770 VENTURE turned to Oliver Smith's family for help in providing for Meg. They readily agreed and sold a 26-acre farm on Stonington-point to their former slave for 60 pounds.

VENTURE bought the farm as an investment but more importantly to provide Meg with a place to live and where he and the boys could visit her while he was working on Long Island. It may seem odd that the Stantons would permit their slaves to live elsewhere, but it saved the expense of feeding them and providing heat in winter.

Deed records indicate that on December 1, 1770,[13] after over five years as a free man, he purchased the 26-acre farm on Stonington-point, located next to his old nemesis, the Stantons.

This was his first real-estate transaction as a free man. It is believed that when he was a slave, in about 1761, he used his free friend Sikes to buy six acres of land on Stonington-point for him. This was the same plot that VENTURE farmed to help earn his freedom. This earlier land and farmhouse were a small part of the 26 acres be bought in 1770.

The decision to purchase his sons, who were then 14 and 9, was a practical one. The boys carried with them potentially higher earning power. Whether white or black, a man's sons were his security for the future, and if they did not work for the home business, they were hired out.

The father and Solomon worked together for more than two years cutting wood, fishing, and farming wherever the opportunities arose around Long Island Sound and off the Rhode Island coast.

With his remaining money, he then *"purchased a negro man"* who had asked VENTURE to take him, evidently so he could work for his own freedom some day. But instead, the slave ran away a short time later, leaving VENTURE 60 pounds in the lurch *"except twenty pounds which he paid me previous to his absconding."*

It was another broken trust. VENTURE had employed a customary African tradition to earn his own redemption and was clearly willing to give that opportunity to others of his race. But in the new world, his faith seemed destined to be betrayed.

A TABLE of the Value and Weight of COINS, as they now pass in England, Pennsylvania, and New-York.		Sterling. £ s. d.	Philad. £ s. d.	N. York £ s. d.	Weight. dwt. gr.	Most Sorts of Spanish Silver are sold in London by the Ounce, and often varies, but seldom or ever exceeds 5s. 5d. In Pennsylvania it sells for 8s. 6d. per Ounce.
	Engl. Guineas at	1 1 0	1 14 0	1 16 0	5 6	
	French Guineas	1 1 0	1 13 6	1 15 0	5 5	
	Moidores - - -	1 7 0	2 3 6	2 6 0	6 18	
	Johannes's - - -	3 12 0	6 0 0	6 6 0	18 8	
	Half Johannes's -	1 16 0	3 0 0	3 3 0	9 4	
	French milled Pistoles	16 6	1 6 6	1 8 0	4 4	
	Spanish Pistoles	0 16 6	1 7 0	1 9 0	4 6	
	Doubloons	3 6 0	5 8 0	5 16 0	17 0	
	English Crowns	0 5 0	0 7 6	0 8 0	19 0	
	French Silver Crowns	5 0	0 7 6	0 8 0	17 6	
	* Spanish Pieces of 8		0 7 6	0 8 0	17 6	
	English Six-pence	0 0 6	0 0 9	0 0 9		

In Boston and Connecticut Pieces of Eight pass for 6s. and Gold by Weight.

Currency table in 1771

If the reader is confused by the constantly changing currencies mentioned in the *Narrative*, one might take solace in the fact that residents of the colonies at this time were almost equally confused. Everything from Spanish coins to English shillings and three kinds of paper currency were used in transactions, and some people carried around a conversion table to get it all straight. The basic currency of Connecticut in the 18th century was the British pound, but it was worth less than the pound sterling. At this particular time, a pound was worth about 2.66 in colonial dollars.[14]

As a new decade opened, the spark of war had been lit with the Boston Massacre on March 5, 1770. Did VENTURE hear about Crispus Attucks, the sailor and fugitive slave of African and Indian descent who became the first man to die for American freedom? Like VENTURE, Attucks was a giant of a man, six feet two inches tall. They chose different paths. VENTURE insulated himself within a world he was trying to shape for himself and his family. But he could not wholly escape.

Death of Crispus Attucks at the Boston Massacre, 5 March 1770
chromolitho by James Wells Champney

In 1772 VENTURE hired out his eldest son, Solomon, to Massachusetts merchant Charles Church *"for one year, on consideration of his giving him* (Solomon) *twelve pounds and an opportunity of acquiring some learning."*

Church, it turned out, had contracted to hire hands for a whaling voyage, and persuaded Solomon, who was then 16, to join up. In addition to his wages, Church promised Solomon *"a pair of silver buckles,"* an enticement that would be equivalent today to a $300 pair of custom Nike sneakers.[15]

When VENTURE heard about it, he rushed to the dock to try to prevent his son from leaving. The father knew the dangers one could encounter on such deep-sea voyages — having himself sailed for seven months on such a precarious mission – especially for an inexperienced youth. The lure of silver shoe buckles must have particularly rankled a man who had no tolerance for frivolities.

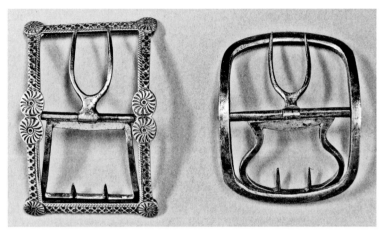

18th-century shoe buckles: at left, a fancy engraved silver dress buckle circa 1760–1770 and at right, a common steel buckle

His eldest son, VENTURE had said, was *"all my hope and dependence for help."* But he got there too late, with the vessel almost out of sight on the horizon. VENTURE's premonition proved true. Solomon died of scurvy on the voyage.

When recalling this tragedy, VENTURE said Church never paid him his son's wages. He also did not get the boy's share of the whale oil or the buckles. He added: *"In my son, besides the loss of his life, I lost equal to seventy-five pounds."* VENTURE would remember how many hours of hard work it had taken to raise the £75, and how he had to pay Stanton double the normal price for Solomon. Now Church had lied to him - behavior that VENTURE could not stand. Church was a Tory and fled at the beginning of the war leaving unpaid debts.

He was talking about what it had cost him to free Solomon three years earlier. While readers might find this a callous and unsentimental appraisal, VENTURE was expressing himself in the terms by which he measured success and failure, triumph and tragedy. One could look

The Transitional Years

more to action than to words when searching for clues to VENTURE SMITH's humanity.

Now about 43 and flush from new profits made delivering wood by boat to the mainland, VENTURE negotiated with former owner Thomas Stanton for the purchase of his wife, Meg. He had been free for 7 years, and the failure to buy his wife's freedom was his greatest frustration. She was now seven months pregnant, so for Stanton it was better to forget revenge and take VENTURE's money. The risks of death in childbirth outweighed his determination to spite VENTURE. Meg cost VENTURE 40 pounds. If he waited until the child was born, he would have had to buy two people. But Stanton still would not sell Hannah, VENTURE's first child.

Their third son was born in 1773, and they named him Solomon Jr. after the deceased first son.[16]

VENTURE also bought two more male slaves and let them both go. Finally, he purchased freedom for Hannah, who was then 21.

The year was now 1774, and the American colonies were embarking on a protracted war for independence. VENTURE's *Narrative* amazingly makes no mention of this. He had just completed a remarkable quest for liberty on his own, and he summarized it succinctly:

I had already redeemed from slavery, myself, my wife and three children, besides three negro men.

He had achieved political independence for his family, and now, on the eve of revolution around him, he embarked on the road of not only financial independence but considerable prosperity.

It was now time to restore his rightful place in society. VENTURE was determined to re-establish his family's position that his father had lost in a war in Africa. He was aligned with the patriot leaders of Connecticut through Oliver Smith and had been doing business with them from Long Island. Now with the winds of war looming, he looked to join them in Connecticut.

VENTURE did not run from war rather he carefully chose the side and the cause he wanted to be part of. VENTURE deliberately decided to join the Patriots' cause and be with them in Connecticut. A third of the people on eastern Long Island made the same choice, many were rejoining family members. Eastern Long Island used to be part of Connecticut, and many Long Islanders still had family ties to the mainland.

We do not know if the following Colonial Act influenced VENTURE's decision to relocate to East Haddam, but it would seem likely he would have thought highly of Connecticut's lead in acting against slavery.

On 13ᵗʰ October 1774, Connecticut ended all forms of the slave trade, including the very Atlantic slave trade from Africa that brought VENTURE to its shores thirty-five year earlier. It would be another thirty-four years before the Government would outlaw the Atlantic Slave Trade to the United States.

General Assembly of the Governor and Company of the English Colony of Connecticut in New England in America,
holden at New Haven 13 October 1774

An Act for prohibiting the Importation of Indian, Negro or Molatto Slaves.

Be it enacted by the Governor, Council and Representatives, in General Court assembled, and by the authority of the same, That no indian, negro or molatto slave shall at any time hereafter be brought or imported into this Colony, by sea or land, from any place or places whatsoever, to be disposed of, left or sold within this Colony.[17]

CERTIFICATE.

STONINGTON, *November* 3d, 1798.

THESE may certify, that VENTURE, is a free negro man, aged about 69 years, and was, as we have ever understood, a native of Africa, and formerly a slave to Mr James Mumford, of Fisher's-Island, in the State of New York ; who sold him to Mr Thomas Stanton 2d, of Stonington, in the State of Connecticut, and said Stanton sold said VENTURE to Col. Oliver Smith, of the aforesaid place. That said VENTURE hath sustained the character of a faithful servant, and that of a temperate, honest and industrious man, and being ever intent on obtaining his freedom, he was indulged by his masters after the ordinary labor on the days of his servitude, to improve the nights in fishing and other employments to his own emolument, in which time he procured so much money as to purchase his freedom from his late master Col. Smith ; after which he took upon himself the name of VENTURE SMITH, and has since his freedom purchased a negro woman, called Meg, to whom he was previously married, and also his children who were slaves, and said VENTURE has since removed himself and family to the town of East Haddam, in this State, where he hath purchased lands on which he hath built a house, and there taken up his abode.

NATHANIEL MINOR, Esq.
ELIJAH PAMMER, Esq.
CAPT. AMOS PALMER,
ACORS SHEFFIELD,
EDWARD SMITH.

"He broke out of the system that enslaved him and triumphed over it."

— David Richardson, Wilberforce Institute, September 2005

✢-◄-◄-◄▣◈▣►-►-►-✢

The Final Years

An interesting area of speculation is whether Venture ever met George Washington. It would initially seem unlikely because such an encounter was not mentioned in the *Narrative*, but neither was the entire Revolutionary War.

It is known that the commander of the Continental Army visited Oliver Smith in Stonington in April 1776 (the same year Smith named his tenth child George). Although Venture had already been a free man for a decade, he maintained close ties with the Smith family, and with the onset of war, moved back to Connecticut in December 1774.

What makes the prospect of these two slave owners and a free black man standing in the same room together so enticing is their physical similarities. They all towered over their contemporaries. Gen. Washington was six feet two inches tall. Col. Smith was over six feet. Venture was six feet one and half inches.[1]

It is noteworthy that most of the stories of Venture's physical prowess came from his later years. The reason is simple: Almost all the testimony to his feats came from witnesses who knew him during that later period in his life in the Connecticut interior. An 80-year-old man from the town of Moodus told a newspaper in 1894 that his father clearly remembered Venture being challenged while in his fifties by a noted wrestler in the area who "found he might as well try to remove a tree." Others talked of his ability to split seven cords of wood in a day.[2]

One can only imagine what the tales might have been like from those who knew Venture in his prime.

But in the areas where he left his greatest marks, there is little mention. Business, he was good at it. Literature, he wrote a master-piece.

Barely a decade out of enslavement, Venture Smith had already made a small fortune by growing and selling huge quantities of water-melons, net fishing, and lobstering at night, and, for one seven-month stint on a whaler arranged by Smith in 1770, sharing in the profits from 400 barrels of oil. That was an enormous haul for a whaling voyage, and taking his share and some savings, Venture was able to purchase the 26-acre farm on Stonington-point from Oliver's family; he bought it for 60 pounds, and three years later sold it for 100 pounds.

Sloop *Providence*, 50 tons, rebuilt in 1976. Sloops were used in the triangular trade, whaling, and as privateers in the Revolution

This was to become a pattern in his business success. Venture would take cash for his labor and, when possible, invest it in real estate that he would later sell at a significantly higher price. He said of this period of his life, *"my temporal affairs were in a pretty prosperous condition."* By 1774 he had already bought and sold a house and land in Stonington twice, had acquired a farm on the eastern end of Long Island, and had considerable cash savings.

This and my industry was what alone saved me from being expelled that part of the island in which I resided, as an act was passed by the select-men of the place, that all negroes residing there should be expelled.

This briefly mentioned incident not only shows that Venture

stood out among other men of his race but also alludes to a period of great turmoil as the northern colonies mobilized for war.

Sentiment for ending the institution of slavery was growing in the North, as the owner class throughout the colonies slaked its own thirst for political independence. John Jay of New York, who would later become the first chief justice of the U.S. Supreme Court, wrote: "It is much to be wished that slavery may be abolished . . . To contend for our own liberty, and to deny that blessing to others, involves an inconsistency not to be excused." Many northern blacks were liberated and the newly freed became refugees. They set up camps outside settled townships, prompting expulsion edicts like the one VENTURE confronted on Long Island.

At the same time, there was a backlash among some slaveholders who tried desperately to protect their property by resurrecting moribund "slave codes" that greatly restricted those still in bondage.[3] Some owners handed over their slaves for safekeeping to friends in distant places in hopes of retrieving them when the conflict was over.[4]

On the eve of the Revolutionary War, the black population in North America numbered 567,000;[5] almost 90 percent were slaves on the plantations of the South. Although much smaller in numbers, blacks had become very much part of the northern fabric. It was against this backdrop that VENTURE set a new course for himself and his family.

But there was something else happening at about the time VENTURE decided to relocate. It was called the War of Independence, and it was spreading south. British forces had their eyes on the abundant livestock throughout the Long Island basin.

VENTURE remembered his history, and his father's death – *"The shocking scene is to this day fresh in my mind"*. VENTURE was determined that history would not repeat itself resulting in him and his family being wiped out by a war. He realized from experience that one could not wait until the actual army invaded to escape.

He saw the signs – March 5, 1770, the Boston Massacre – June 9,

1772, the burning of the British customs schooner Gaspee by Providence Patriots – August 26, 1772, King George's proclamation ordering the capture of the perpetrators – December 16, 1773, the Boston Tea party.

Then in the spring of 1774, British Vice-Admiral Samuel Graves was sent to help control Boston and blockade the harbor. Connecticut called for the First Continental Congress to meet in Philadelphia from September 5 to October 26, 1774, to address "the intolerable act" passed by Parliament to punish Boston for its "tea party".

For VENTURE, it was obvious that the colonies could not effectively continue to do business under the new British Trade restrictions and also be taxed to pay for the expanded British Empire. Shedding themselves of British rule would have to come at some point and would only be achieved by a war.

Although he was too old to join the Continental Army, he could support the cause. Further, he was a master trader and it was clear that this region would be a major supply center for the revolution and thus a good place to do business.

For VENTURE it was obvious that the British Army, in need of food, would soon be coming to Long Island – time to leave.

Gen. Washington was also well aware of the situation, and within four months after war ignited at Lexington and Concord, he issued a warning that the British were likely to raid the offshore islands "to plunder them and bring off what Cattle they may find." In a July 27, 1775, letter from Boston to the Continental Congress, he reported a

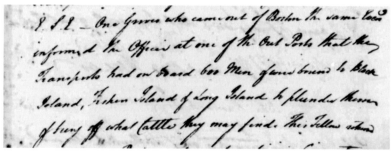

Detail of George Washington's letter to the Continental Congress in July 1775

"great Scarecity of fresh Provisions in the Enemy's Camp."

He was right, but not soon enough. The British had already dispatched six ships from Boston that landed on Fishers Island on August 6, 1775, and plundered the livestock. Records show that they took "1,139 sheep, 3 milch Cows, one pair of Working Oxen, about

NEW - LONDON, Auguſt 11.
Laſt Lord's-Day Morning about 6 o'Clock, we diſcovered nine Ships, one Snow, one Brig, one Schooner, and two Sloops beating up this Harbour, with the Wind at N. E. which greatly alarmed the Inhabitants of this Town, and they immediately ſent off an Expreſs to alarm the neighbouring Towns, that they might get themſelves in Readineſs to march wherever they might be wanted ;— but in a few Hours it was diſcovered that they were bound to Fiſher's Iſland, to take off the Stock, which they effected by the next Morning :—It conſiſted of 1139 Sheep, three milch Cows, one pair of Working Oxen, about 25 young Cattle, and ten Hogs. (All the Beef that was fit for Market were taken off the Day before.) As ſoon as they came to Anchor, an Expreſs was ſent off to thoſe Towns that had before been notified, to let them know the ſituation of the Fleet, and to recommend their being in Readineſs.

Article in the
New London Journal
about British supply raid
August 11, 1775

25 young Cattle, and ten Hogs,"[6] which they brought back through the blockade to the starving Tories and troops.

The patriots also played the game. After the Battle of Bunker Hill, in 1775 Thomas Mumford, a nephew of George Mumford, and New London merchant Nathaniel Shaw loaded up a ship with cattle and sailed it to the West Indies, where they traded the beef for badly needed gunpowder for the army.[7]

After numerous British raids for supplies in the Long Island basin, Gen. Washington repeated his call for preventive action nearly a year later. In a letter to Gov. Jonathan Trumbull Sr. of Connecticut on July 9, 1776, he urged that the "great Quantities" of livestock and provisions on Fishers, Block, Plumb, Elizabeth islands, and on Martha's Vineyard "be removed quite out of the reach of the Enemy."[8]

The residents, however, remained slow to respond. The British launched aggressive forays, clashed with American militias, and finally captured the whole of Long Island and Manhattan in August 1776 and held them until the end of the war.

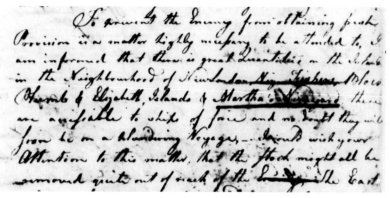

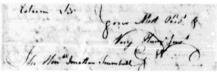

Detail of signed letter
from George Washington to
Gov. Trumbull of Connecticut
July 1776

The British attached such importance to this area as a continuing source of provisions for the West Indian colonies, as well as for their troops, that the English Parliament passed a special law exonerating all Caribbean governors of treason for trading with the New England plantations.

As for VENTURE SMITH, now in his late forties, he had his entire family together, purchased by his own hand. After ten years of non-stop itinerant work, it was time for stability.

VENTURE may have not mentioned the war directly in his *Narrative*, but the conflict impacted his life and family, as it did nearly every one else's. In fact, he took advance steps to deal with it. He and his family joined the mass evacuation of Long Island a good year before it became occupied by the British. Some slaves and free blacks linked up with the Tory exodus to New Brunswick and Nova Scotia. Some stayed in their homes and awaited the arrival of the British. VENTURE chose the route of the Patriots across the sound to Connecticut.[9]

But, always the consummate businessman, he managed to "*dispose*" of his property before the British seized it, and, with family in tow, arrived in a part of the world with which he had already become quite familiar.

East Haddam on the Connecticut River, drawing by J. W. Barber

When he got to Connecticut, VENTURE chose to settle in the lightly populated, but commercially active communities of East Haddam and Haddam on the Connecticut River.

Haddam, East Haddam, and Haddam Neck were at the center of the patriot cause. Generals Henry and Epaphroditus Champion would run the supply operation for the Continental Army. On Haddam Neck, at least three ships were built and sailed from there as war ships or privateers. Also, six long boats were launched to attack the British at Point Judith. It is likely that VENTURE, who had sailed the waters around Point Judith for years, would have provided strategic information

This may have seemed an odd settlement choice for a man whose experience in Connecticut had been exclusively along the southeastern coast. East Haddam was 18 miles upriver and a day's ride from the New London and Stonington areas. But VENTURE always kept his eyes and ears open for new opportunities, and this part of the Connecticut River south of Hartford, where the wider and deeper waters

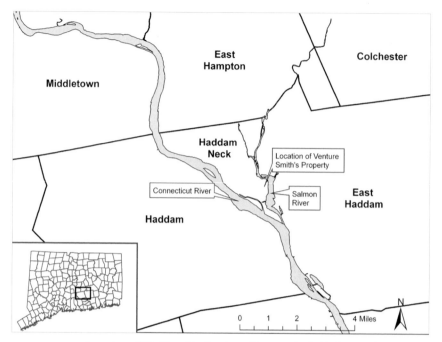

Location of Haddam Neck, where VENTURE built his farm and home

were tidal and ideal for boat traffic and trade, had already proved its mercantile worth.

An example of the kind of provisioning activity occurring in East Haddam at the time could be found in the cargo record of a ship bound for Grenada, a new British colony in the Caribbean, in 1764. The ship carried an entire prefabricated house of white oak, two outbuildings, horses, oxen, sheep, geese, ducks, hay, and several carpenters with enough foodstuffs for them while they erected the house on the West Indian island.[11]

For years, the area had been shipping livestock, mainly mules and some horses, to work the sugar plantations of the West Indies. Also in great demand, was firewood to stoke the fires that made the sugar, and white oak to make the barrels for shipping the sugar.

The Connecticut River area was known for the wood trade. In one year the Northern Dock in East Haddam shipped 3,000 cords of firewood.

He knew the key role this area played in the colonial economy.

Next door in the Connecticut town of Salem was the enormous Browne plantation, owned by Col. William Browne of Massachusetts. As Browne was branded a Tory sympathizer, the colonial government confiscated his 9,536-acre plantation in 1779, thus taking possession of one of the most important northern provisioners of the West Indies. Coincidentally, it had been managed by members of the prolific Mumford family, Browne's cousins. Col. Browne ended up governor of the British island of Bermuda.

From the outset, VENTURE knew what he wanted. He had his eye on a piece of high ground (Bald Hill) on Haddam Neck overlooking a cove on the Salmon River, a tributary of the Connecticut River.

Boundaries of VENTURE's farm at Haddam Neck in March 1778
with overlays by Cameron Blevins

Because of its isolated location, commerce at Haddam Neck operated with little government oversight. Haddam's government on the western side of the river was only interested in collecting taxes and recruiting soldiers from its remote neighbor. So, for VENTURE, Haddam Neck was the perfect place to base his farm and business. A

THE FINAL YEARS

natural loner, he wanted as much independence as possible – isolated but next door to a center of commerce.

As evidence from his choice of Ram Island as his redoubt five years earlier, VENTURE opted for isolated land and water to protect his privacy

Mouth of the Salmon River by J. W. Barber: VENTURE's Haddam Neck farm is on the ridge "Bald Hill" to the left of the sailboat in the center background

Two centuries later, the Connecticut Yankee Nuclear Power Plant would also find Haddam Neck to be an ideal location to operate – producing electricity for nearly 30 years (1968-1996) without the mishaps or controversy that often hit others.

Another clear indication that VENTURE was determined to control his own destiny was his apparent decision not to register as a "Freeman,"

Geo. Bradford Brainerd

This remarkable photo was taken in 1878 from VENTURE's farm
looking south toward East Haddam
The middle water is Salmon Cove, which abuts VENTURE's property.
To the south, the Salmon River empties into the Connecticut River

This photo, taken in 1877 by George Bradford Brainerd, looks north
from East Haddam up the Connecticut and Salmon rivers towards VENTURE's
farm (Some damage to the negative is apparent)

THE FINAL YEARS

which would have given him the right to vote at town meetings. There is no record that he ever voted. One reason may have been that voting was a public affair, not a secret ballot, and was often used by local leaders as a way to monitor public support or dissent – definitely not an appealing prospect for a proud and private man. Connecticut also did not require Freeman status to own property or conduct business, as was the case elsewhere. VENTURE clearly was not a joiner, he avoided adding his name to public lists. If he joined anything, it would have been the Masons and they did not publish lists of their members.

Instead of using his capital, VENTURE would work for it. He hired himself out to others for about 11 weeks, and with the proceeds, on March 3, 1775, purchased his first 10 acres from a local farmer, Abel

Detail: March 3, 1775 deed for VENTURE's first land purchase at Haddam Neck

Bingham. VENTURE summarized what happened next as if he were cutting butter with his ax:

> On this land I labored with great diligence for two years, and shortly after purchased six acres more of land contiguous to my other. One year from that time I purchased seventy acres more of the same man, and paid for it mostly with the produce of my other land. Soon after I bought this last lot of land, I set up a comfortable dwelling house on my farm, and built it from the produce thereof.

VENTURE is explaining that he picked the first ten-acre piece for what was on it. First growth trees would have been what he was looking for, ones that were very tall, tight grained, straight and long trunks with branches only at the top. Before putting up his money, he would have secured a contract to supply someone with beams for a building, or best, there would be trees that would make tall masts, the most valuable wood. The remains he would cut and split for firewood and ship it to New York or Newport. From the deed we know that he secured a right-of-way down to a location on the shore where he could load his produce onto ships. As soon as he cut, harvested and got paid for the wood products, he would buy an adjoining six-acre piece of land with more trees to be cut and sold, repeating this process until he owned about 140 acres.

While still winter, on the 3rd of March 1775, he bought the first ten acres so he could fell the trees before the sap started running. Then he could spend the spring and summer cutting, trimming and readying the product for market.

VENTURE went on to build houses for each of his sons, and barns for the large farm operation, which included grain fields, livestock, and orchards. He added a dry dock and all the support sheds and buildings needed to trade with nearby New England towns and off-shore buyers. He also had valuable fishing rights on the Salmon River, which he worked with a partner, William Ackerly, from East Haddam.

Since my residence at Haddam neck, I have owned of boats, canoes and sail vessels, not less than twenty. These I mostly employed in the fishing and trafficking business, . .

"VENTURE pursued the American dream of freedom and success, symbolized in the early republic by land. He charted a course that, through hard work and shrewd land purchases, would define him as a renowned and prosperous member of his community. Land equated to freedom in the concept of the American Dream."[12]

The George Bradford Brainerd[13] photo on page 105, taken from VENTURE's farm looking south in 1878, shows why East Haddam was where he conducted most of his affairs. He even said in his *Narrative* that he moved from Long Island to East Haddam, not Haddam. For VENTURE to get to the East Haddam landings, to do business, was a quick boat ride down the Salmon River. When he chose the location as the war was breaking out, he saw a place very secure from any potential British naval attack.

If British war ships did come up the Connecticut River, they would not see his compound nor would an attack be easy. The Salmon River wraps around VENTURE's farm, and any ships anchored in the northern cove would be out of sight of anyone in Haddam, East Haddam, or on the Connecticut River. People like the British navy or customs agents would not be able to see what VENTURE was doing.

Picking Haddam Neck fit a pattern. VENTURE seemed to like places that were not on the way to anywhere else – remote enough to discourage passers-by, but still near centers of commerce. His farm at Stonington-point was just such a place. Ram Island in Southampton, too, was only accessible by boat, yet it enjoyed easy access to the commercial and shipping centers on eastern Long Island, like North Sea and Sag Harbors, and Southold.

Not all was well, however. His eldest child, Hannah, fell into bad health. She was free now, and married to another free black by the name of Isaac, whom VENTURE called "*a dissolute and abandoned wretch*" who let her languish in her illness.

I therefore thought it best to bring her to my house and nurse her there. I procured her all the aid mortals could afford, but notwithstanding this she fell a prey to her disease, after a lingering and painful endurance of it.

In reporting his daughter's death, VENTURE could not help but mention that the attending doctor charged him £40. VENTURE knew how long he would have to work to raise £40 and how much more work he had done to rescue her from slavery.

Five years later, he faced another event that sheds more light on his nature and abilities. With Cuff in the Army, VENTURE needed more help.

In his mid-fifties, he hired two freed slaves to work for him. One, named Mingo, overspent his wages and borrowed eight dollars from VENTURE. He then ran away. VENTURE procured an arrest warrant from a local judge and tracked Mingo down. Mingo refused to accompany VENTURE to the judge's chambers, and the *Narrative* described what happened next:

Bronze plaque showing slave Jordan Freeman killing a British Officer

I took him on my shoulders, and carried him there; distant about two miles. The justice asking me if I had my prisoner's note with me, and replying that I had not, he told me that I must return with him and get it. Accordingly I carried Mingo back on my shoulders, but before we arrived at my dwelling, he complained of being hurt, and asked me if this was not a hard way of treating our fellow creatures. I answered him that it would be hard thus to treat our honest fellow creatures. He then told me that if I would let him off my shoulders, he had a pair of silver shoe-buckles, one shirt and a pocket handkerchief, which he would turn out to me. I agreed, and let him return home with me on foot; but the very following night, he slipped from me, stole my horse and has never paid me even his note.

Time and time again VENTURE would give his trust, only to have it broken. This he could never abide, and he would seek justice and resolution, usually with a Justice of the Peace. His kind heart would prevail again. It might seem strange that VENTURE did not talk about those trusts that were kept, although we know there were some. For example, two free black men, identified as Whacket Freeman and Peter (also probably Freeman, they married their wives in a joint ceremony in the East Haddam Congregational church), bought land from VENTURE and conducted other transactions. VENTURE helped them try to set up a free black enclave on Haddam Neck. They proved themselves to be honest men. But, for VENTURE, that was expected behavior and, perhaps that is why he chose not to mention it.

The same with Sawney Anderson who VENTURE purchased and freed in 1778, with a bill-of-sale/mortgage. ^{illust.} page 198-199 Anderson paid the balance due in 1782. Clearly, VENTURE was not setting out to prove and brag about helping other Africans have the chance to be free. He did it from his heart, with his hard-earned money. These three men proved to be honorable, earning VENTURE's respect.

We learn at the end of VENTURE's *Narrative* that his sons also broke his heart, but we do not know how. He does not talk much about his relationship with them. It is important to note here that VENTURE dictated his *Narrative* seven years before his death, so there is that unrecorded period during which he might have changed his mind. We do know from other testimony that his second living son, Solomon, cared for both parents in their final years and is buried with them.

It is known from records and oral histories that his oldest living son, Cuff, enlisted in the Continental Army for three years on December 4, 1780, when he was 19, and served against the British from January 29, 1781 until the war ended late in 1783. It is interesting that he enlisted in East Haddam, not Haddam/Haddam Neck. Was he living in East Haddam or did he enlist in place of someone else for a bounty? Cuff may have already started to live partly on his own, not under his father's wing.

In the early days of the war, Congress had sought to remove

blacks from the army, but later recanted because of the dire need for manpower and because the British forces were recruiting blacks with the promise of freedom.[14] Connecticut was a leader in the campaign to recruit black soldiers for the colonial cause. In the end, some 5,000 men of African descent had joined the colonial forces, while some 800 had signed on with the British. The latter figure does not include the thousands who deserted from slavery to the British lines.[15]

On 9 February 1778, the Rhode Island General Assembly declared that any slaves, black or Native American, who joined the First Rhode Island Regiment would be freed; many slaves joined and the state government compensated their former owners. They became famous during the war as the "Black Regiment."[16]

Cuff joined the regular army, one of an estimated 400-plus blacks in service from Connecticut, but he did not enlist in either of the colony's two all-black regiments. His regiment had at least 10 negros out of over 300 soldiers.[17] Exactly how much action he personally experienced is not known. His unit was involved in some skirmishes with British patrols in the Hudson Valley. There was plenty going on at the time. In 1781 Benedict Arnold led a British force up the Thames River and burned to the ground New London and part of Groton. In the Battle of Groton Heights, a slave by the name of Jordan Freeman fought alongside his owner and killed the British major leading the charge before he himself was slain. Freeman's owner, Col. William Ledyard, the commander of the patriot forces in the battle, died while surrendering.

The turncoat Arnold, himself from the New London area, used the occasion to settle some scores. He ordered his troops to torch certain houses, including that of David Mumford in New London and his brother Thomas Mumford in Groton, a war-time adviser to Gov. Trumbull and the man who helped procure the precious gunpowder for the cause early in the war.

The hypocrisy of an oppressed colony going to war for freedom that it was denying to others was not lost on all in the white community. In 1774, Abigail Adams wrote to her husband, John: "I wish most sincerely there was not a slave in the province – it always appeared a most iniquitous scheme to me – fight ourselves for what we are daily robbing and plundering from those who have as good a right to freedom as we have – you know my mind upon this subject."[18]

Abigail Adams

Most blacks who joined up did so in exchange for their freedom, but Cuff was already a freeman. But in Connecticut, service was no guarantee of freedom. In New Haven, Brister Baker, a slave joined and served for over 6 years. His discharge is signed by General Washington and he was decorated with the Badge of Merit for his faithful service;[19] but he went home a slave. Six months later his owner, Joshua Austin wrote, *"thinking that it is reasonable that he should be set free as he has been fighting tor the Liberties of the Country"*, freed him. He then petitioned the General Assembly to confirm it.[20] If the General Assembly freed Baker, then Austin would not be responsible for Baker if he could longer support himself.

Given, VENTURE's skepticism and highly practical nature, he may

Excerpt from Abigail Adams' 1774 letter to her husband John Adams not have ap proved of his son's enlistment. But it would be unfair to assume that his heart did not speak in a conversation that fathers and sons have had since wars began. The parting had to have been wrenching. By 1781 a number of Haddam Neck residents had already died in the War. But Cuff returned from the war apparently unscathed and joined his father and brother in the quest for civilian prosperity.

An interesting side note – memorials to the Revolutionary War dead commonly listed them all, including African Americans, in alphabetical order, sometimes with the word "Negro" after the name.

Jeff Liberty, Judeah Cemetery
Washington, Connecticut

It appears that the only time men of color achieved equality was in death.

In late 1784, sitting on his estate and looking over Salmon Cove, VEN-TURE must have been satisfied with what he and the United States had achieved with their independence. The war years had been economically difficult for many of the farmers and traders. With a weak central government in Philadelphia that did not have the power to tax and pay for the cost of the war, the Continental Congress

Detail of plaque honoring those killed, wounded, and captured in the battle of Groton in 1781, listing "negros" Jordan Freeman and Lambo Latham alphabetically with the others

THE FINAL YEARS

resorted to issuing payment vouchers and other financial instruments that came due one year after the end of the War. These instruments were not readily tradable at face value for cash or other goods. The individual States also issued payment documents which had a higher value. By 1781 in Connecticut, many farmers looked rich on paper but no longer had any money to plant crops or buy livestock to fatten and sell to the Government for the troops. There was widespread inflation, so the smartest financial move was to be in assets like land, ships and tangible goods.[21]

Since his land holdings increased from 10 acres in 1775 to 134 acres in 1778, and some of these land purchases involved partners and notes payable at a future date, VENTURE must have been converting what paper he received into real estate. He may have had to discount them to convert them into cash or land. These were all good business moves in a period of inflation. Buy the land, finance it, and hope to pay for it with depreciated currency in the future. VENTURE seems to have succeed during this period better than many of his neighbors.

His son Cuff was now home from the war, and would be trying to fit back into the family and daily life. Military service, especially during wartime, changes people. Cuff had been on his own for three years, with his comrades, fighting to survive in often harsh conditions. Continental soldiers were frequently underequipped and had to do whatever they could to stay warm and to eat. Drinking, swearing, and other similar behavior would have become norms for Cuff, but not well received by VENTURE. The military taught him to survive, but sometimes in ways that would not conform to VENTURE's high standards. Over time, small things would have led to conflicts between father and son. Furthermore, Solomon was only ten and probably had become somewhat favored.

We know that both Cuff and Solomon sometimes worked at the Brainerd Quarry, loading stone on the boats to earn cash. VENTURE may have seen this as a betrayal. The boys should have devoted all their time on the farm, building VENTURE's vision of a family compound like the one his father died trying to save in Ouangara. If they used

View across Salmon Cove from VENTURE SMITH's farm on Haddam Neck today

their money to buy fancy clothing, tobacco, or alcohol, it would have been another act of contention. It appears that in 1794 Cuff committed an act that VENTURE could never forgive – taking someone else's firewood.

Most peoples' homes, also included a separate "wood lot" for their firewood. These wood lots were usually land that could not be farmed or had difficult access. People cut their firewood and stacked it on site, then left it to season sometimes fot a year or more.

In 18th century Connecticut, it was inconceivable that anyone would touch another person's stacked wood. We do not know when Cuff crossed the line, and took the first piece – it must have been very cold, since taking the wood was an inconceivable act of violating the trust of his neighbors and everyone he lived and worked with. From the official court paper, it's clear that during the fall of 1794 he took wood, piece by piece, for a total of two cords. Each time, thinking no one would notice a few missing pieces from a large stack, he would have probably told himself he was borrowing it, and would replace it in the spring.

An analogy is when young people steal a small drink of their parent's liquor. At the start, taking half a shot does not show. But after a few weeks of imbibing another half shot every few days, the pilferer would not see the difference, but the parents would when after a few weeks they find a mostly full bottle only one-third full. This is what happened to Cuff: a few logs every night to heat his place, thinking it would not show, became two cords; and when the owner did finally walk by, he exploded.

He was caught before he could replace the wood and ended up in front of Justice of the Peace Ezra Brainerd on 9 January 1795. He was found guilty - fined, and ordered to be whipped. [22] see JP Brainerd's ruling C v

Photograph, taken in 1874 by George Bradford Brainerd, identifies the site as "Bald Hill", Haddam Neck. It was part of VENTURE's farm until 1788.

For VENTURE, the promises of the Patriots and the Declaration of Independence had been realized. Without the economic opportunities delivered by political independence, he would never have been able to achieve what he did. Slavery was ending in the north, led by Connecticut ending the slave trade to the Colony in 1774. Then in 1783, a ruling by the Massachusetts Supreme Court freed all its slaves. The following year, Connecticut and Rhode Island legislated the gradual ending of slavery within their own states.

In the post war period, the Continental Congress and the States had to figure out how to pay for the war and whether there would be a strong central government, or that the power would remain with the states. Meantime, the British Act blocking access to its West Indies sugar colonies was making it difficult for the New England traders like the Mumfords, Oliver Smith, and VENTURE, to return to trading with the West Indies at pre-war levels. Combined with severe inflation caused by all the notes from the Revolution, the economic climate was difficult. However, VENTURE seems to have adapted - he was good at finding new products and new markets.

In the 23 years between his arrival at Haddam Neck and recording his story in 1798, VENTURE SMITH had amassed more than 130 acres of land, "*three habitable dwelling houses*," no fewer than 20 boats and canoes, and dry docks, barns, and warehouses. He was the equivalent of a millionaire in today's terms.

But the situation with his son Cuff must have gradually deteriorated over the years. Clearly, Solomon became the son VENTURE relied on and favored. By the time of VENTURE's death, the Haddam Neck land and buildings were all in Solomon's name. Meg lived on the farm for another four years and then was buried beside her husband of fifty years. Solomon and one of his daughters are also buried with VENTURE. Missing is Cuff. Since Solomon outlived Cuff by almost twenty years, he was either fulfilling his father's orders or made the decision himself to not bury Cuff with the family.

The cemetery plot was laid out with spaces for VENTURE's wife and children in order by age - VENTURE, Meg, (oldest son, Cuff), and

Solomon. Later Solomon's, daughter Eliza Roy, took the open space. As an old man, VENTURE's memory was plagued by disappointments. He dwelled toward the end of his story on incidents where he was *"cheated out of considerable money by people whom I traded with taking advantage of my ignorance of numbers."* He also related the humiliation of being forced in court in 1790 to pay damages for a lost hogshead of molasses that was not his fault. However, by including this story, he was also making the case that he had succeeded to the point where on the dock he was singled out from the crowd as the most prominent person and the one who could pay a large settlement. However, the last word was VENTURE's; in print, he showed the world Captain Hart's true character.

He summarized his life as follows:

I am now sixty nine years old. Though once strait and tall, measuring without shoes six feet one inch and an half, and every way well proportioned, I am now bowed down with age and hardship. My strength which was once equal if not superior to any man whom I have ever seen, is now enfeebled so that life is a burden, and it is with fatigue that I can walk a couple of miles, stooping over my staff.

Other griefs are still behind, on account of which some aged people, at least, will pity me. My eye-sight has gradually failed, till I am almost blind, and whenever I go abroad one of my grand-children must direct my way; besides for many years I have been much pained and troubled with an ulcer on one of my legs. But amidst all my griefs and pains, I have many consolations; Meg, the wife of my youth, whom I married for love, and bought with my money, is still alive. My freedom is a privilege which nothing else can equal.

What VENTURE SMITH neglected to say in this conclusion is that through dint of hard work, legendary accomplishments, and unyielding adherence to his principles, he had earned unprecedented respect from a society acculturated against giving it.

By the end of his life, VENTURE SMITH was the equal of any man in community status and was regarded by many as without peer. It was not in his nature to publicly concede that. But he knew it.

The five men who certified his *Narrative* were leading citizens of New London County, including Col. Smith's son, Edward.

VENTURE SMITH died on September 19, 1805. The cause of death is not known, but his late life ailments were considerable. Meg outlived him by four years.

It is both intriguing and frustrating for historians that VENTURE's *Narrative* makes no mention of his religious beliefs or origins. Scholars now believe that his father's people were animists and that the raiding army was Islamic. Whatever they were, it would have been difficult for him, especially during his 14 years with the Mumfords on isolated Fishers Island, to practice the beliefs of his ancestors.

There is no evidence that VENTURE formally joined the Christian faith in his new homeland. Did Daniel Edwards take VENTURE to Church in Hartford; did he use the Bible to teach VENTURE to read or, to utilize the all-important Bible in observing the faith? VENTURE does not say. Tantalizingly, there are several Biblical references in VENTURE's *Narrative*[22], and on his tombstone is inscribed *"sacred to . . . "*. The evidence clearly suggests that this man was a believer, but a private one.[23]

After being attacked while sitting on his own property , VENTURE filed a complaint and writ to the local Justice of the Peace, on 14 March 1785 on Haddam Neck.[24] He was seeking damages for his injuries sustained, and charges against the three men. VENTURE in his statement made it clear he believed there is a God. The Justice of the Peace, Ezra Brainerd, repeated VENTURE's words in his ruling, (see the original document by the judge - color plate C i). VENTURE said, *"being Sabbath or Lords / Day he was in Haddam at or near a place Called Bald Hill / in the peace of God. . ."*. J. P. Brainerd was a neighbor and probably a friend and business associate, so he would have understood what VENTURE was doing on Bald Hill on the Sabbath. In his ruling he found the three men guilty as charged, and ordered them to pay VENTURE for the injuries he suffered in the attack and also fined them.

VENTURE and Meg are buried side by side in the cemetery of the First Congregational Church of East Haddam, which from 1792 to this day has been the final resting place of the white establishment in that community.

First Church of Christ East Haddam, Connecticut
designed by Lavius Fillmore and dedicated on November 27, 1794

The church was built 11 years before VENTURE died. Because he was such a successful member of the community by then, it is likely that he was approached for a donation if not also solicited for membership. The head of the building committee was Epaphroditus Champion,

a leading businessman of East Haddam who had been crucial, as a Commissary General of the Continental Army in the supply effort during the Revolution. He served two terms as the local Representative to the US Congress. He would later provide a pallbearer for VENTURE's funeral (he was too old to carry the coffin himself). What exactly the

Gen. Epaphroditus Champion

burial plot agreement was we may never know, but clearly Champion had the power and the respect for VENTURE to provide a prime location in the new cemetery – a family plot for this former slave.

For VENTURE, this may have been his most important real estate transaction.

Probably around 1790, when VENTURE turned about 60, he began to shape his legacy. HE saw himself as a Connecticut gentleman and patriarch. He had succeeded in reclaiming his position in society that had been lost in a West African war in 1739.

As befit his status, he required a proper Christian burial. He needed to be buried with his peers in the First Church of East Haddam cemetery. By acquiring a family plot in a prominent location, and commissioning a tombstone with an epitaph, VENTURE was linking his African station as heir to a king, to his achieved American status. Drawing on memory and evidence, VENTURE selected New Year's Day 1729 as his birth date[25] for the stone, the date he would later use for his autobiography.

The family plot in East Haddam Cemetery, showing gravestones for, from left, Solomon, granddaughter Eliza, Marget, and VENTURE

Ninety years later, in a published retrospective about VENTURE SMITH's life, an elderly Haddam resident, Robert Cone, said his father, Colonel Cone, had told him about VENTURE's funeral, where he served as a pallbearer.

THE FINAL YEARS

The pallbearers included Uri Gates, a prominent local business-man; Col. Cone; Hannawell, a slave provided by Dr. Thomas Moseley, whose son was also a US Congressman from East Haddam; and a servant of Gen. Epaphroditus Champion. Obviously, both Dr. Mosely and General Champion (both Masons and founders of the local lodge) were not fit to carry a coffin bearing a large heavy man for three miles and sent their substitutes. The two pallbearers in front were white and the two in back were black, one a slave and one free. From the weight, one of the black men complained: "It makes the gravel stones crack under my feet."[26]

The four pallbearers honored VENTURE's African heritage, his current standing as a peer in the community, and his status as a Connecticut gentleman. The funeral procession from VENTURE's home to the cemetery was typical of one for a prominent Mason or leader of the community. His coffin was of hardwood and included a "viewing door", so people could see his face as the procession passed – a striking image, the face of a black man bearing African ritual scarification.

The heavy body of the deceased was conveyed in a boat across the cove and carried on a bier the distance of three miles to the Wicket Lane cemetery (First Congregational Church Cemetery).

VENTURE was laid to rest under a brown tombstone carved by John Isham,[27] with a winged cherub's head at the crest. This angel of immortality is graced with an African nose. Likely, VENTURE would have commissioned John Isham to do the carving, since he was the premier tombstone carver in the area, and then chose Isham's best design, to reflect his American status, but including the African face

Tombstones in the Newport Cemetery left 1740 and right 1772 [28]

Susannah Scott 1779

from Newport designs in it, to reafirm his African heritage. VENTURE would have been familiar with the tombstones in the African section of the Newport Cemetery.[29] More than a hundred of these stones survive today, with similar angels of immorality with an African nose, and some have curly hair. The earliest surviving dated one is 1723. Several tombstones are carved by Zingo, aka Pompe Stevens, the first identified African American stone carver.[30]

VENTURE's inscription, still clearly legible in the stone, reads:

Sacred to the Memory
of Venture Smith an
African tho the son of a
King he was kidnapped
& sold as a slave but by
his industry he acquired
Money to purchase his
Freedom who Died Sept 19th
1805 in ye 77th Year of his
Age

VENTURE succeeded

in a world

in which he was not meant to succeed.

GEORGE A. KRIMSKY, 2014

*"My freedom is a privilege which nothing else can equal ...
It gives me joy to think that I have and that I deserve so good
a character, especially for truth and integrity."*

– VENTURE SMITH, 1798

CONCLUSION

What made VENTURE SMITH so special? He was, after all, only one of nearly half a million Africans forcibly brought to these shores. Other slaves had told their stories for posterity. Others had earned their freedom long before it became the law of the land. Others, as well, left a lineage of descendants.

Historians say VENTURE SMITH put a rare human face on an anonymous, oppressive, and unconscionably long institution in America. They also say he contributed greatly to the knowledge of an American slave's African origins and capture, because of his *Narrative*. And they say he provided an invaluable glimpse into the specific practice of northern slavery, a reality that had largely been suppressed in the flush of northern victory in the Civil War.

All this is true, but there is more to it than that. What makes VENTURE SMITH special is the man himself, and what he was able to accomplish by dint of his own perseverance, abilities, and self-created opportunities.

It is too easy to attribute VENTURE's success to just "hard work." His unwavering determination, extraordinary constitution, good health, brains, savvy, Africa-rooted sense of honor, and dominant physical presence – all contributed to the process. VENTURE never gave up, despite all his setbacks.

By the time VENTURE SMITH died on September 19, 1805, he had become a fully vested and respected American. It was an earned status, not a conferred one. VENTURE succeeded in a world in which he was not meant to succeed. How he accomplished that is what makes his story so exceptional.

In a sense VENTURE achieved the promised life in America. But what a gentle phrase for such an arduous journey. Unlike so many immigrants to these shores, he began his journey as another man's property and not as a recognized member of the society he entered. Yet he overcame that overwhelming obstacle and became a property owner himself.

Although the core of his *Narrative* shows that "property" was important to him, the deeper evidence shows that a sense of *"truth* and *integrity"* – qualities he never abandoned – defined his essence.

There are many mysteries about VENTURE SMITH left unsolved, and one must admit that they have inspired continuing curiosity to this day about the man and his times. But he was not one to be coy – dangling tantalizing clues that would keep his name alive.

VENTURE omitted from his *Narrative* the public events of his lifetime – a time when even those who were experiencing these tumultuous years realized it was a crucial period in American history. It was, more likely, his own intention. Everything in his autobiography revolved around his own personal experiences. Most writers bring in comments about their surroundings and events, even those that indirectly affected their lives. VENTURE was telling *his* story, what he had done and who he was; it was someone else's job to document the history of America's birth.

VENTURE's failure to mention the American Revolution, or the Declaration of Independence that served as the new country's philosophical foundation, or even his son Cuff having served in that conflict may have been his way of expressing some disappointment. To him, they were broken promises.

We hold these truths to be self-evident, that all men are created equal,

He knew that in many ways "all men are created equal" was not meant to apply to him. He would have to make it so. And he did. By the 1790s VENTURE and the new nation had both succeeded, and despite his earlier skepticism, the nation had kept its promise to him. Although slavery would remain a stain on America for another seven decades, VENTURE could not have accomplished what he did if the political climate had disallowed it.

He believed in the Revolution and the American promise of opportunity – he joined with the Patriots when leaving Long Island for Connecticut in 1774-5 – but toward the end of his life when he told his story, there was no evidence of it. He did not talk of the promise of achieving equality. Rather, when people disappointed him, he let examples of their broken word and trust speak for themselves. He died less than 18 months before Congress outlawed the Atlantic slave trade, and it would be another 60 years before Lincoln and the Civil War freed the enslaved people. But his adopted state had legislated the gradual end of slavery in 1784.

VENTURE's *Narrative* ends on a negative note. Clearly he was tired of life, a crippled, semi-blind, and embittered man when he published it. He was a man who had lived his whole life on his own as a loner – relying on no one but his beloved wife, Meg. The young tended to take care of and venerate their elders in those days, but there was little mention in the *Narrative* that his own children did so. The role Solomon played in helping his parents had to be sketched from other sources. Because of his solitary nature, VENTURE perhaps brought this on himself.

He also judged himself, his children, the people he did business with, and his adopted country against a standard impossible to achieve – the image of his father that he had created from a youth's memories. To VENTURE, his father was perfection. The son remembered him as "*a man of remarkable strength and resolution, affable, kind and gentle, ruling with equity and moderation.*"

For reasons he did not articulate, VENTURE was disappointed by his children. Clearly they did not, nor could they have ever lived up to the standards by which he judged them – the standards he applied to his father and himself. He lived his life working dawn to dusk seven days a week to create a better life for his wife and children, and yet, like many first-generation immigrants, he was resentful when his children enjoyed the life of privileged offspring of a wealthy and successful peer of the community. We can only speculate about how Solomon disappointed him. We have had to search in archives and uncover "lost" records, to learn of Cuff's fall from grace. On the other hand, in 1802, land records show that Solomon paid off his father's mortgage on the farm. A descendant (very likely Solomon) kept VENTURE's legacy alive by republishing his *Narrative* in 1835, but the following closing section was omitted: *"O! that they had walked in the way of their father. But a father's lips are closed in silence and in grief! – Vanity of vanities, all is vanity!"*

The unanswered questions of his religion and its absence from VENTURE's *Narrative*, we have largely attributed to the man's private and practical-minded character. Sunday may have been the Sabbath and thus a day of rest for the white establishment believers, but for VENTURE as a slave, it would have been a day to work on his own account. Indeed, it would have been his principal day of personal work until he regained his freedom. He would have regarded time in church as lost time in the quest for freedom.

A slave, even one believing in God, would have found it proper to work on the sabbath if it was to gain his and his family's freedom (all children of God). In rural New England the neighbors would have known why he was working and as long as he was not disturbing others or doing it in public, they would have accepted it.

However once he and his family were free, he would have observed the Sabbath to thank God. This did not require going to the Meeting house every Sunday, but rather in his own way quietly thanking the Lord. Even George Washington, a devote Christian, when retired at Mount Vernon, only went every third or fourth Sunday.

VENTURE never mentioned the religion practiced by his African family. During the 18th century, the two dominant religions in West Africa were the traditional, which Europeans called "animism" after the Latin word for "soul," and Islam, which had gradually been introduced by Arab traders and adopted by some ethnic groups. The two belief systems co-existed and intermingled throughout the region, with a common tenet that the spiritual and temporal worlds are unified. We now think VENTURE's people were animists. King Boukar (in the *Narrative* Baukurre), who we believe raided and killed VENTURE's father, converted to Islam in 1715 and then began a Jihad and conquest going West.

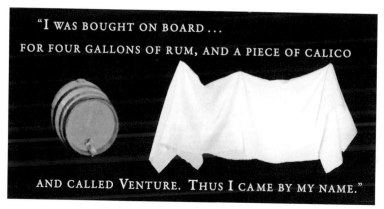

"I WAS BOUGHT ON BOARD . . . FOR FOUR GALLONS OF RUM, AND A PIECE OF CALICO AND CALLED VENTURE. THUS I CAME BY MY NAME."

Stripping the identity of the victims of the Middle Passage was one of the cruelest acts of the slave trade, turning a human being into a commodity to be traded like material goods. Knowing who we are and where we come from are basic issues for all people.

Overcoming slavery, gaining economic freedom, and retaining his identity were VENTURE's three great struggles. VENTURE knew who he was and worked his entire life to retain his African and American identities.

The definition of what it means to be "American" was first explored in detail by a French-American writer, Hector St. John de Crèvcoeur in his 1782 essays entitled *Letters from an American Farmer* – half-a-century before Alexis de Tocqueville published *Democracy in America*. Crèvecoeur described the principles of equal opportunity, self-determination, ingenuity, and the acceptance of religious freedom, in a society of diverse ethnic and cultural backgrounds. He invoked the practical Latin maxim "Ubi panis ibi patria" – *Where there is bread, there is my country* – as being the motivating force of this emerging country.

Overcoming slavery, gaining economic freedom, and retaining his identity were VENTURE's three great struggles. VENTURE knew who he was and struggled his entire life to retain his African and American identities.

VENTURE saw his *Narrative* as the writing of a gentleman recording his personal history – he was producing a memoir in the manner of a Franklin. In the *Narrative* he defines his status as an American of African birth. The *Narrative* offered him a way to redress past acts against him by publicly calling out all the perpetrators. By doing this he was taking the high moral ground against people like Capt. Hart, by describing the loss of the molasses and Hart's behavior in a sarcastic and sophisticated way. If Hart tried to counter, he would be recognizing VENTURE as a gentleman and a peer. At the same time VENTURE was leaving a record of who he was, what he had done, and his worthiness in this life and the next.

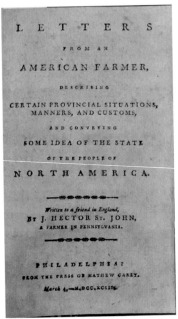

First American edition, 1793

For thirty years after regaining his freedom in 1765, VENTURE had been defining himself as an American. This process entailed a struggle between two cultures on how to live and behave. VENTURE was trying to rebuild on American soil, to the standards of his father and under the rules of his African heritage, what his family lost in an African war in 1738/39. He sought to establish himself as a respected figure judged by the rules and customs of his new society. At the same time he was able to enrich his new culture with practices from the former one, but at other times the cultures conflicted.

Finally in 1795, Cuff's fall from grace forced VENTURE to confront his identity and decide which system and codes he was living under.

What Cuff had done, under VENTURE's African heritage, would have banned Cuff and brought disgrace on VENTURE and the entire family for generations. VENTURE would no longer have been able to say he was a peer of his community. However, as an American in the new society, although Cuff's conviction would have been a stain on the family, it did not destroy what VENTURE had created and accomplished. VENTURE simply left Cuff out of the *Narrative*, not mentioning his birth or his military service – something VENTURE would have been very proud of as an heir to the ruler of an African kingdom, where military prowess was held in high esteem. By leaving him out of the *Narrative* and the cemetery, the stain of what Cuff had done would not affect VENTURE's and the family's legacy.

The problem of adopting and choosing between two cultures is highlighted by how VENTURE describes the other Africans who he tried to help and who violated his trust. They disgraced both the codes of their African heritage and those of their adopted land, and therefore in writing VENTURE publicly called them out.

In writing the *Narrative*, VENTURE finally comes to terms with his conflict and realizes, if he is to be judged as a peer of the community, he has to completely adopt his new country. He states this clearly on the title page – "*resident above sixty years in the United States of America*", and then for 30 pages describes how he has come to be an African American.

In his final act in the East Haddam cemetery, this African-educated man accomplished what none of his traditionally educated owners were able to do – he left an identity and a legacy that would survive him through the ages. The SMITH family plot, in a cemetery adjacent to one of the most important churches in Connecticut, is an anomaly. Unlike almost everyone else buried there, VENTURE did not belong to the church. Even today people belong to the church just so they can be buried in historic East Haddam Cemetery.

VENTURE saw himself as an American and a respectable middle-class one at that. He was underlining his freedom in terms his contemporary associates would recognize. As with his *Narrative*, his burial and gravestone are statements about his freedom as an African-born

V E N T U R E,

A NATIVE OF AFRICA:

But resident above sixty years in the United States of America.

American. For many 18th-century abolitionists, freedom was identified with religion, and VENTURE's burial in a place of significance in East Haddam Cemetery underlines how much he had internalized this philosophy and that he recognized some ultimate higher being.

The last page of VENTURE SMITH's *Narrative* over the years, has generated extensive discussion and debate. Many people have suggested elaborate explanations with complex meanings, when with a careful reading a straight forward interpretation makes sense. We need to remember how the writer, VENTURE SMITH, presented things – simply, honestly, and directly. VENTURE was not about hidden meanings or presenting facts in a nice way to please. He recognized from the start his *Narrative* was an autobiography and that meant recounting *truthfully* and factually - what he had done and what he believed.

In his last paragraph he sums up everything that is important. These include age; physical size; the current state of his health; the things he is blessed by; his Freedom; Meg his wife who he married for "love"; the principles he has lived by: "truth" and "integrity". Things that have disappointed him; his children, and the people he has tried to help and who have let him down. We know how his son Cuff disappointed him and was nolonger part of his story; but so far we have not been able to determine what Solomon may have done that did not come up to VENTURE's high standard.

Venture makes it clear that he is looking for an afterlife: "looking to the grave as my home, my joy for this world would be full – ..." It makes sense that when he turned 60, around 1790, he would have organized his resting place; starting with a prime location – near to the church and its steeple, a place that everyone coming to the church and the cemetery would see, the design and wording of his tombstone, and the layout of the individual plots (now with a gap in the space intended for Cuff).

He ended with the famous Biblical verse from Ecclesiastes 1:2: "Vanity of vanities, all is vanity!" Clearly he was wounded by his children's failures: the first Solomon who squandered his life for the sparkle of a silver shoe-buckle; Cuff, who fell from grace; and Solomon, whose offense may have been not completely believing in his father's dream. But it may be that, facing eternity, VENTURE realized that the dream of rebuilding what was lost in Africa was itself a fool's errand.

The scriptural quote, the *Narrative*, and the tombstone inscription framed an account of VENTURE for people who never knew him, and an accounting before his "Almighty protector."

Then there is also the question of the Freemasons – did VENTURE join or did he just align himself with them? Did he go to meetings? Certainly his code of truth and integrity, in which he so prided himself, fit well with the beliefs of the Masons, and may have stirred memories of the men's societies common in West Africa. We have found no record of VENTURE joining any group or institution. He does not show as a member in any church records, and Haddam has no surviving records of voter registration or who voted at Town Meetings (the "Standing Order" was essentially a one-party system, so at the Annual Meeting the list of those appointed to office was adopted without the formality of a vote count). If he joined anything, it seems likely it would have been the Freemasons; however, they did not circulate membership lists. But this would have suited VENTURE.

The Masons used the judicial process to settle disputes rather than getting bogged down in government processes or personal battles. Fellow Masons accepted the rulings of the JP or the Courts and then moved on. The disputing parties could now go back to working together, a practice that VENTURE would have embraced and recognized from childhood. In most of West Africa, people would go to the chiefs for a ruling, and whatever the outcome, be satisfied that they had their chance to present their side of the story. Masons are usually very well educated, erudite and wordly. All these values that describe how VENTURE lived his life were instilled in him by his formal education in Africa.

It is important to note here that residents of post-Colonial America referred to themselves as "Americans," or "residents" of the United States not as American citizens.[2] That would come later.

VENTURE was unusual in his capacity to rebuild a new life, to reinvent himself in a new world focused on the future, while not forgetting where he came from. His own *Narrative* and words on his tombstone were a way of confirming his acceptance of the written word as a substitute for the oral traditions of his African heritage. Yet he never compromised his basic principles, learned from his father: *Truth*, *integrity*, and his word.

VENTURE was permanently reaffirming who he was, where he came from, and what he accomplished – his final statement carved in stone. VENTURE commissioned an American masterpiece to make this statement – an extraordinary tombstone, a major work of folk art by carver John Isham, now recognized as the earliest public memorial to the Middle Passage. To this day, to everyone who comes to the Church and the cemetery, it delivers Venture's statement that in the latter part of the 18th century in East Haddam, a black man [a former African and slave] could achieve success equal to any of the peers of the community.

It is fitting that the work of art protecting VENTURE's legacy was the product of another man's hard work. VENTURE's size and strength had made him ideal as a builder of post-and-beam buildings and probably constituted a major reason why both Thomas Stanton and then Oliver Smith bought him. Most important, these qualities helped VENTURE earn his freedom.

In 1765, after regaining his freedom, VENTURE was able to put race and his own experiences of enslavement aside to build a future and legacy for his family. He truly began from scratch, for unlike most immigrants, he started with absolutely no capital, and began with no hereditary family support group. But he managed to acquire an understanding of American shipping, trading, and business practices from observing his owners, particularly the Mumfords and Smiths, and turning this knowledge into his "capital", and, after freeing himself from the bonds of slavery, succeeded in achieving success as the ultimate self made man. By aligning himself with Oliver Smith and the Denisons, he created a "family" support group, then used his intellectual "capital" to form connections with Freemasons in the business and political community.

VENTURE, who came to this country as a traded commodity, another man's property and investment, achieved success by becoming a trader in commodities with the very people and system that had subjugated him.

Archbishop Desmond Tutu, head of the Truth and Reconciliation Commission in South Africa, speaking at the *Wilberforce Institute for the study of Slavery and Emancipation* on the bicentenary of the end of the British Slave Trade, addressed the need for the victims and the perpetrators of crimes against humanity to heal. He emphasized that victims must put hatred and a desire for retaliation behind them and join with the perpetrators, working together to build a common future. VENTURE SMITH and his sons accomplished this enlightened relationship with Oliver Smith and his offspring. All put slavery behind them and joined together for 40 years as successful businessmen and neighbors – truly one of the great lessons VENTURE has taught us.[3]

One cannot leave this story without harking back to the striking name of our subject. Shakespeare noted that a rose would "smell as sweet" by any other name. What about "VENTURE?" The name is clearly a caricature, bestowed insensitively by a white man who viewed another human being as a property investment. Mockingly contrived as labels rather than identities, such names were commonly imposed on slaves to relegate them to the status of lesser beings. So why did VENTURE choose to retain this name after gaining his independence and not select one of greater dignity?

First, he was not ashamed of his name. If he ever had doubts, perhaps provoked by the snickering of strangers, it was his nature not to succumb. He would wear his name as a badge of honor.

On Haddam Neck, where he left his mark, he was known as "VENTURE" and his sons were often refered to as "Cuff Venture" and "Solomon Venture" not Cuff or Solomon Smith.[4] Further, beyond

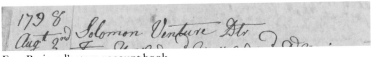

Ezra Brainerd's store account book.

any question of pride, the concept of "venture" became his true identity. It is a name he grew into, and he shaped his life by it. It is not an exaggeration to say he was a venture capitalist before the phrase became part of America's lexicon: he invested in himself; he invested in the earth and its productive power, in real estate, in shelter, and in many other utilitarian things. He also invested in his sons and in his African-American brethren, although these were investments that often disappointed him.

VENTURE made the name fit him. No greater testimony to that can be found than what is carved in the stone of his grave marker:

"Venture Smith an African."

We know of no other survivor of the Middle Passage to North America in the 17th or 18th century who has left us so much.

"He is richest whose honor outlives him."

– MARILYN NELSON, Connecticut Poet Laureate, 2005

"This extraordinary problem which sooner or later the entire world has to face up to, is how people of very different ethnic backgrounds can learn to live together on this earth."

-PETE SEEGER, March 2001

EPILOGUE

VENTURE SMITH lives on foremost in his family, some of whom still reside just a few miles from his Haddam Neck farm more than 200 years later. To date, genealogists have documented more than 9,000 descendants of VENTURE and Meg, spanning 11 generations. It is not known exactly how many are alive, but family members as far away as California are stepping forward.

One has only to visit the cemetery in East Haddam on any September 19th, the anniversary of VENTURE's death, to see his descendants and others from the area gathered together to honor VENTURE and Meg.

Now, the *Documenting VENTURE SMITH Project*, initially inspired by the family, is spreading VENTURE's legacy to a wider world. This project has been described by scholars as the largest research enterprise ever mobilized to trace a survivor of the Middle Passage from his birth in Africa to enslavement and on to freedom in the Americas.

VENTURE's magnificent tombstone, his remarkable *Narrative*, and the legendary stories about him, added further inspiration and motivation to this effort. But, beyond that, what has struck this unusual coalition of scholars, scientists, poets, archaeologists, historians, and civil rights activists is the story of a slave who reinvented himself. VENTURE decided that he and his family would become free, be successful – economically, socially, and politically – and become fully vested Americans. To do this, he had to set aside past persecution, injustice, and inequality to work with the very people who had enslaved him.

As his story unfolded, it became clear that VENTURE was as much a founder of this country as were his owners – the Smiths, the Edwards, the Stantons, and the Mumfords – many of whose descendants also still live in Connecticut. On July 4, 1776, whether he knew it or not, VENTURE embarked on a journey to build a new country. Although the full promise of equality and freedom for him and other African Americans had not yet been achieved, the new country delivered an unprecedented opportunity.

Among the tangible legacies left to us by VENTURE's story are the numerous physical sites that still exist today. These include:

The slave fort at Anomabo on the Gold Coast in present-day Ghana. What was called Annamaboe Fort, a major fortress of that period, has been preserved and can be seen today.

The homes of his owners. Robert Stanton's Stonington house is largely untouched since VENTURE's time, even down to much of the original furniture. The site of Thomas Stanton's house is in a State sanctuary area,[1] and Oliver Smith's house, which VENTURE helped build, can also still be seen today in Stonington.

Venture's first farm. The land VENTURE farmed and owned, first as a slave, and then again as a freeman, with the foundation of his first house located in the same State sanctuary.[1]

Venture's farm on Haddam Neck. The home and farm that VENTURE built for his family after they were freed is a pristine archaeological site, ironically because a nuclear power plant was built there in the 20th century. The owner, for many years, Connecticut Yankee Atomic Power, has recognized the importance of VENTURE's farm site and its place in American history. The corporation, which decommissioned the plant in 2006, has striven to preserve the site and has financed years of intensive digging and documentation by American Cultural Specialists LLC of Shelton, Connecticut. In January 2013, CY Atomic Power sold 38 acres to the US Fish & Wildlife Service, constituting about one-quarter of VENTURE's holdings.

The family's burial site in East Haddam Cemetery. The excavations and gravestone carvings have provided a wealth of information that has only begun to be interpreted.

Annamaboe Fort early 18th century print, Gold Coast (Ghana)

Robert Stanton house 1670 - 1700 Stonington-point

Oliver Smith house built 1761 Stonington

Foundation on VENTURE's Farm Stonington-point

Looking south from VENTURE's Farm Haddam Neck 1874

Bald Hill on VENTURE's Farm Haddam Neck 1874

VENTURE SMITH family gravesite East Haddam

The *Beecher House Center* and the *Wilberforce Institute* are working to earn formal recognition by UNESCO for both of VENTURE SMITH's family farms and his East Haddam gravesite as UNESCO World Heritage Sites, and linking them to its World Heritage Site in Anomabo, the sugar plantations in Barbados, and the William Wilberforce House Museum in Hull, UK. This would create a new UNESCO World Heritage Transnational Serial Site – *A Shared History and a Common Humanity: Slavery and Emancipation in the English Speaking Atlantic World.*

Then there is the science. Archeology and modern genetics research are helping us learn more about the origins of people like VENTURE and Meg. For example, we do not know the exact location of VENTURE's birth (only the general area in the West African interior) or anything about Meg's origins, not even her country of origin. DNA tracking may help provide answers.

View of East Haddam cemetery and church
during 2006 excavation project

At the family's request, the *Documenting VENTURE SMITH Project* opened the East Haddam graves in July 2006, a project supervised by Connecticut State Archaeologist Nicholas Bellantoni. VENTURE, Meg, and Soloman's remains had mostly disintegrated, but samples recovered from Meg's grave were taken to the University of Connecticut's Center of Applied Genetics and Technology for analysis. In addition, DNA research on the Smiths' living descendants is also being

Excavation project leaders: Chandler Saint and Nicholas Bellantoni

conducted; the *Project* is mapping the full genetic landscape of VENTURE, his family, and his descendants.

In explaining some of the DNA conclusions, the center's director, Dr. Linda Strausbaugh, reported in September 2006: "From the family tree of Meg and VENTURE's descendants, we can infer back to one 5th generation female founder who has a mitochondrial type that moved in early human history out of the Near East to explore surrounding areas. It is, interestingly, not typically associated with the main African types, but is currently found in a wide distribution including Europe, northern Africa, India, Arabia, northern Caucasus Mountains, and the Near east. In addition to this lineage, the family includes other genetic components from across the world, including

EPILOGUE

The excavation at the VENTURE SMITH Family gravesite
East Haddam, Connecticut, August 2, 2006

six different African types that represent each of the major human lineages within the continent, as well as the major european mitochondrial type. These results represent only a fraction of the family tree and we expect that as additional family members are identified and better databases become available, future research will reveal Venture's genetic legacy to be even more diverse."

But like history, science cannot tell us everything. We may never know, for example, exactly where VENTURE was born in the interior of West Africa. Despite extensive research by contemporary scholars, entire places, people, and even languages were evidently wiped out in the fight over territory, religion, resources, and slave populations during the 18th century and later. No written record of VENTURE's homeland, Dukandarra or what we now believe was designated "d'Ouangara," has been found, except for the description in his *Narrative*, although a French map of the period indicates he was likely born in the area near Lake Chad, where the modern-day countries of Chad, Cameroon, Nigeria, and Niger converge. Scholars now believe that VENTURE's people are a "lost tribe."

This is also an area we cannot presently visit. It appears Broteer

Furro was born very near the current headquarters of Boko Haram. History is repeating itself, 275 years after King Baukurro went on a Jihad across interior West Africa, Boko Haram is repeating it, in the same place with the same results. At a recent summit in Hull, modern campaigners against human trafficking and terrorism, said a new phenomenom is happening – the terrorists like ISIS and Boko Haram are capturing whole villages, killing off the men and trafficking the women and children to raise money for their wars. Actually this is what happened 275 years ago to Sigmun Furro and his people. What VENTURE called an *invading army* was a terrorist group who wiped out the kingdom, captured the livestock, killed the men and marched the women and children to the Gold Coast to sell them to the slave traders. VENTURE's people were simply the victims of terrorism.[2]

The assumption that DNA alone can give instant answers, as purveyed in television programs and the mass media, is a fiction, but science can help confirm or deny genealogical records. The family tree loses much of its accuracy as one traces along each branch — often because the listed father of a child is not always the real father.

We mentioned previously about VENTURE being owned by the "right" people. Every American success story requires something that one might call chance, luck, or opportunity. The individual must recognize it, seize it, and then utilize his own assets (brains, strength, energy, and determination) to capitalize on the opportunity. VENTURE took advantage of the social capital and business knowledge he accumulated while living as a slave on Fishers Island with the Mumfords to start reinventing himself and ultimately freeing himself and his family. He looked to the future, not the past, and changed his status from a piece of property to a working businessman and finally to a builder of partnerships that cemented his and his family's future.

Will people continue to remember and admire VENTURE SMITH? The enthusiasm generated by VENTURE's story on the 200th anniversary of his death and recently on the 250th anniversary of his regained freedom, and on the continuing work to share his story with the public, strongly suggest they will.

Public outreach under the *Documenting VENTURE SMITH Project* gained a major boost in February of 2011 when Connecticut Congresswoman Rosa L. DeLauro (New Haven, CT-3) co-sponsored an event on Capitol Hill in Washington D.C. for the Congressional Black Caucus and the Descendants of VENTURE SMITH and his owners, featuring an early version of the exhibition *Making Freedom - The Life of Venture Smith: In His Own Voice.* The exhibit then went to the *Connecticut State Library* and *Museum of Connecticut History* on 17 February to 4 May, 2011; the Hull History Center, Hull, UK, 23 August through to 31 October 2011; the Marcus Garvey Library, London, UK, 6 October to 9 December 2012; and Annamaboe Fort, Ghana, September 2014.

Under the leadership of Congresswoman DeLauro, the *Project* has conducted a number of public school programs in Connecticut.

Connecticut State Capitol, Hartford, February 2013.
Congressman Joe Courtney, Congresswoman Rosa L. DeLauro,
Chandler Saint, Senator Richard Blumenthal, Congressman Jim Himes,
and Congresswoman Elizabeth Esty

In 2013, she sponsored a program with the *Connecticut State Library* to bring VENTURE's story to every public school and library in the State, with gift copies of the book, *Making Freedom: The Extraordinary Life of Venture Smith* and the CD reading of his 1798 *Narrative*.

In 2014, it was 275 years since a youth named Broteer Furro left Africa in 1739. To mark the occasion, VENTURE's descendants shared the story of his odyssey with his homeland. In September, 2014, a version of the exhibit *Making Freedom – The Life of VENTURE SMITH: In His Own Voice* was donated to the people of Anomabo, forming a link among the living from North America to the West Indies and to Africa, completing the modern triangular trade route.

The Royal Palace, Anomabo, Ghana October 2013. Chandler Saint meeting with Chief Amonu XI and his Council of Elders
Nana Baffoe IV-Kontihene, Chandler Saint, Nana Bassaw-Tufuhene, Nana Awer-Akwamuhene, Kantamanto Amonoo-Omanahene, Nana Owiansah-Guatuahene, Nana Otisiwah Kumah-Ankobeahene

The Chief of Anomabo and the Anomabo Traditional Council said they will place the exhibit in the Fort.

The exhibition *Making Freedom – The Life of Venture Smith: In His Own Voice*, retraces VENTURE's life, using his own words from his 1798 autobiography.

In 2015, on the 250th Anniversary of VENTURE regaining his freedom, the exhibit returned to Connecticut at the Hartford History Center, Hartford Public Library (see C-Span show[3]); and then at the Torrington Historical Society for Black History Month (February 2016); and in April, in conjunction with a major international conference, *Confronting Slavery – Venture Smith to the Present: 1765–1865–1965 –Today*, at the Connecticut Department of Energy and Environmental Protection.

To date the *Project* has inspired a book of poetry by Marilyn Nelson (*The Freedom Business*); a biography, *Making Freedom: the Extraordinary Life of Venture Smith*; a collection of papers, *Venture Smith and the Business of Slavery and Freedom*; this book; a handstitched reprint of the *Narrative*; a BBC documentary, *A Slave's Story*; five C-SPAN shows; two C-NET shows; a United States Senate Proclamation honoring VENTURE, by Connecticut Senator Christopher Dodd on September 13, 2010; and a traveling exhibition, *Making Freedom–The Life of Venture Smith: In His Own Voice*. There have been five conferences devoted to understanding this story.

The 250th anniversary of VENTURE's liberation (in 1765) was also the 150th anniversary of the end of the Civil War. These events were followed by the opening of the new *National Museum of African American History and Culture at the Smithsonian Institution* in 2016. The museum director, Lonnie G. Bunch, recently said about the *Project*, "One of the joys of history is to uncover and make accessible compelling stories that inform us about the past and illuminate the important issues of our times. Venture Smith is just such a story – one that we hope will inspire people to see the world around them in new ways."

In April 2015, on the 250th anniversary of his liberation, "VENTURE's Freedom Day" was celebrated in the UK with events in Kingston-upon-Hull by a luncheon at City Hall, a lecture at the Wilberforce Institute, and an announcement that annually there will be youth sport programs for the Venture Smith Trophy in boys rugby and the Meg Smith Trophy for girls football.

In the United States, Connecticut Governor Dannel Malloy recognized April 23 as "Venture Smith Freedom Day". On April 28, 2015 the Connecticut Department of Energy and Environmental Protection placed a sign on VENTURE SMITH's farm, on Stonington-point, that he owned and worked to help earn his freedom.[4] Two hundred years earlier, VENTURE SMITH's son Solomon celebrated the fiftieth anniversary of VENTURE's regained freedom, by naming his son after his father's last owner and the founder of the country – George Oliver Washington Smith. The name passed down for many generations. Just as Oliver and VENTURE had figured how to turn owned and owner into equals their sons were able to live and work together.

We anticipate that new information uncovered in historical societies, libraries, town records, and attics – information previously ignored because it's significance was unrecognized – will increase our understanding of VENTURE's story. A good example are the Ezra Brainerd court records, which were "lost" in church records. Recently we were asked to look at them, and see if they were important to understanding VENTURE. Other documents, concerning people like Daniel Edwards who clearly played a decisive role in VENTURE's life, but has remained obscure in Connecticut history, will be "discovered" by their owners or custodians as important to the story of VENTURE SMITH and Connecticut. Also, now someone is likely to study Daniel Edwards and write on his role in VENTURE's life and in Connecticut history, especially on its slavery past. Edwards is very complex, he represented Chief Uncas in Court, baptized slave children, educated them in God, and yet in his will he leaves his "servants" (slaves) to his wife. This man's story needs to be uncovered and told.

Up to this point, the *Documenting VENTURE SMITH Project* has focused on historical documentation of the facts of VENTURE's life and will continue working to discover new information and refine what we know. From now, on the focus will be on public awareness and effecting social change. We expect that VENTURE's story will have a broader influence – an influence that will help us stimulate popular interest in the history of slavery in Africa, the Atlantic, the Caribbean, New England, and the Long Island basin.

David Eltis, co-author of the *Atlas of the Transatlantic Slave Trade*, wrote "Venture's life thus embodies the virtues of liberal North American society as they later came to be defined. His life can be interpreted as reaching toward pluralism, democracy, and human rights well before these three fused together. Within a very few years his story, we predict, will likely have displaced that of Equiano's as the best known personal memoir of the African Diaspora".[5]

Most importantly, the *Project* will use VENTURE's experience to explain contemporary slavery and work to eradicate it.

So, VENTURE's story lives on.

———

"I'd like to see VENTURE in the history books, but in the *school* history books. I think slavery is a very painful subject for America and we need to start healing, and perhaps VENTURE can be one of those vehicles to help in the healing process."

–FLORENCE P. WARMSLEY, 8th-generation descendant of VENTURE SMITH

Appendix Contents

1798 NARRATIVE FACSIMILE

❧ ◄ ◄ ◄◈◗◆◖◈► ► ► ❧

The following is a facsimile of VENTURE SMITH's original *Narrative*, printed by *The Bee* in New London, Connecticut, in November/December 1798. It was 32 pages (with a plain blue cover and an additional blank sheet).

The final page is a certificate attesting to the veracity of the *Narrative* by five leading citizens of Stonington, Connecticut, dated November 3, 1798.

The title page (it often is improperly referred to as "the cover") is from a copy in the Beinecke Rare Book and Manuscript Library Yale University and pages 3-32 are from a copy at the Connecticut Historical Society, all are full size. This title page is particularly interesting because it appears to have been Venture's or his family's own copy. Handwritten corrections to the spelling of several of the African names are on the title page with what scholars believe are calculations of sales; and on page 32 of this copy, the name "Venture Smith" is written in the location where owners often put their names.

Readers unfamiliar with pre-19th-century printed text may be confused by some of the type characters, especially the use of the long "s" (f), which looks almost like an "f", and was a holdover from earlier manuscript writing. In VENTURE's *Narrative* we find both the long "s" and the normal "s". The normal "s" is used at the end of words, and also when a word is capitalized. In other places, the long "s" is used. Example: The modern form of "seamstress" becomes "feamftrefs," but in the beginning of a sentence it is, "Seamftrefs".

Throughout the *Narrative*, at the bottom right of each page, the printer added the first word from the next page.

A
NARRATIVE
OF THE
LIFE AND ADVENTURES
OF
VENTURE,

A NATIVE OF AFRICA:

But resident above sixty years in the United States of
America.

RELATED BY HIMSELF.

New-London:

PRINTED BY C. HOLT, AT THE BEE-OFFICE.
1798.

PREFACE.

THE following account of the life of VENTURE,
is a relation of simple facts, in which nothing is
added in substance to what he related himself. Many
other interesting and curious passages of his life might
have been inserted ; but on account of the bulk to
which they must necessarily have swelled this narrative,
they were omitted. If any should suspect the truth of
what is here related, they are referred to people now
living who are acquainted with most of the facts mentioned in the narrative.

The reader is here presented with an account, not
of a renowned politician or warrior, but of an untu-
tored African slave, brought into this Christian country
at eight years of age, wholly destitute of all education
but what he received in common with other domesti-
cated animals, enjoying no advantages that could lead
him to suppose himself superior to the beasts, his fellow
servants. And if he shall derive no other advantage
from perusing this narrative, he may experience those
sensations of shame and indignation, that will prove
him to be not wholly destitute of every noble and generous feeling.

The subject of the following pages, had he received
only a common education, might have been a man of
high respectability and usefulness ; and had his education been suited to his genius, he might have been an
ornament and an honor to human nature. It may perhaps, not be unpleasing to see the efforts of a great
mind wholly uncultivated, enfeebled and depressed by
slavery, and struggling under every disadvantage.——

A 2   The

The reader may here see a Franklin and a Washington, in a state of nature, or rather in a state of slavery. Destitute as he is of all education, and broken by hardships and infirmities of age, he still exhibits striking traces of native ingenuity and good sense.

This narrative exhibits a pattern of honesty, prudence and industry, to people of his own colour; and perhaps some white people would not find themselves degraded by imitating such an example.

The following account is published in compliance with the earnest desire of the subject of it, and likewise a number of respectable persons who are acquainted with him.

A nar-

A narrative of the life, &c.

❖◄◄◦◗◯◖◦►►►❖

CHAPTER I.

Containing an account of his life, from his birth to the time of his leaving his native country.

I WAS born at Dukandarra, in Guinea, about the year 1729. My father's name was Saungm Furro, Prince of the Tribe of Dukandarra. My father had three wives. Polygamy was not uncommon in that country, especially among the rich, as every man was allowed to keep as many wives as he could maintain. By his first wife he had three children. The eldest of them was myself, named by my father, Broteer. The other two were named Cundazo and Soozaduka. My father had two children by his second wife, and one by his third. I descended from a very large, tall and stout race of beings, much larger than the generality of people in other parts of the globe, being commonly considerable above six feet in height, and every way well proportioned.

The first thing worthy of notice which I remember was, a contention between my father and mother, on account of my father's marrying his third wife without the consent of his first and eldest, which was contrary to the custom generally observed among my countrymen. In consequence of this rupture, my mother left her husband and country, and travelled away with her three children to the eastward. I was then five years old. She took not the least sustenance along with her, to support either herself or children. I was able to
travel

travel along by her fide ; the other two of her offspring fhe carried one on her back, and the other being a fucking child, in her arms. When we became hungry, my mother ufed to fet us down on the ground, and gather fome of the fruits which grew fpontaneoufly in that climate. Thefe ferved us for food on the way. At night we all lay down together in the moft fecure place we could find, and repofed ourfelves until morning. Though there were many noxious animals there ; yet fo kind was our Almighty protector, that none of them were ever permitted to hurt or moleft us. Thus we went on our journey until the fecond day after our departure from Dukandarra, when we came to the entrance of a great defert. During our travel in that we were often affrighted with the doleful howlings and yellings of wolves, lions, and other animals. After five days travel we came to the end of this defert, and immediately entered into a beautiful and extenfive interval country. Here my mother was pleafed to ftop and feek a refuge for me. She left me at the houfe of a very rich farmer. I was then, as I fhould judge, not lefs than one hundred and forty miles from my native place, feparated from all my relations and acquaintance. At this place my mother took her farewel of me, and fet out for her own country. My new guardian, as I fhall call the man with whom I was left, put me into the bufinefs of tending fheep, immediately after I was left with him. The flock which I kept with the affiftance of a boy, confifted of about forty. We drove them every morning between two and three miles to pafture, into the wide and delightful plains. When night drew on, we drove them home and fecured them in the cote. In this round I continued during my ftay there. One incident which befel me when I was driving my flock from pafture, was fo dreadful to me in that age, and is to this time fo frefh in my memory, that I cannot help noticing it in this place. Two large dogs fallied out of

a certain

a certain house and set upon me. One of them took me by the arm, and the other by the thigh, and before their master could come and relieve me, they lacerated my flesh to such a degree, that the scars are very visible to the present day. My master was immediately sent for. He came and carried me home, as I was unable to go myself on account of my wounds. Nothing remarkable happened afterwards until my father sent for me to return home.

Before I dismiss this country, I must just inform my reader what I remember concerning this place. A large river runs through this country in a westerly course. The land for a great way on each side is flat and level, hedged in by a considerable rise of the country at a great distance from it. It scarce ever rains there, yet the land is fertile; great dews fall in the night which refresh the soil. About the latter end of June or first of July, the river begins to rise, and gradually increases until it has inundated the country for a great distance, to the height of seven or eight feet. This brings on a slime which enriches the land surprisingly. When the river has subsided, the natives begin to sow and plant, and the vegetation is exceeding rapid. Near this rich river my guardian's land lay. He possessed, I cannot exactly tell how much, yet this I am certain of respecting it, that he owned an immense tract. He possessed likewise a great many cattle and goats. During my stay with him I was kindly used, and with as much tenderness, for what I saw, as his only son, although I was an entire stranger to him, remote from friends and relations. The principal occupations of the inhabitants there, were the cultivation of the soil and the care of their flocks. They were a people pretty similar in every respect to that of mine, except in their persons, which were not so tall and stout. They appeared to be very kind and friendly. I will now return to my departure from that place.

My

My father sent a man and horse after me. After settling with my guardian for keeping me, he took me away and went for home. It was then about one year since my mother brought me here. Nothing remarkable occured to us on our journey until we arrived safe home.

I found then that the difference between my parents had been made up previous to their sending for me. On my return, I was received both by my father and mother with great joy and affection, and was once more restored to my paternal dwelling in peace and happiness. I was then about six years old.

Not more than six weeks had passed after my return, before a message was brought by an inhabitant of the place where I lived the preceding year to my father, that that place had been invaded by a numerous army, from a nation not far distant, furnished with musical instruments, and all kinds of arms then in use; that they were instigated by some white nation who equipped and sent them to subdue and possess the country; that his nation had made no preparation for war, having been for a long time in profound peace that they could not defend themselves against such a formidable train of invaders, and must therefore necessarily evacuate their lands to the fierce enemy, and fly to the protection of some chief; and that if he would permit them they should come under his rule and protection when they had to retreat from their own possessions. He was a kind and merciful prince, and therefore consented to these proposals.

He had scarcely returned to his nation with the message, before the whole of his people were obliged to retreat from their country, and come to my father's dominions.

He gave them every privilege and all the protection his government could afford. But they had not been there longer than four days before news came to them
that

that the invaders had laid waste their country, and were coming speedily to destroy them in my father's territories. This affrighted them, and therefore they immediately pushed off to the southward, into the unknown countries there, and were never more heard of.

Two days after their retreat, the report turned out to be but too true. A detachment from the enemy came to my father and informed him, that the whole army was encamped not far out of his dominions, and would invade the territory and deprive his people of their liberties and rights, if he did not comply with the following terms. These were to pay them a large sum of money, three hundred fat cattle, and a great number of goats, sheep, asses, &c.

My father told the messenger he would comply rather than that his subjects should be deprived of their rights and privileges, which he was not then in circumstances to defend from so sudden an invasion. Upon turning out those articles, the enemy pledged their faith and honor that they would not attack him. On these he relied and therefore thought it unnecessary to be on his guard against the enemy. But their pledges of faith and honor proved no better than those of other unprincipled hostile nations; for a few days after a certain relation of the king came and informed him, that the enemy who sent terms of accommodation to him and received tribute to their satisfaction, yet meditated an attack upon his subjects by surprise, and that probably they would commence their attack in less than one day, and concluded with advising him, as he was not prepared for war, to order a speedy retreat of his family and subjects. He complied with this advice.

The same night which was fixed upon to retreat, my father and his family set off about break of day. The king and his two younger wives went in one company, and my mother and her children in another. We left our dwellings in succession, and my father's company

B   went

went on firſt. We directed our courſe for a large ſhrub plain, ſome diſtance off, where we intended to conceal ourſelves from the approaching enemy, until we could refreſh and reſt ourſelves a little. But we preſently found that our retreat was not ſecure. For having ſtruck up a little fire for the purpoſe of cooking victuals, the enemy who happened to be encamped a little diſtance off, had ſent out a ſcouting party who diſcovered us by the ſmoke of the fire, juſt as we were extinguiſhing it, and about to eat. As ſoon as we had finiſhed eating, my father diſcovered the party, and immediately began to diſcharge arrows at them. This was what I firſt ſaw, and it alarmed both me and the women, who being unable to make any reſiſtance, immediately betook ourſelves to the tall thick reeds not far off, and left the old king to fight alone. For ſome time I beheld him from the reeds defending himſelf with great courage and firmneſs, till at laſt he was obliged to ſurrender himſelf into their hands.

They then came to us in the reeds, and the very firſt ſalute I had from them was a violent blow on the head with the fore part of a gun, and at the ſame time a graſp round the neck. I then had a rope put about my neck, as had all the women in the thicket with me, and were immediately led to my father, who was likewiſe pinioned and haltered for leading. In this condition we were all led to the camp. The women and myſelf being pretty ſubmiſſive, had tolerable treatment from the enemy, while my father was cloſely interrogated reſpecting his money which they knew he muſt have. But as he gave them no account of it, he was inſtantly cut and pounded on his body with great inhumanity, that he might be induced by the torture he ſuffered to make the diſcovery. All this availed not in the leaſt to make him give up his money, but he deſpiſed all the tortures which they inflicted, until the continued exerciſe and increaſe of torment, obliged him to ſink and expire. He

He thus died without informing his enemies of the place where his money lay. I saw him while he was thus tortured to death. The shocking scene is to this day fresh in my mind, and I have often been overcome while thinking on it. He was a man of remarkable stature. I should judge as much as six feet and six or seven inches high, two feet across his shoulders, and every way well proportioned. He was a man of remarkable strength and resolution, affable, kind and gentle, ruling with equity and moderation.

The army of the enemy was large, I should suppose consisting of about six thousand men. Their leader was called Baukurre. After destroying the old prince, they decamped and immediately marched towards the sea, lying to the west, taking with them myself and the women prisoners. In the march a scouting party was detached from the main army. To the leader of this party I was made waiter, having to carry his gun, &c.—As we were a scouting we came across a herd of fat cattle, consisting of about thirty in number. These we set upon, and immediately wrested from their keepers, and afterwards converted them into food for the army. The enemy had remarkable success in destroying the country wherever they went. For as far as they had penetrated, they laid the habitations waste and captured the people. The distance they had now brought me was about four hundred miles. All the march I had very hard tasks imposed on me, which I must perform on pain of punishment. I was obliged to carry on my head a large flat stone used for grinding our corn, weighing as I should suppose, as much as 25 pounds; besides victuals, mat and cooking utensils. Though I was pretty large and stout of my age, yet these burthens were very grievous to me, being only about six years and an half old.

We were then come to a place called Malagasco.—When we entered the place we could not see the least

B 2   appearance

appearance of either houses or inhabitants, but upon
stricter search found, that instead of houses above ground
they had dens in the sides of hillocks, contiguous to
ponds and streams of water. In these we perceived they
had all hid themselves, as I suppose they usually did upon such occasions. In order to compel them to surrender, the enemy contrived to smoke them out with fag-
gots. These they put to the entrance of the caves and
set them on fire. While they were engaged in this business, to their great surprise some of them were desperately wounded with arrows which fell from above on
them. This mystery they soon found out. They perceived that the enemy discharged these arrows through
holes on the top of the dens directly into the air.—
Their weight brought them back, point downwards on
their enemies heads, whilst they were smoking the inhabitants out. The points of their arrows were poi-
soned, but their enemy had an antidote for it, which
they instantly applied to the wounded part. The smoke
at last obliged the people to give themselves up. They
came out of their caves, first spatting the palms of their
hands together, and immediately after extended their
arms, crossed at their wrists, ready to be bound and
pinioned. I should judge that the dens above mentioned were extended about eight feet horizontally into
the earth, six feet in height and as many wide. They
were arched over head and lined with earth, which
was of the clay kind, and made the surface of their
walls firm and smooth.

The invaders then pinioned the prisoners of all ages
and sexes indiscriminately, took their flocks and all their
effects, and moved on their way towards the sea. On
the march the prisoners were treated with clemency, on
account of their being submissive and humble. Having
come to the next tribe, the enemy laid siege and immediately took men, women, children, flocks, and all their
valuable effects. They then went on to the next district

trict which was contiguous to the sea, called in Africa, Anamaboo. The enemies provisions were then almost spent, as well as their strength. The inhabitants knowing what conduct they had pursued, and what were their present intentions, improved the favorable opportunity, attacked them, and took enemy, prisoners, flocks and all their effects. I was then taken a second time. All of us were then put into the castle, and kept for market. On a certain time I and other prisoners were put on board a canoe, under our master, and rowed away to a vessel belonging to Rhode-Island, commanded by capt. Collingwood, and the mate Thomas Mumford. While we were going to the vessel, our master told us all to appear to the best possible advantage for sale. I was bought on board by one Robertson Mumford, steward of said vessel, for four gallons of rum, and a piece of calico, and called VENTURE, on account of his having purchased me with his own private venture. Thus I came by my name. All the slaves that were bought for that vessel's cargo, were two hundred and sixty.

CHAPTER II.

Containing an account of his life, from the time of his leaving Africa, to that of his becoming free.

AFTER all the business was ended on the coast of Africa, the ship sailed from thence to Barbadoes. After an ordinary passage, except great mortality by the small pox, which broke out on board, we arrived at the island of Barbadoes: but when we reached it, there were found out of the two hundred and sixty that sailed from Africa, not more than two hundred alive. These were all sold, except myself and three more, to the planters there.

The

The vessel then sailed for Rhode-Island, and arrived there after a comfortable passage. Here my master sent me to live with one of his sisters, until he could carry me to Fisher's Island, the place of his residence. I had then completed my eighth year. After staying with his sister some time I was taken to my master's place to live.

When we arrived at Narraganset, my master went ashore in order to return a part of the way by land, and gave me the charge of the keys of his trunks on board the vessel, and charged me not to deliver them up to any body, not even to his father without his orders. To his directions I promised faithfully to conform. When I arrived with my master's articles at his house, my master's father asked me for his son's keys, as he wanted to see what his trunks contained. I told him that my master intrusted me with the care of them until he should return, and that I had given him my word to be faithful to the trust, and could not therefore give him or any other person the keys without my master's directions. He insisted that I should deliver to him the keys, threatening to punish me if I did not. But I let him know that he should not have them let him say what he would. He then laid aside trying to get them. But notwithstanding he appeared to give up trying to obtain them from me, yet I mistrusted that he would take some time when I was off my guard, either in the day time or at night to get them, therefore I slung them round my neck, and in the day time concealed them in my bosom, and at night I always lay with them under me, that no person might take them from me without being apprized of it. Thus I kept the keys from every body until my master came home. When he returned he asked where VENTURE was. As I was then within hearing, I came, and said, here sir, at your service. He asked me for his keys, and I immediately took them off my neck and reached them out to him. He took them, stroked my hair, and commended me, saying in presence of his father that

his

his young VENTURE was so faithful that he never would have been able to have taken the keys from him but by violence ; that he should not fear to trust him with his whole fortune, for that he had been in his native place so habituated to keeping his word, that he would sacrifice even his life to maintain it.

The first of the time of living at my master's own place, I was pretty much employed in the house at carding wool and other houshold business. In this situation I continued for some years, after which my master put me to work out of doors. After many proofs of my faithfulness and honesty, my master began to put great confidence in me. My behavior to him had as yet been submissive and obedient. I then began to have hard tasks imposed on me. Some of these were to pound four bushels of ears of corn every night in a barrel for the poultry, or be rigorously punished. At other seasons of the year I had to card wool until a very late hour. These tasks I had to perform when I was about nine years old. Some time after I had another difficulty and oppression which was greater than any I had ever experienced since I came into this country. This was to serve two masters. James Mumford, my master's son, when his father had gone from home in the morning, and given me a stint to perform that day, would order me to do *this* and *that* business different from what my master directed me. One day in particular, the authority which my master's son had set up, had like to have produced melancholy effects. For my master having set me off my business to perform that day and then left me to perform it, his son came up to me in the course of the day, big with authority, and commanded me very arrogantly to quit my present business and go directly about what he should order me. I replied to him that my master had given me so much to perform that day, and that I must therefore faithfully complete it in that time. He then broke out into a great rage, snatched
a pitchfork

a pitchfork and went to lay me over the head therewith; but I as soon got another and defended myself with it, or otherwise he might have murdered me in his outrage. He immediately called some people who were within hearing at work for him, and ordered them to take his hair rope and come and bind me with it. They all tried to bind me but in vain, tho' there were three assistants in number. My upstart master then desisted, put his pocket handkerchief before his eyes and went home with a design to tell his mother of the struggle with young VENTURE. He told her that their young VEN-TURE had become so stubborn that he could not controul him, and asked her what he should do with him. In the mean time I recovered my temper, voluntarily caused myself to be bound by the same men who tried in vain before, and carried before my young master, that he might do what he pleased with me. He took me to a gallows made for the purpose of hanging cattle on, and suspended me on it. Afterwards he ordered one of his hands to go to the peach orchard and cut him three dozen of whips to punish me with. These were brought to him, and that was all that was done with them, as I was released and went to work after hanging on the gallows about an hour.

After I had lived with my master thirteen years, being then about twenty two years old, I married Meg, a slave of his who was about my age. My master owned a certain Irishman, named Heddy, who about that time formed a plan of secretly leaving his master. After he had long had this plan in meditation he suggested it to me. At first I cast a deaf ear to it, and rebuked Heddy for harboring in his mind such a rash undertaking. But after he had persuaded and much enchanted me with the prospect of gaining my freedom by such a method, I at length agreed to accompany him. Heddy next inveigled two of his fellow servants to accompany us. The place to which we designed to go was the Missisippi. Our

next

next business was to lay in a sufficient store of provisions
for our voyage. We privately collected out of our
master's store, six great old cheeses, two firkins of butter, and one whole batch of new bread. When we
had gathered all our own clothes and some more, we
took them all about midnight, and went to the water
side. We stole our master's boat, embarked, and then
directed our course for the Mississippi river.

We mutually confederated not to betray or desert
one another on pain of death. We first steered our
course for Montauk point, the east end of Long-Island.
After our arrival there we landed, and Heddy and I
made an incursion into the island after fresh water, while
our two comrades were left at a little distance from the
boat, employed at cooking. When Heddy and I had
sought some time for water, he returned to our companions, and I continued on looking for my object. When
Heddy had performed his business with our companions
who were engaged in cooking, he went directly to the
boat, stole all the clothes in it, and then travelled away
for East-Hampton, as I was informed. I returned to
my fellows not long after. They informed me that
our clothes were stolen, but could not determine who
was the thief, yet they suspected Heddy as he was missing. After reproving my two comrades for not taking
care of our things which were in the boat, I advertised
Heddy and sent two men in search of him. They
pursued and overtook him at Southampton and returned him to the boat. I then thought it might afford some
chance for my freedom, or at least a palliation for my
running away, to return Heddy immediately to his master, and inform him that I was induced to go away by
Heddy's address. Accordingly I set off with him and
the rest of my companions for our master's, and arrived
there without any difficulty. I informed my master
that Heddy was the ringleader of our revolt, and that
he had used us ill. He immediately put Heddy into

C   custody

custody, and myself and companions were well received and went to work as usual.

Not a long time passed after that, before Heddy was sent by my master to New-London gaol. At the close of that year I was sold to a Thomas Stanton, and had to be separated from my wife and one daughter, who was about one month old. He resided at Stonington-point. To this place I brought with me from my late master's, two johannes, three old Spanish dollars, and two thousand of coppers, besides five pounds of my wife's money. This money I got by cleaning gentlemen's shoes and drawing boots, by catching musk-rats and minks, raising potatoes and carrots, &c. and by fishing in the night, and at odd spells.

All this money amounting to near twenty-one pounds York currency, my master's brother, Robert Stanton, hired of me, for which he gave me his note. About one year and a half after that time, my master purchased my wife and her child, for seven hundred pounds old tenor. One time my master sent me two miles after a barrel of molasses, and ordered me to carry it on my shoulders. I made out to carry it all the way to my master's house. When I lived with Captain George Mumford, only to try my strength, I took up on my knees a tierce of salt containing seven bushels, and carried it two or three rods. Of this fact there are several eye witnesses now living.

Towards the close of the time that I resided with this master, I had a falling out with my mistress. This happened one time when my master was gone to Long-Island a gunning. At first the quarrel began between my wife and her mistress. I was then at work in the barn, and hearing a racket in the house, induced me to run there and see what had broken out. When I entered the house, I found my mistress in a violent passion with my wife, for what she informed me was a mere trifle; such a small affair that I forbear to put my mistress

treſs to the ſhame of having it known. I earneſtly re-
queſted my wife to beg pardon of her miſtreſs for the
ſake of peace, even if ſhe had given no juſt occaſion
for offence. But whilſt I was thus ſaying my miſtreſs
turned the blows which ſhe was repeating on my wife to
me. She took down her horſe-whip, and while ſhe
was glutting her fury with it, I reached out my great
black hand, raiſed it up and received the blows of the
whip on it which were deſigned for my head. Then I
immediately committed the whip to the devouring fire.

When my maſter returned from the iſland, his wife
told him of the affair, but for the preſent he ſeemed
to take no notice of it, and mentioned not a word about
it to me. Some days after his return, in the morning
as I was putting on a log in the fire-place, not ſuſpecting
harm from any one, I received a moſt violent ſtroke on
the crown of my head with a club two feet long and as
large round as a chair-poſt. This blow very badly
wounded my head, and the ſcar of it remains to this day.
The firſt blow made me have my wits about me you may
ſuppoſe, for as ſoon as he went to renew it, I ſnatched
the club out of his hands and dragged him out of the
door. He then ſent for his brother to come and aſſiſt
him, but I preſently left my maſter, took the club he
wounded me with, carried it to a neighboring Juſtice
of the Peace, and complained of my maſter. He finally adviſed me to return to my maſter, and live contented
with him till he abuſed me again, and then complain.
I conſented to do accordingly. But before I ſet out for
my maſter's, up he come and his brother Robert after
me. The Juſtice improved this convenient opportunity
to caution my maſter. He aſked him for what he treated his ſlave thus haſtily and unjuſtly, and told him what
would be the conſequence if he continued the ſame
treatment towards me. After the Juſtice had ended
his diſcourſe with my maſter, he and his brother ſet out
with me for home, one before and the other behind me.

When

When they had come to a bye place, they both dismounted their respective horses, and fell to beating me with great violence. I became enraged at this and immediately turned them both under me, laid one of them across the other, and stamped both with my feet what I would.

This occasioned my master's brother to advise him to put me off. A short time after this I was taken by a constable and two men. They carried me to a blacksmith's shop and had me hand-cuffed. When I returned home my mistress enquired much of her waiters, whether VENTURE was hand-cuffed. When she was informed that I was, she appeared to be very contented and was much transported with the news. In the midst of this content and joy, I presented myself before my mistress, shewed her my hand-cuffs, and gave her thanks for my gold rings. For this my master commanded a negro of his to fetch him a large ox chain. This my master locked on my legs with two padlocks. I continued to wear the chain peaceably for two or three days, when my master asked me with contemptuous hard names whether I had not better be freed from my chains and go to work. I answered him, No. Well then, said me, I will send you to the West-Indies or banish you, for I am resolved not to keep you. I answered him I crossed the waters to come here, and I am willing to cross them to return.

For a day or two after this not any one said much to me, until one Hempsted Miner, of Stonington, asked me if I would live with him. I answered him that I would. He then requested me to make myself discontented and to appear as unreconciled to my master as I could before that he bargained with him for me; and that in return he would give me a good chance to gain my freedom when I came to live with him. I did as he requested me. Not long after Hempsted Miner purchased me of my master for fifty-six pounds lawful. He

took

took the chain and padlocks from off me immediately after.

It may here be remembered, that I related a few pages back, that I hired out a fum of money to Mr. Robert Stanton, and took his note for it. In the fray between my mafter Stanton and myfelf, he broke open my cheft containing his brother's note to me, and deftroyed it. Immediately after my prefent mafter bought me, he determined to fell me at Hartford. As foon as I became apprized of it, I bethought myfelf that I would fecure a certain fum of money which lay by me, fafer than to hire it out to a Stanton. Accordingly I buried it in the earth, a little diftance from Thomas Stanton's, in the road over which he paffed daily. A fhort time after my mafter carried me to Hartford, and firft propofed to fell me to one William Hooker of that place. Hooker afked whether I would go to the German Flats with him. I anfwered, No. He faid I fhould, if not by fair means I fhould by foul. If you will go by no other meafures, I will tie you down in my fleigh. I replied to him, that if he carried me in that manner, no perfon would purchafe me, for it would be thought that he had a murderer for fale. After this he tried no more, and faid he would not have me as a gift.

My mafter next offered me to Daniel Edwards, Efq. of Hartford, for fale. But not purchafing me, my mafter pawned me to him for ten pounds, and returned to Stonington. After fome trial of my honefty, Mr. Edwards placed confiderable truft and confidence in me. He put me to ferve as his cup-bearer and waiter. When there was company at his houfe, he would fend me into his cellar and other parts of his houfe to fetch wine and other articles occafionally for them. When I had been with him fome time, he afked me why my mafter wifhed to part with fuch an honeft negro, and why he did not keep me himfelf. I replied that I could not give him the reafon, unlefs it was to convert me into cafh, and

speculate

speculate with me as with other commodities. I hope
that he can never justly say it was on account of my ill
conduct that he did not keep me himself. Mr. Edwards told me that he should be very willing to keep
me himself, and that he would never let me go from
him to live, if it was not unreasonable and inconvenient for me to be parted from my wife and children ;
therefore he would furnish me with a horse to return to
Stonington, if I had a mind for it. As Miner did not
appear to redeem me I went, and called at my old mafter Stanton's first to see my wife, who was then owned
by him. As my old master appeared much ruffled at
my being there, I left my wife before I had spent any
considerable time with her, and went to Colonel O.
Smith's. Miner had not as yet wholly settled with
Stanton for me, and had before my return from Hartford given Col. Smith a bill of sale of me. These men
once met to determine which of them should hold me,
and upon my expressing a desire to be owned by Col.
Smith, and upon my master's settling the remainder of
the money which was due to Stanton for me, it was
agreed that I should live with Col. Smith. This was
the third time of my being sold, and I was then thirty-
one years old. As I never had an opportunity of redeeming myself whilst I was owned by Miner, though
he promised to give me a chance, I was then very ambitious of obtaining it. I asked my master one time if he
would consent to have me purchase my freedom. He
replied that he would. I was then very happy, knowing that I was at that time able to pay part of the purchase money, by means of the money which I some time
since buried. This I took out of the earth and tendered to my master, having previously engaged a free
negro man to take his security for it, as I was the property of my master, and therefore could not safely take
his obligation myself. What was wanting in redeeming
myself, my master agreed to wait on me for, until I
could

could procure it for him. I still continued to work for Col. Smith. There was continually some interest accruing on my master's note to my friend the free negro man above named, which I received, and with some besides which I got by fishing, I laid out in land adjoining my old master Stanton's. By cultivating this land with the greatest diligence and economy, at times when my master did not require my labor, in two years I laid up ten pounds. This my friend tendered my master for myself, and received his note for it.

Being encouraged by the success which I had met in redeeming myself, I again solicited my master for a further chance of completing it. The chance for which I solicited him was that of going out to work the ensuing winter. He agreed to this on condition that I would give him one quarter of my earnings. On these terms I worked the following winter, and earned four pounds sixteen shillings, one quarter of which went to my master for the privilege, and the rest was paid him on my own account. This added to the other payments made up forty four pounds, eight shillings, which I had paid on my own account. I was then about thirty five years old.

The next summer I again desired he would give me a chance of going out to work. But he refused and answered that he must have my labor this summer, as he did not have it the past winter. I replied that I considered it as hard that I could not have a chance to work out when the season became advantageous, and that I must only be permitted to hire myself out in the poorest season of the year. He asked me after this what I would give him for the privilege per month. I replied that I would leave it wholly with his own generosity to determine what I should return him a month. Well then, said he, if so two pounds a month. I answered him that if that was the least he would take I would be contented.

Accordingly

Accordingly I hired myself out at Fisher's Island, and earned twenty pounds; thirteen pounds six shillings of which my master drew for the privilege, and the remainder I paid him for my freedom. This made fifty-one pounds two shillings which I paid him. In October following I went and wrought six months at Long Island. In that six month's time I cut and corded four hundred cords of wood, besides threshing out seventy-five bushels of grain, and received of my wages down only twenty pounds, which left remaining a larger sum. Whilst I was out that time, I took up on my wages only one pair of shoes. At night I lay on the hearth, with one coverlet over and another under me. I returned to my master and gave him what I received of my six months labor. This left only thirteen pounds eighteen shillings to make up the full sum for my redemption. My master liberated me, saying that I might pay what was behind if I could ever make it convenient, otherwise it would be well. The amount of the money which I had paid my master towards redeeming my time, was seventy-one pounds two shillings. The reason of my master for asking such an unreasonable price, was he said, to secure himself in case I should ever come to want. Being thirty-six years old, I left Col. Smith once for all. I had already been sold three different times, made considerable money with seemingly nothing to derive it from, been cheated out of a large sum of money, lost much by misfortunes, and paid an enormous sum for my freedom.

CHAPTER

CHAPTER III.

Containing an account of his life, from the time of his purchasing his freedom to the present day.

MY wife and children were yet in bondage to Mr. Thomas Stanton. About this time I lost a chest, containing besides clothing, about thirty-eight pounds in paper money. It was burnt by accident. A short time after I sold all my possessions at Stonington, consisting of a pretty piece of land and one dwelling house thereon, and went to reside at Long-Island. For the first four years of my residence there, I spent my time in working for various people on that and at the neighboring islands. In the space of six months I cut and corded upwards of four hundred cords of wood. Many other singular and wonderful labors I performed in cutting wood there, which would not be inferior to those just recited, but for brevity sake I must omit them. In the aforementioned four years what wood I cut at Long-Island amounted to several thousand cords, and the money which I earned thereby amounted to two hundred and seven pounds ten shillings. This money I laid up carefully by me. Perhaps some may enquire what maintained me all the time I was laying up money. I would inform them that I bought nothing which I did not absolutely want. All fine clothes I despised in comparison with my interest, and never kept but just what clothes were comfortable for common days, and perhaps I would have a garment or two which I did not have on at all times, but as for superfluous finery I never thought it to be compared with a decent homespun dress, a good supply of money and prudence. Expensive gatherings of my mates I commonly shunned, and all kinds of luxuries I was perfectly a stranger to ; and during the time

D.   I was

I was employed in cutting the aforementioned quantity of wood, I never was at the expence of six-pence worth of spirits. Being after this labour forty years of age, I worked at various places, and in particular on Ram-Island, where I purchased Solomon and Cuff, two sons of mine, for two hundred dollars each.

It will here be remembered how much money I earned by cutting wood in four years. Besides this I had considerable money, amounting in all to near three hundred pounds. When I had purchased my two sons, I had then left more than one hundred pounds. After this I purchased a negro man, for no other reason than to oblige him, and gave for him sixty pounds. But in a short time after he run away from me, and I thereby lost all that I gave for him, except twenty pounds which he paid me previous to his absconding. The rest of my money I laid out in land, in addition to a farm which I owned before, and a dwelling house thereon. Forty four years had then completed their revolution since my entrance into this existence of servitude and misfortune. Solomon my eldest son, being then in his seventeenth year, and all my hope and dependence for help, I hired him out to one Charles Church, of Rhode-Island, for one year, on consideration of his giving him twelve pounds and an opportunity of acquiring some learning. In the course of the year, Church fitted out a vessel for a whaling voyage, and being in want of hands to man her, he induced my son to go, with the promise of giving him on his return, a pair of silver buckles, besides his wages. As soon as I heard of his going to sea, I immediately set out to go and prevent it if possible.— But on my arrival at Church's, to my great grief, I could only see the vessel my son was in almost out of sight going to sea. My son died of the scurvy in this voyage, and Church has never yet paid me the least of his wages. In my son, besides the loss of his life, I lost equal to seventy-five pounds.

My

My other fon being but a youth, ftill lived with me. About this time I chartered a floop of about thirty tons burthen, and hired men to affift me in navigating her. I employed her moftly in the wood trade to Rhode-Ifland, and made clear of all expences above one hundred dollars with her in better than one year. I had then become fomething forehanded, and being in my forty-fourth year, I purchafed my wife Meg, and thereby prevented having another child to buy, as fhe was then pregnant. I gave forty pounds for her.

During my refidence at Long-Ifland, I raifed one year with another, ten cart loads of water-melons, and loft a great many every year befides by the thievifhnefs of the failors. What I made by the water-melons I fold there, amounted to nearly five hundred dollars. Various other methods I purfued in order to enable me to redeem my family. In the night time I fifhed with fet-nets and pots for eels and lobfters, and fhortly after went a whaling voyage in the fervice of Col. Smith.— After being out feven months, the veffel returned, laden with four hundred barrels of oil. About this time, I become poffeffed of another dwelling-houfe, and my temporal affairs were in a pretty profperous condition. This and my induftry was what alone faved me from being expelled that part of the ifland in which I refided, as an act was paffed by the felect-men of the place, that all negroes refiding there fhould be expelled.

Next after my wife, I purchafed a negro man for four hundred dollars. But he having an inclination to return to his old mafter, I therefore let him go. Shortly after I purchafed another negro man for twenty-five pounds, whom I parted with fhortly after.

Being about forty-fix years old, I bought my oldeft child Hannah, of Ray Mumford, for forty-four pounds, and fhe ftill refided with him. I had already redeemed from flavery, myfelf, my wife and three children, befides three negro men.

D 2 About

About the forty-seventh year of my life, I difpofed
of all my property at Long-Ifland, and came from thence
into Eaft-Haddam. I hired myfelf out at firft to Timothy Chapman, for five weeks, the earnings of which
time I put up carefully by me. After this I wrought
for Abel Bingham about fix weeks. I then put my money together and purchafed of faid Bingham ten acres
of land, lying at Haddam neck, where I now refide.——
On this land I labored with great diligence for two years,
and fhortly after purchafed fix acres more of land contiguous to my other. One year from that time I purchafed feventy acres more of the fame man, and paid
for it moftly with the produce of my other land. Soon
after I bought this laft lot of land, I fet up a comfortable
dwelling houfe on my farm, and built it from the produce
thereof. Shortly after I had much trouble and expence
with my daughter Hannah, whofe name has before been
mentioned in this account. She was married foon after
I redeemed her, to one Ifaac, a free negro, and fhortly after her marriage fell fick of a mortal difeafe; her
hufband a diffolute and abandoned wretch, paid but little attention to her in her illnefs. I therefore thought it
beft to bring her to my houfe and nurfe her there. I
procured her all the aid mortals could afford, but not-
withftanding this fhe fell a prey to her difeafe, after a
lingering and painful endurance of it.

The phyfician's bills for attending her during her illnefs amounted to forty pounds. Having reached my
fifty-fourth year, a hired two negro men, one named
William Jacklin, and the other Mingo. Mingo lived
with me one year, and having received his wages, run
in debt to me eight dollars, for which he gave me his
note. Prefently after he tried to run away from me
without troubling himfelf to pay up his note. I procured
a warrant, took him, and requefted him to go to Juftice
Throop's of his own accord, but he refufing, I took
him on my fhoulders, and carried him there, diftant
about

about two miles. The juftice afking me if I had my prifoner's note with me, and replying that I had not, he told me that I muft return with him and get it. Accordingly I carried Mingo back on my fhoulders, but before we arrived at my dwelling, he complained of being hurt, and afked me if this was not a hard way of treating our fellow creatures. I anfwered him that it would be hard thus to treat our honeft fellow creatures. He then told me that if I would let him off my fhoulders, he had a pair of filver fhoe-buckles, one fhirt and a pocket handkerchief, which he would turn out to me. I agreed, and let him return home with me on foot ; but the very following night, he flipped from me, ftole my horfe and has never paid me even his note. The other negro man, Jacklin, being a comb-maker by trade, he requefted me to fet him up, and promifed to reward me well with his labor. Accordingly I bought him a fet of tools for making combs, and procured him ftock. He worked at my houfe about one year, and then run away from me with all his combs, and owed me for all his board.

Since my refidence at Haddam neck, I have owned of boats, canoes and fail veffels, not lefs than twenty. Thefe I moftly employed in the fifhing and trafficking bufinefs, and in thefe occupations I have been cheated out of confiderable money by people whom I traded with taking advantage of my ignorance of numbers.

About twelve years ago, I hired a whale-boat and four black men, and proceeded to Long-Ifland after a load of round clams. Having arrived there, I firft purchafed of James Webb, fon of Orange Webb, fix hundred and fixty clams, and afterwards, with the help of my men, finifhed loading my boat. The fame evening, however, this Webb ftole my boat, and went in her to Connecticut river, and fold her cargo for his own benefit. I thereupon purfued him, and at length, after an additional expence of nine crowns, recovered the
boat;

boat; but for the proceeds of her cargo I never could obtain any compensation.

Four years after, I met with another loss, far superior to this in value, and I think by no less wicked means. Being going to New-London with a grand-child, I took passage in an Indian's boat, and went there with him. On our return, the Indian took on board two hogsheads of molasses, one of which belonged to Capt. Elisha Hart, of Saybrook, to be delivered on his wharf. When we arrived there, and while I was gone, at the request of the Indian, to inform Captain Hart of his arrival, and receive the freight for him, one hogshead of the molasses had been lost overboard by the people in attempting to land it on the wharf. Although I was absent at the time, and had no concern whatever in the business, as was known to a number of respectable witnesses, I was nevertheless prosecuted by this conscientious gentleman, (the Indian not being able to pay for it) and obliged to pay upwards of ten pounds lawful money, with all the costs of court. I applied to several gentlemen for counsel in this affair, and they advised me, as my adversary was rich, and threatened to carry the matter from court to court till it would cost me more than the first damages would be, to pay the sum and submit to the injury; which I according did, and he has often since insultingly taunted me with my unmerited misfortune. Such a proceeding as this, committed on a defenceless stranger, almost worn out in the hard service of the world, without any foundation in reason or justice, whatever it may be called in a christian land, would in my native country have been branded as a crime equal to highway robbery. But Captain Hart was a *white gentleman*, and I a *poor African*, therefore it was *all right, and good enough for the black dog*.

I am now sixty nine years old. Though once strait and tall, measuring without shoes six feet one inch and

an

an half, and every way well proportioned, I am now
bowed down with age and hardſhip. My ſtrength
which was once equal if not ſuperior to any man whom
I have ever ſeen, is now enfeebled ſo that life is a burden, and it is with fatigue that I can walk a couple of
miles, ſtooping over my ſtaff. Other griefs are ſtill
behind, on account of which ſome aged people, at leaſt,
will pity me. My eye-ſight has gradually failed, till I
am almoſt blind, and whenever I go abroad one of my
grand-children muſt direct my way; beſides for many
years I have been much pained and troubled with an
ulcer on one of my legs. But amidſt all my griefs and
pains, I have many conſolations; Meg, the wife of my
youth, whom I married for love, and bought with my
money, is ſtill alive. My freedom is a privilege which
nothing elſe can equal. Notwithſtanding all the loſſes
I have ſuffered by fire, by the injuſtice of knaves, by
the cruelty and oppreſſion of falſe hearted friends, and
the perfidy of my own countrymen whom I have aſſiſt-
ed and redeemed from bondage, I am now poſſeſſed of
more than one hundred acres of land, and three habitable dwelling houſes. It gives me joy to think that I
have and that I *deſerve* ſo good a character, eſpecially
for *truth* and *integrity*. While I am now looking to
the grave as my home, my joy for this world would be
full—IF my children, Cuff for whom I paid two hundred dollars when a boy, and Solomon who was born
ſoon after I purchaſed his mother—If Cuff and Solomon
—O! that they had walked in the way of their father.
But a father's lips are cloſed in ſilence and in grief!—
Vanity of vanities, all is vanity!

F I N I S.

CERTIFICATE.

STONINGTON, *November* 3, 1798.

THESE certify, that VENTURE, a free negro man, aged about 69 years, and was, as we have ever understood, a native of Africa, and formerly a slave to Mr. James Mumford, of Fisher's-Island, in the state of New-York; who sold him to Mr. Thomas Stanton, 2d, of Stonington, in the state of Connecticut, and said Stanton sold said VENTURE to Col. Oliver Smith, of the aforesaid place. That said VENTURE hath sustained the character of a faithful servant, and that of a temperate, honest and industrious man, and being ever intent on obtaining his freedom, he was indulged by his masters after the ordinary labour on the days of his servitude, to improve the nights in fishing and other employments to his own emolument, in which time he procured so much money as to purchase his freedom from his late master Col. Smith; after which he took upon himself the name of VENTURE SMITH, and has since his freedom purchased a negro woman, called Meg, to whom he was previously married, and also his children who were slaves, and said VENTURE has since removed himself and family to the town of East-Haddam, in this state, where he hath purchased lands on which he hath built a house, and there taken up his abode.

NATHANIEL MINOR, Esq.
ELIJAH PALMER, Esq.
Capt. AMOS PALMER,
ACORS SHEFFIELD,
EDWARD SMITH.

NARRATIVE
PUBLICATION HISTORY

✦·◄·◄·◄◉◈◉►·►·►·✦

VENTURE's *Narrative* was first published in late 1798 as a hand-stitched booklet of 32 pages (22 by 13 centimeters in size) with a blank page front and back, and a plain blue cover. Starting on December 26, 1798 it was advertised for sale in *The Bee* of New London for six weeks. There is no record of how many copies were sold. From February 20 through May 14, 1799 the *Journal of the Times* in Stonington, Connecticut, advertised it for sale. (not in edition #26-April 2nd or #27-April 9th, 1799)

In 1835, on the 30th anniversary of VENTURE's death, the *Narrative* was re-published by an unidentified descendant, probably his only living son, Solomon, who was 62 at the time. The format was similar but type size smaller. It was 24 pages (20cm by 11cm) and hand-stitched with a plain blue cover, number printed unknown. Interestingly, the following final passage in the original *Narrative* had been excised from the text:

> *While I am now looking to the grave as my home, my joy for this world would be full — if my children, Cuff for whom I paid two hundred dollars when a boy, and Solomon who was born soon after I purchased his mother — If Cuff and Solomon — O! that they had walked in the way of their father. But a father's lips are closed in silence and in grief! — Vanity of vanities, all is vanity!*

The *Narrative* was next re-published in 1897 in Middletown, Connecticut, along with information taken from oral histories of those who knew VENTURE or had heard relatives talk about him. The format was a 42-page (24cm by 15cm), wire-stapled booklet, number printed unknown. This re-publication occurred one year short of a century after the Smith family first produced the *Narrative*, reflecting continued local interest in VENTURE. In the late twentieth century, the full *Narrative* has been included in several printed anthologies and on-line sites. If one finds reading the original typeface difficult, several modern versions are available:

1. New London County Historical Society has published the *Narrative* set in modern type.
2. In *Five Black Lives*, Wesleyan University Press, 1987, (in print).
3. A transcription can be seen or downloaded from the University of North Carolina's web site: http://docsouth.unc.edu/neh/venture/venture.html
4. An audio version on the CD *The Narrative of an African American: VENTURE SMITH (1798)*, by the *Beecher House Center for the Study of Equal Rights* and the *Wilberforce Institute for the study of Slavery and Emancipation*, 2010.
5. A reproduction booklet identical to the 1798 1st edition, except for replacing the long "*f*" with a modern "s", by the *Beecher House Center for the Study of Equal Rights* and the *Wilberforce Institute for the study of Slavery and Emancipation*, 2010.

A NARRATIVE

OF THE

LIFE & ADVENTURES

OF

VENTURE,

A NATIVE OF AFRICA;

BUT RESIDENT ABOVE SIXTY YEARS IN THE
UNITED STATES OF AMERICA.

RELATED BY HIMSELF.

NEW LONDON :—PRINTED IN 1798.

RE-PRINTED, A. D. 1835,

AND PUBLISHED BY A

DESCENDANT OF VENTURE.

A NARRATIVE

—OF THE—

LIFE AND ADVENTURES

—OF—

VENTURE

A NATIVE OF AFRICA,

But Resident Above Sixty Years in the United States of America.

RELATED BY HIMSELF.

New London: Printed in 1798. Reprinted A. D. 1835, and Published by a Descendant of Venture.

Revised and Republished with Traditions by H. M. SELDEN, *Haddam, Conn., 1896.*

MIDDLETOWN, CONN.:
J. S. STEWART, PRINTER AND BOOKBINDER.
1897.

New England Sloops

❖┄◄┄◄◉◉◉◈◉◉◉►┄►┄❖

No drawing or painting is known to exist of the *Charming Susanna*,
the ship that brought VENTURE to America in 1739. But it would have
looked very much like the *Sloop Providence* (shown on page 96).

Sloops were the workhorses of the New-England based cargo,
whaling, and slave trade in the 17th and 18th centuries. The larger ones,

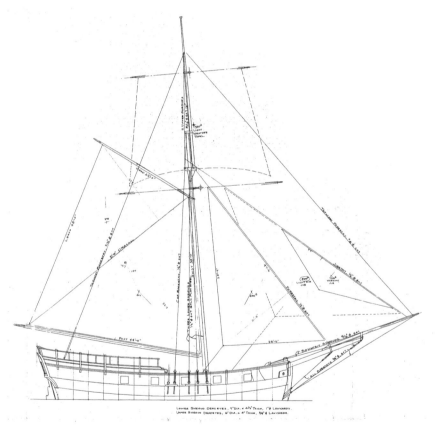

Drawing showing the *Sloop Providence*

between 35 and 50 tons, plied the oceans, while the smaller ones worked the coasts and rivers.

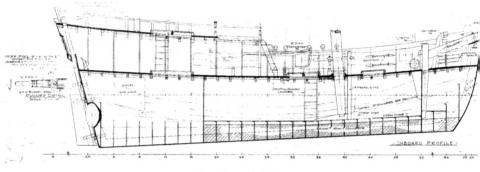

Cutaway drawing of the *Sloop Providence*

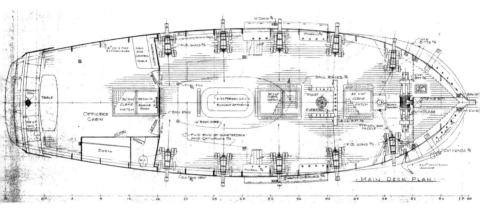

Deck of the *Sloop Providence*

Sloops were not designed for specific tasks, but were "fitted out" for each voyage and type of cargo. When provisioning the West Indies, for example, a ship's cargo containing such supplies as wood shingles, bricks, and foodstuffs were stored in the hold, while horses, oxen, and other livestock were secured on deck under tents.

Leaving Newport, the *Charming Susanna* would have carried mainly hogsheads of rum. When arriving off the coast of Africa, she would have traded rum for other goods with ships from Britain and other European countries, so as to have a good selection to trade for slaves and for provisions on the return voyage from the Gold Coast. The ship was configured to carry slaves in two main holds below decks on the return trip. One hold would be for men and the other for women, girls, and boys (probably under age 15).

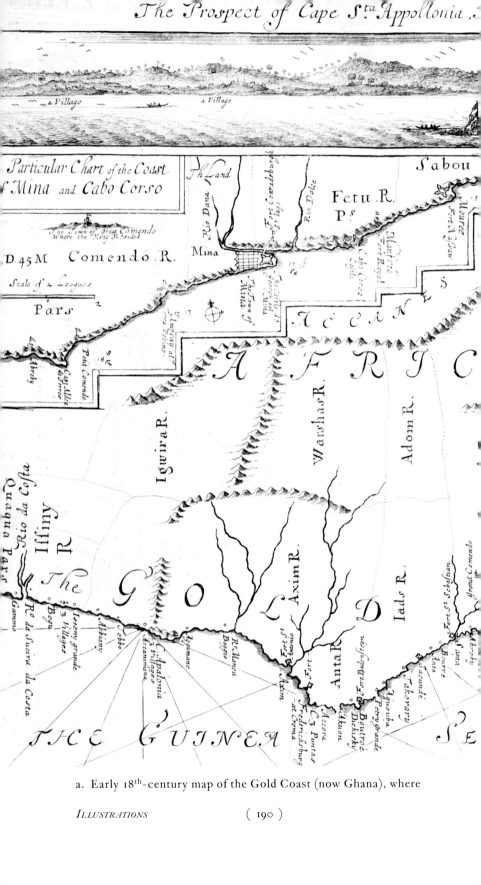

The Prospect of Cape S.ta Appollonia.

a Village   a Village

Particular Chart of the Coast of Mina and Cabo Corso

Th Land

Rio Dana

Fort Conradburgh

Rio Dolce

Fetu R.
P.s

Sabou

The Town of great Comendo where the King Resided

D. 45 M   Comendo R.   Mina

Cabo Corso Castle

Scale of 2 Leagues

Pars   2

The Town of Mina

Petit Comendo   Cape Allee de Torros

A   F   R   I   C

Iguira R.

Warshas R.

Adom R.

Quanqua Pars

Rio da Costa

Iffiny R.

Rio da Suera da Costa

Gamou

Eboe

Albany

3 Villages

Atpalonia 4 Villages Accanume

Agamane

R.e Mancu Bogoe

The   G   O   L   D

Axim R.

Iads R.

Anta R.

Fort S.t Antonio

Fort Axim

Frederickshurg de Crema

C. 3 Puntas

Fort St Sebastian

Grand Comendo

THE   GUINEA   S   E

a. Early 18th-century map of the Gold Coast (now Ghana), where

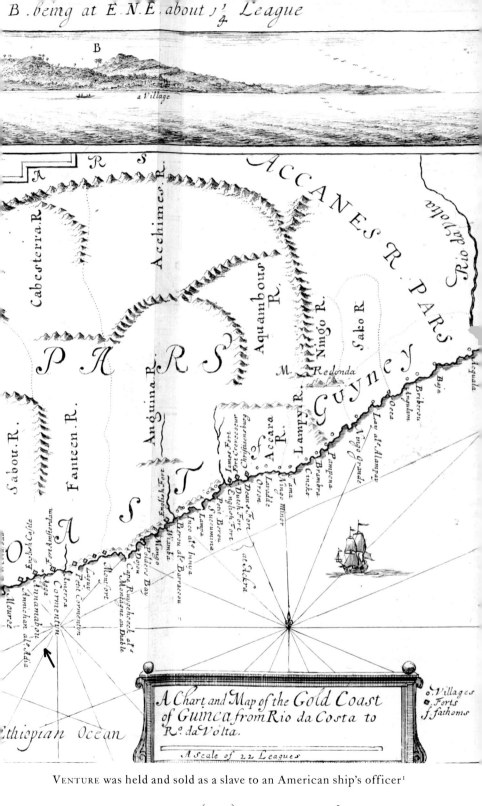

VENTURE was held and sold as a slave to an American ship's officer[1]

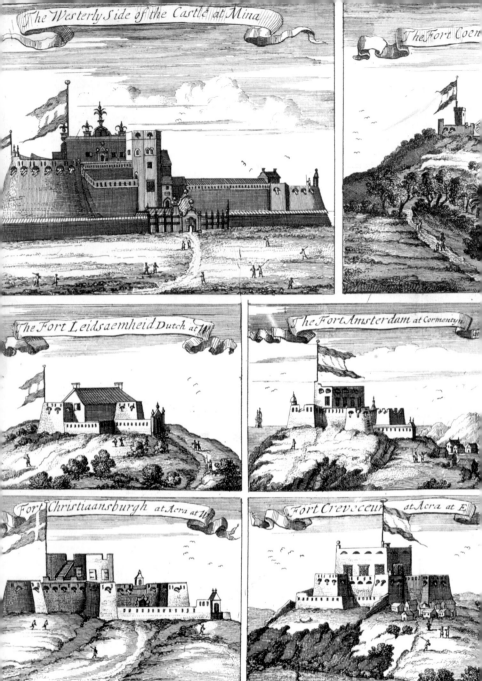

b. European-owned castles and forts on Guinea's Gold Coast (now Ghana),

Gardens at W

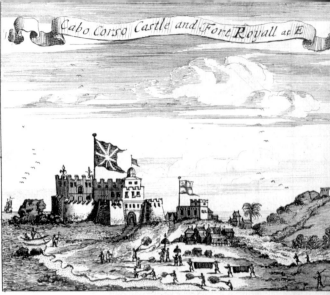

Cabo Corso Castle and Fort Royall at E

The English Castle at Anamaboe at E

The Fort Nassau Dutch at W

Fort Iames at Acra at E

The English Fort at Simpa at W

where African captives were held and sold to foreign slave-ship captains
Annamaboe Fort – middle left

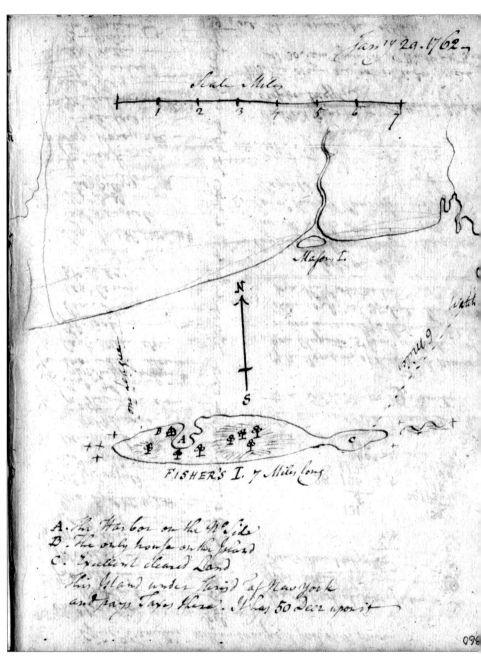

Map of Fishers Island drawn by Ezra Stiles in 1762,
from his sketch book

RUN away from George Mumford, of Fisher's-Island, the 27th Instant, four Men Servants, a white Man and three Negroes, who hath taken a large two-Mast Boat, with a square Stern, and a large white Pine Canoe; the Boat's Timbers are chiefly red Cedar. The white Man named Joseph Heday, says he is a Native of Newark, in the Jerseys; a short well set Fellow, of a rudy Complection; his Cloathing when he went away was a red Whitney Great Coat, red and white flower'd Serge Jacket, a Swan-Skin strip'd ditto, lapell'd, a Pair of Leather Breeches, a Pair of Trowsers, old Shoes, &c. The Negroes are named Fortune, Venture, and Isaac; Fortune is a tall slim comely well spoken Fellow, had on a Kersey Great Coat, three Kersey Jackets, and Breeches of a dark Colour, a new Cloth colour'd Fly-Coat, with a red Lining, a blue Serge Jacket, with red Lining, a new Pair of Chocolate colour'd corded Drugget Breeches, a Pair of blue and white check'd Trowsers, two Pair of Shoes, one of them new, several Pair of Stockings, a Castor and a new Felt Hat. Venture had a Kersey dark colour'd Great Coat, three Kersey Jackets, two Pair of Breeches of the same, a new Cloth colour'd Fly-Coat, with red Shalloon Lining, a green Ratteen Jacket almost new, a trimson birded Stuff ditto, a Pair of large Ozmabrigs Trowsers, a new Felt Hat, two Pair of Shoes, one Pair new, several Pair of Stockings; he is a very tall Fellow, 6 Feet 2 Inches high, thick square Shoulders, large bon'd, mark'd in the Face, or scar'd with a Knife in his own Country. Isaac is a Muslee, a short Fellow, seemingly clumsy and stiff in his Gate, bushy Head of Hair, sower Countenance, had on a Kersey Great Coat, Jacket and Breeches as aforesaid, a new Cloth colour'd Fly-Coat, with Lining, a Pair of Trowsers, of Guinea Cloth, a new Felt Hat, Shoes and Stockings as above. Stole and carried away with them, a Firkin of Butter, weighs about 60 Pound, two Cheeses weighs 64 Pounds, and Bread for the same. Whoever takes up and secures said Run-aways, so that their Master may have them again, shall have TWENTY POUNDS, New-York Currency, Reward and all reasonable Charges paid, or equivalent for either of them; or secure the Boat, that the Owner may have her again, shall be well rewarded, by

GEORGE MUMFORD.

Newspaper advertisement placed by George Mumford for the capture and return of VENTURE SMITH and three other escapees in 1754[2]

(195)

Deed for the first Haddam Neck land purchased by VENTURE SMITH
"a free negro Resident in Haddam", from Abel Bingham in 1775

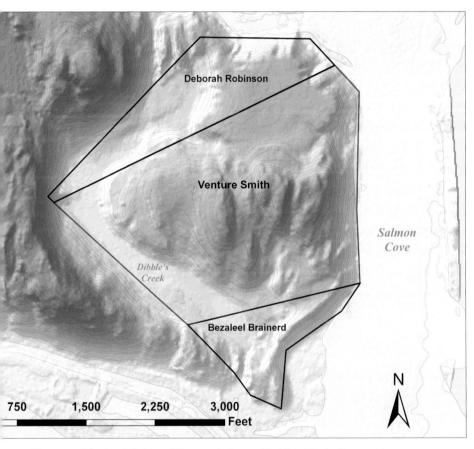

Topographical aerial view of Venture's farm at Haddam Neck, Connecticut
with overlay of 1778 boundaries, by Cameron Blevins

Illustrations

To all People to whom these Presents shall [come] Greeting. Know ye, that We, Guy Richards & Richard Dishon, both New-London, Administrators on the Estate of Capt. Peter Harris, late of New-London. deceas'd. by and with the Consent of the Heirs of said Estate, and For, and in the Consideration of the Sum of Forty Pounds in Money, and Ten Bushels

206.   1750.

Corn, & Ten Bushels Rye to us in Hand paid by Venture Smith, of East-Haddam, in Hartford County, received to our full Satisfaction: have Bargained, Sold, Set-over, & Delivered, & by these Presents; do Bargain, Sell, Set-over, & deliver unto the said Venture Smith a certain Negro Man, Named Sawney, which was the Property of said Capt. Peter Harris, Deceas'd.

To have and to Hold, the said bargained Premises, with the Appurtenances, & the proper Use and Behoof of him, the said Venture Smith, & his Heirs and Assigns forever. And we, the said Richards & Dishon, do for ourselves & Heirs, covenant

Venture purchased Sawney form the estate of Sawney's former owner, Capt. Peter Harris. Venture put up the money, but significantly gave Sawney his freedom immediately and then recorded the money still due as a mortgage.

& warrant and defend for ever, the said Bar-
gained Premises, unto the said Venture Smith,
with his Heirs & Assigns, against all, and
all manner of Persons, by these Presents.
In Witness whereof, with the Delivery of said
Negro Man, named Sawney, have hereunto set our
Hands & Seals, the Seventh day of December,
Annoque Domini 1778.

Signed, sealed & delivered.   Guy Richards, a Seal.
in Presence of
Marvin Ward.   Rich'd Dishon, a Seal.
Marvin G. Ward.

                    1781.   207.

East. Haddam, Octr. 26, 1778:
The within Bill of sale was given upon Condition,
in Nature of Mortgage, for a small sum that I
was bound for Sawney, and he having paid
the same, I do this Day Deliver this Bill of
Sale to s'd Sawney, having no further claims
upon him.

In presence of   his
Dyar Throop.   Venture X Smith.
Thos. Moseley.   mark

A true Copy of the Original.
              Test, Josiah Hale, Regr.

To All Persons to whome it may Concern — Know ye that I Winthrop Saltonstall of New London in the County of New London at a Publick Vendue purchased Sundry Articles at the Sign Post — Vizt. Two Plows One Saddle Horse Taking ye Joke Oxen, Cart, Negro Will, parcel Pots, ptonques & Shovel, ff Handirons, ff Doz. Looking Glass, Brass Kettle, Bedd & Furniture, Ax, Skillet, parcel Pewter Plates Dishes & Basons, Two Tables, Cow, Two Horses, Rowlingstone — Clock, ____ Ten Tons Hay, Negro Flora, Anchor, parcel Plank Fourteen Cannon, ____ Struck of to my self — Also Three Looking Glasses, Three Brass Kettles, Two Dozen Chairs & One Horse Cart — Struck of to Mr. John Richards ff my request to him for my Acco. Also a par=cel Basons Struck of to Mr. Joseph Hurlbut ff my request for my Acco. Also one Saddle Struck of to Capt. David Mumford ff my request for my Acco. also ff Tonques & Shovel, Skillet & ff Handirons Struck of to Jeremiah Miller Esqr. ff my request for my Acco. Also 1 Skillet Struck of to Mr. ____ David Manwaring ff my request for my Acco. And Negro Neptune Log Chain & Four Tables, ff Trux, Scale Beem Scales & Ten half hund. Weights, Two Tons Wheat Straw & Four Swivel Guns Struck of to Mr. Thomas Mumford ff my request for my Acco. — Which said Articles ____ Amounting to £346.7.9 were levied upon by Christopher Christophers Dept. Sheriff in part of Satisfaction of an Execution against Colo. Gurdon Saltonstall in favour of Dudley Saltonstall dated 18 Decr. 1771 which said Articles were purchased for him the said Dudley Saltonstall & are now indorsed on the Execution aforesd. And that no Person by from or under me might have any Right Claim or Pretence thereto I the said Winthrop Saltonstall do hereby for ever Quit Claim to him the said Dudley Saltonstall all right Title or Interest that might any ways accrue to me my Heirs or Assigns by Virtue of the Purchase aforesd. in Witness whereof I have here=unto sett my Hand & Seal in New London on this 15 Day of July A Domini 1772 —

Witnesses.
Nathaniell Chappell
Daniell Coit

Wm. Saltonstall

Bill of sale from Winthrop Saltonstall for goods bought at auction
July 15, 1772, New London, Connecticut

Venture Smith of Haddam in Hartford County Having this 8th of November 1784 Taken out an Attachment against Amos Ranny of P. Haddam to the Value of 4 Lawful Money to be prosecuted before Ezra Brainerd Justice of peace for P. County Dudly Brainerd of P. Haddam acknowledged himself bound in a Recognisance of P. Lawful Money payable to the said Amos Ranny Conditioned that the P. Venture Smith Shall prosecute his Attachment at P. Court to Effect and answer all Damage in Case he make not his plea Good

Acknowledged the 8th of November 1784

Before me Ezra Brainerd Justice of peace

At a Court for the Trial of Small Causes Holden at Haddam in the County of Hartford 9ber 16th 1784 present Ezra Brainerd Justice of peace for P. County. Venture Smith of Said Haddam plantiff Versus Amos Ranny of P. Haddam Defendant in an Action or plea Demanding the Sum of four pounds Lawful money Due by book & also Damages in neglecting to build a Scowboat. As by the writ on file Dated the 8th of 9ber 1784 may appear. The parties Appeared and the Defendt

VENTURE SMITH sues Amos Ranny in Haddam Small Causes court held by Justice of the Peace Ezra Brainerd of Haddam Neck, October 16, 1784

in the County of Middlesex pleaded that he Owed the plantiff Nothing in manner and form as the plantiff in his Declaration hath alledged and upon this the parties were at Issue this Court having heard the pleas is of Opinion the Defendt Owes the plantiff whereupon it is Considered the plantiff Shall Recover of the Defendt the Sum of one pound four Shillings and ten pence Lawful money Debt and Cost of Suit Taxed at Six Shilling and Eight pence and that Execution go forth accordingly

per me Ezra Brainerd Justice of peace

Damages for Neglecting the Boat	1:0:0
Due on Book	0:4:10
Justice's fees	0:4:6
Constables fees	.:1:1
plantiff fees	.:1:1
	1:11:6

Mr Ranny on hearing the Judgment paid the Cost in Order to appeal

January 26th 1785 Execution granted on the above Judgment

C - ii

To the honorable General Assembly now
sitting at New Haven

Whereas Brister a Negro man Servant of mine
that has served in the Connecticutt Line during the
late War, and has been a good Soldier and frugal of
his Interest and capable of Business, Equal to most while
Man in Way of Husbandry, and being as he says but about 38
Years old, Thinking that it is reasonable that he Should be set
free as he has been fighting for the Liberties of the Country,
and I being willing that he Should be Emansipated I freely
give up all my Right to Sd Servant and humble Request
that your Honors would set Sd Servant free as your humble
Memorialist prays,

                                        Joshua Austin

New Haven Jany the 21. 1784.

                                  New Haven Jany 21 1784

This Certifies that Brister Baker Soldier in the late
4th Connt Regt has served faithfully while in public
Service for the term of Six Years — Never appeared to be
very careful of the pay he recd from the public,
I believe that he would if liberated, be very Industrious &
able to render himself a Sufficient Support in the
Character of a free Citizen

he was transpd to the 2nd Conn Regt
where he was recd his discharge

                                  R Sherman P M
                          Jno Trowbridge late 4t Connt Regt
                                        Lieut 4 Connt Regt

C - iii

10

At a Justice Court Holden at Haddam for the Tryal of
Small Causes March 14th 1785.

Present Ezra Brainerd Justice of the peace for the County
of Hartford: Venture Smith of E Haddam Confess'd
a Judgment against himself of being Guilty of pro-
phane Swearing.   and paid fine Six Shillings

Justice of the Peace Ezra Brainerd, Haddam Neck – March 14, 1785
top – VENTURE pleads guilty to public swearing
below – VENTURE was assaulted and is charging the perpetrators, lead by Ranny see c4

At a Court held at haddam in the County of Hartford on the
14th Day of March 1785 Present Ezra Brainerd Esqr a Justice of
peace for Said County Amos Ranny & Elisha Day Both of Said
Haddam and Jonathan Bowers of Chatham were brought be
fore this Court by a writ to answer to the Complaint of Venter
Smith which writ & Complaint are Dated the 14th Day of
March instant Setting forth that in the night Season preceed
ing the 13th Day of March instant it being Sabbath or Lords
Day he was in Haddam at or near a place Called Baldhill
in the peace of God and of this State and about his own Law
ful Business and that then and there three men Assaulted
Beat wounded maimed and Greatly Terrified and put his life
in Danger whereby he was Damaged the Sum of forty Shillings
Lawful money and that he Suspected the Said Amos Elisha
and Jonathan to have Committed the Said Act praying that
they might be proceeded against according to one Law of
this State Entitled an Act for preventing & punishing Dis
orders Committed in the night Season as per Said Com
plaint and writ on file may more fully appear — To which
Complaint the Said Amos Elisha and Jonathan being Ar
raigned pleaded not Guilty this Court having Examined the
witnesses and heard the parties is of the Opinion that the Said
Amos Elisha & Jonathan are Guilty whereupon it is Consider
ed by this Court that the Said Amos Elisha and Jonathan
pay the Said Venture the Sum of nine Shillings Lawful
money Damages and be further punished by Each of them paying
to the Treasurer of the Town of Haddam a fine of five Shil
lings Lawful money and Cost of Suit Taxed at Taxed at Eight
Shillings and one penny   per me Ezra Brainerd Justice of peace
On hearing the above Judgment the S Amos Elisha & Jonathan paid Damages fine &

C - iv

At a justice Court Holden in Haddam on the 9th
Day of January 1795 present Ezra Brainerd Justice of
peace for Said County Cuff a Negro of Said Haddam
was brought before Said Court by a writ Dated Janry
9th AD 1795 to answer to a Complaint made and Exhi-
bited against him by Sam Northum one of the
Grandjurors of Said Haddam for being Guilty of a
breach of one Law of this State Entitled an Act for the
punishment of Theft in that the Said Cuff Negro
did on or about the middle of December Last
Steal two cords of Oak wood and Conceal the Same
to which Complaint the Defendant plead not gui-
ty Whereupon the Evidence in Said Case was Sworn
and Examined which this Court having heard
Considered with the pleas of the parties is of Opinion
that the Said Cuff Negro is Guilty in Manner &
form as Set forth in Said Complaint whereupon
the Said Cuff Negro is Sentenced by this Court to be
whipped Ten Stripes on his Naked Body and pay
a fine of forty Shillings for the use of the Town
of Haddam and pay Cost of prosecution Taxed at
one pound Lawful money and to Stand Committed till this Judgment is Complied with
                    By me   E B.   J P

Complaint   1
Writ   1
C Selden Jnr P's
  Northum   3:6   Evidences   Elijah Brooks   0:2:0
    Eddy   3:6   Asa Brooks   0:2:0
                                                    ½ 0
                                                   16
                                                  1: 0: 0

                                          Cuff to Goal

Fishers Island 1741/42 lease between Madm Anne Winthrop of New London, Connecticut, agent for her husband John Winthrop, who resided in London, England, and was the owner of Fish Island, and George Mumford. Leasing the Island, buildings, and livestock, an entire working provisioning plantation. A transcription is included in the endnotes pages 197-200, note # 49.

Expell Remove & Cast out and the Same to have again Retain & Repossess as in their former Estate, this Indenture or any thing herein Contained to the Contrary thereof in any wise Notwithstanding, & further the Lessor doth reserve the Liberty of one Chamber in the Best house for his own Use only, also ten Acres of Land on the North hill with Liberty of Setting up Fences warehouses Stables, & out houses with free Egress & Regress to & from ye premises or any part thereof. & the said John Winthrop his heirs Execut[ors] Administrat[ors] or Assigns shall have Liberty to Come upon the demised Land & premises to Live there and to Make Preparation for Improvement against another year two Months before the Expiration of this Lease, and it is further agreed that no Swine is to run at Large on ye said premises, but are to be Kept Suitable Pastures or Inclosures where they may do the Least Dammage and are all to be Ring'd, to prevent their rooting & Spoiling the ground, and that the Said George Mumford shall at no time Break up Any of the Meadow or Mowing Land but what hath been Usual & Accustomary or Such an Equivolent And to lay down what is now or shall be hereafter broken up, in good order and not to Leave the Same in Indian Hills, and ye said George Mumford his Execut[or] or Administrat[or] shall at no time Make over this Lease or any part thereof to any person or persons, without the approbation & free Consent of the Lessor, and also all ye Deer, Patridges peacocks, Quails, rabbitts or any other Sort of wild Creatures with their Increase are to run at Liberty, & Remain there for the Use of the Lessor, & that the Lessor shall Have Liberty to Continue on ye premises, to Fodder and Look after the Creatures untill the first day of May next after the Expiration of this Lease, in Wittness where of the parties to these presents above Written have Interchangeably Set to their hands and Seals the Day & year first above Written

N[ota]. Interlined on ye fir[st] side between 4th & 3[d] lines this word (Late)
between 5th & 6th line the first side these words / now of Fishers Island in the Province of New York /
above first line on this side these words / first &/ all were wrote before
Signing & Sealing

George Mumford

Signed Sealed and Delivered
In Presence of

J. Hempsted
Geo. Rotherstall

April the 29th 1746 It is Covenanted and agreed by the Lessor & Lessee that this Lease shall be & it hereby is Lengthned out one year after the Expiration of the Same & to Stand in full force in Every part thereof Excepting in the Sum pay- able for the Rent. & the Sum to be paid for Rent this Current year in the Same Manner as Expressd in the Lease is Two Hundred & Seventy five Hundreds in Currant money of NewYork or Bills of Credit on this Colony or any of the Neighbouring Govern- =ments that are good & passable Equivolent to the afores[ai]d N.York Currancy as wittness our hands the Day abov[e]s[ai]d

George Mumford

Wittness
Basill Winthrop
Margrett Miller

Sub Stock of Neat on Fishers Island
before Mr. — in this Lease
4 Four Sucks Grown oxen one year
Eight years old or other Litter
11 Twenty two Cows
2 Two five years old Steers
4 four five year old Steers
1 Ditto
3 Three 3 yr[s] old Stock
1 Three years old Bull
4 Three yr[s] old Heif[e]rs
1 one Three years old Bull
7 Seven two year old Heif[e]rs
12 Twelve yearlings
81 — These be Neat Cattle

8 Breeding Mares
120 Twenty horse kind
1350 Thirteen Hundred & fifty Sheep with their fleeces and their Lambs

Inventory of the Estate of the Hon.ble Daniel
Edwards Esq.r Late of Hartford Dec.d

taken August 1775

1 Looking Glass 7/		3..10
1 Chest & 4 Drawers 25/		1..5
1 Dressing Table 6/		6
1 Small Round Table 4/6		4..6
6 Chairs @ 5/		1..10
1 Trunk 6/		6
1 Bed, Bolster & pillow, Bed Quilt and Bedstead & Curtains	100/	5
2 Glass Servers 3/ 1 pr Glass Candlesticks 1/		10
3 pint Glasses 2/ 2 Salts & 1 Cream pot 1/		3
1 Silver Tankard w.t 22.. oz 6/8	7..6..8
1 Silver porringer, 5 Table Spoons & 6 Tea Spoons, 1 pepper Box, Sugar Tongs, Clasp and Buckle all 25 oz 6/8	8..4
1 Toilet Table 10/ 7 Sheets @ 7/each	2..19..0
28 Diaper Napkins @ 4/3	1..6..3
6 Holland Do 3/ 25 pillow cases & Towels 7..3..10
7 Coarse Towels 4/3 2 Diaper Table Cloths 10/	15..3
4 Sheets 28/ 1 Table Cloth 3/	1..11
8 Table Cloths @	2
5 Home Spun Towels @ 9	3..9
2 pillow Cases 9/6	1..6
41 Pewter Platters @ 9/6	1..10..9
29 Do Plates & Basons @ 9	1..2..1½
7 Do Plates @ 9/	17
1 Large Bringer & Cover	2
1 Bed, Bolster & pillows	2..10
purple & white bed Quilt 18/ Old Curtains 5/	1..3
3 Old Brass Candlesticks 4/ Small Coffee pot 3/	6
1 Small Brass Kittle 3/	3
2 pott Covers & 2 Dish Covers	2
1 Small Copper Coffee Kittle	2..6
1 Br Brass Skimmer & Ladle	2
Block tin & coffee pot & Collender & Tunnel 4/6	2..6
5 Brass pall pans 4/6 1 Stone Jarr 2/	2..10
1 Old Duck & Book Case	3..3
1 Large Black Walnut Table	12
1 Ditto 8/ 1 Ditto 5/	13
1 Looking Glass Cleat	15
1 Great Chair 4/ 1 Commode 2/	18

Carried Over

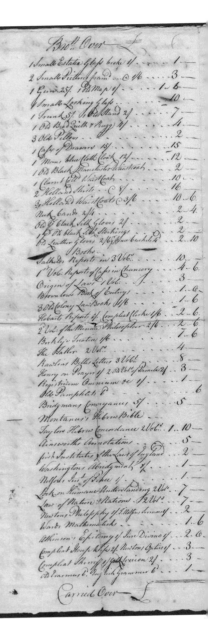

Br.t Over

1 Small Estate Glass books 4/		1
2 Small Pictures framed @ 6		3
1 Gun 25/ 1 old Map 1/		1..6
4 Small Looking Glass		10
1 Trunk 5/ 1 old Stand 2/		7
1 Old Bed Quilt & Rugg 4/		4
3 Old Pillows		2
1 Case of Drawers 15/		15
1 Mans blue Cloth Coat 12/		12
1 Old Black Manchester Waistcoat		2
1 Claret Cold Waistcoat		10
2 Holland Shirts @ 8/		16
3 Holland Waistcoats 3/6		10..6
Neck Cloth 2/4		2..4
Old p.r black Silk Gloves 2/		2
1 p.r Old black silk Stockings		2
Old Leather Gloves 2/6 Shoe buckle 4		2..10

Books

Salked's Reports in 3 Vol.		10
1.st Vol. Reports of Cases in Chancery		4..6
Origin of Laws 1 Vol.		3
Brownlow's Book of Entries		1..6
3 Old Colony Law Books 1/6		1..6
Hobart Report of Compleat Clerke 1/6		2..6
2 Vol. of the Minute Philosopher 2/6		2..6
Birkly's Oration 9/6		7..6
The Hitler 2 Vol.		4
Rawlins Bells Letters 3 Vol.		8
Henry on Prayer 1/ 2 old Vol. of Swifts 2/		3
Negotium Omnium &c 1/		1
Old Pamphlets &c		6
Bridgmans Conveyances 5/		5
Montanus Hebrew Bible		
Taylors Hebrew Concordance 2 Vol.	1..10
Ainsworths Annotations		5
first Institutes of the Laws of England		2
Washingtons Abridgmt 7/		1
Nelsons Just of Peace 1/		1
Lock on Humane Understanding 2 Vol.		7
Law of Nature & Nations St 2 Vol.		7
Newtons Philosophy of 5 Vol. in Summary		2
Wards Mathematicks		1..6
Athinson's Epitomy of Law Divine 4/		2..0
Compleat Surv.r whole of Newtons Optics 4/		3
Compleat History of England 2/		3
Old Erasmus & English Grammar &c		1

Carried Over

C - viii

el Edwards' Probate inventory page 3   Daniel Edwards' Probate inventory page 4

Daniel Edwards died in New Haven September 6, 1765 and his probate inventory
was done after his wife Sarah died July 31, 1775

Daniel Edwards' Probate inventory page 5   Sarah Edwards' Probate inventory page 1

ILLUSTRATIONS

Brot Over   £

7 Aprons . . . . @ 3/ . . . . 1..1..
2 Cambrick Handkr @ 1/ . . . .. 2 —
Silver Chain Buckle Stay Hook }
Hairpins &c Wt 1st 7½ ℔ . . . . 9..2
1 ps old Silver Shoe buckles . . . . 6..0
Gold Sleeve buttons & things . . . 1..5
1 Gold Neck Lace . . . . 1..15..0
4 Stone Ring . . . . 14..—

The Above & Within Apprized by us the
Subscribers Under Oath

     Samuel Church
     James Hooker

Added by the Administrators Money recd
for Skyman Jacob Baanheahs Note
Carried to Mr Edwards Inventory

Hartford County ss
Hartford Aug 12 1776
Messrs Sa. Church & Ja. Hooker made
Oath to the truth of the above & foregoing —
before me Oliv Ellsworth Just Pe

added by the administrators Indian Corn that grass
raised at the Blue Hills Sold for

11th Sept 1777 Then Solomon Smith &
Sarah Tassett Jun administrators
made oath in form, & accepted by me
J. Talcott Judge

Inventory of the Estate of Mrs Sarah
Edwards late of Hartford Decd
taken August 11th 1775

2 Negros Cuff & Kate @ 25 Each 50..0..0
1 Negro Girl Jenny 25..—
1 Ditto Kate 16..—
1 Ditto Mabel 9..—
1 Table M:H .. 0..8..0
6 Chairs M:H @ 2/6 .. 0..15..0
1 Silver Can & 2 Spoons Mark M:H wt 3..19..0
2 Diaper Napkins M:H @ 1/6 .. 0..3..
4 Towels M:H 1/ .. 0..4..
1 Diaper Table Cloath .. 0..6
7 Home Made Towels @ 1/4 0..9..4
1 Sheet 6/ 1 Diaper Table Cloath 6/ 0..12..
1 pillow Case 2/ 1 ps Sheets 7/ 0..9
1 ps Sheats 3/ 5 Diaper Towls 4/ 0..9..
2 pewter Platters wt 11 @ 1/ 0..11..0
1 Round Tea Table 0..15
1 Bunk Bolster & quilt 3..10
1 Blanket 5/ 1 ps Sheats 10/ 15
1 Vol Henrichs Sermons 1/ 1..—
1 Large Bible 1..0
Lectern on Gun Middlemads 0..1
1 Note of Hand agt Joseph Lee for 2..0
1 Ditto agt Solomon Earles Dated 1 June
1775 on Interest pay't 6 June 1776 £260 60..14..0
1 Forty Shilling Bill 2..—
1 ox Cart 80/ 1 ox Sled 20/ 5..—
1 Yoak of Cattle 14..—
2 pitch forks 3/ 2 Rakes 1/6 4..6
2 Cows @ 65/ 6..10..0
1 Heifer 2..0..0
1 ps of Sheats 20/ ps pillos Case 5/ 1..5
C of Hay in the Barn @ 2/6 ℔
Flax in the Barn not Dresst
Wheat in the Barn not Thrasht
1 Cheespress 3/ 0..3..0

Carried Over   £

Sarah Edwards' Probate inventory page 2   Sarah Edwards' Probate inventory page 3

Sarah Edwards' Probate inventory page 4

In the Name of God, Amen. I Daniel
Edwards of Hartford Town and County in the Colony
of Connecticut, being now confin'd by Sickness, yet of
Sound Mind and Memory, do make this my last Will &
Testament — I do now in the first place renewedly and
heartily devote myself and my all to the eternal God,
hoping for his Acceptance and everlasting Favour, of
his infinite Mercy, in Jesus Christ, the Lord: And
touching my worldly Interest, which God has been —
pleased to put into my Hands, (my just Debts and
Funeral Expences being first paid) my Will is as —
follows. —

Imprimis. I give to my dear and loving Wife Sarah —
Edwards, all my four Servants absolutely and to
her own Disposal; and also the Use and improvement
of all my Estate, both real and personal, in Old —
England and New, during her natural Life, except
so much personal Estate as shall be necessary to
answer the particular Legacies hereafter mentioned.

Item. I give to the Rev.d M.r Edward Dorr of Hartford
as an Acknowledgement for his special Kindness to
me and mine in times of Distress and Sorrow the
Sum of Thirty Pounds, to be paid by my Ex.rs hereafter named.

Item. I give to the Rev.d M.r Elnathan Whitman of —
Hartford the Sum of Ten Pounds, to be paid him by
my Ex.rs hereafter nam'd

Item. I give to my well-beloved Son in Law, M.r George
Lord my Sword and Belt; and also the Use of
my Shop and such other Apartments & Accommodations
in or about my House, as shall be needful for carrying
on his Trade and Business, together with the Liberty
of the House, so long as he shall continue a single
Man.

Item. I give and bequeath all the Rest and Residue of
my Estate, both real and Personall to my tenderly —

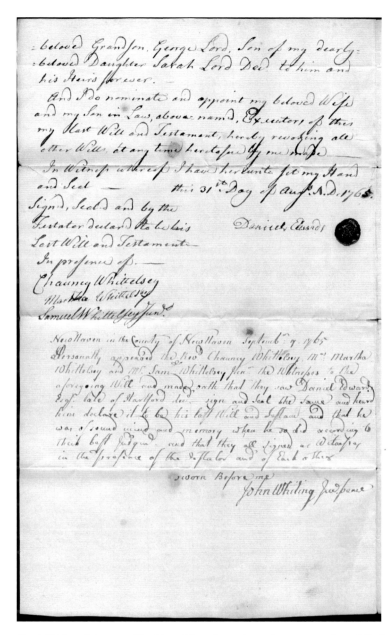

Daniel Edwards became ill with a violent fever about August 27, 1765 and died
11 days later on September 6, while in New Haven. He executed this will on
the 31st of August 1765.

TIME LINE
THE LIFE OF VENTURE SMITH

✠·◄·◄·◄◉✜◉►·►·►·✠

Legend:

- **Entries** - that are confirmed by documented records
  Entries - on which there is general agreement
  (Entries) - that are being researched, documented, or refined

The date in the *Narrative* that VENTURE gives for his birth is *"about the year 1729."* The age/date on the tombstone and the title page of the *Narrative*, cross-referenced to the slave voyage and the runaway notice, put his birth within a range of 1727 – 1729, probably 1729. His own estimates of dates, recounted when he was about 70 years old and in failing health, are sometimes in conflict with each other or historical records. Even the sons, Cuff and Solomon, often did not use the actual dates of their births. It appears that VENTURE settled on January 1, 1729 as his birth date when planning his burial and then used it for the *Narrative*.

1729 –
> "Broteer Furro," the first son of the prince of "Dukandarra" is born. Probably in the Royaume d'Ouangara (Kingdon of Ouangara).

1737 – [November-December]
> Mother leaves with her three children after a dispute with her husband, returning to her own family. She leaves Broteer with a prominent farmer, likely for some form of apprenticeship.
> *VENTURE is now 8 - 9*

• **1738** – [October 6]
Charming Susanna departs from Rhode Island for Africa.

1738-1739 – [December-January]
> Broteer returns home.
> *VENTURE is now 9 - 10*

1739 – [January-February]
> A raiding army kills Broteer's father, and the youth is captured. Army is led by Baukurre (probably King Boukar).

1739 – [March-April-early spring]
> The army raids the village of Malagasco.
> *VENTURE is now 10 - 11*

1739 – [spring]
> Broteer is taken to Annamaboe District on the Gold Coast of West Africa (now Ghana). It is unclear which slave castle (likely a

remaining part of Annamaboe Fort) he was kept in or how long he was held there.

1739 — [late May or early June]
Broteer and other slaves are purchased by American slavers operating the Rhode Island ship *Charming Susanna*. Broteer was purchased by the steward Robinson Mumford, "*with his own private venture*" and was named VENTURE for "*four gallons of rum, and a piece of calico.*"

1739 — [around June]
Charming Susanna sails from the Gold Coast. Mumford starts training VENTURE during the voyage, so probably he had the run of the ship.
slavevoyages.org - voyage #36067.

• **1739** — [late August]
Charming Susanna arrives in Bridgetown Harbor, Barbados; on August 23 all but four of the captives are sold by agent David Minvielle, taxes paid on the sale of 74 slaves £ 18 10s.

1739 — [late August or early September]
Charming Susanna sails from Barbados.

1739 — [September]
Ship arrives in Rhode Island. Robinson Mumford places the youth with one of his sisters (likely Mercy Dyer, his oldest, who lived in Newport) to learn some English and how to be a manservant.
   VENTURE is now about 11

(1740 - 1741) — [late 40 or early 41]
VENTURE is taken from Rhode Island to the Mumford homestead on Fishers Island.

1741 —
Robinson Mumford dies at sea; his father, Capt. George Mumford, inherits VENTURE. VENTURE goes from the Big House to the fields.

1753 - 1754 — [late in 53 or January/February 54]
VENTURE marries Meg (Marget), another Mumford slave.
   VENTURE is now 25

• **1754** — [March 27] (newspaper ad appears on April 1st)
VENTURE runs away with two other slaves and an indentured servant, then returns voluntarily within a few days. They were headed for the Massepe River on the South Shore of Long Island (misspelled in *Narrative* as "Mississippi").

1754 —
After runaway attempt George Mumford transfers ownership of VENTURE and Meg to his son James.

1754 — [November or slightly earlier]
Meg gives birth to their first child, Hannah.

- **1754** – [close of year]
  VENTURE is sold to Thomas Stanton of Stonington-point and separated from Meg and his month-old baby.

  1756 – [late spring]
  Thomas Stanton buys Meg and Hannah for £700 old tenor.

  1756 – [in late 56 or early 57]
  VENTURE and Meg's first son, Solomon, is born.

  1759 – [winter of 1758-1759]
  Hempstead Miner of Stonington contracts to buy VENTURE for £56 from Thomas Stanton and then hires him out to Daniel Edwards of Hartford for £10. Edwards is a lawyer, Supreme Court Judge, Member Upper House of the Colonial Legislature, and Hartford Probate Judge; and it is likely he taught VENTURE to read. Edwards is baptizing other slaves in 1760.

  In the Narrative ages given before 1754 are consistently short by 3 years.

  Going forward all ages given align.

  1760–
  VENTURE is sold for the last time to Oliver Smith Jr., who has moved to Stonington Long Point from Groton. Smith agrees to let VENTURE purchase himself for £85, to be paid in installments. Oliver Smith moved into his newly built house in spring 1761.

  VENTURE is now 31

  1760–
  1ˢᵗ payment £30 16s
  VENTURE makes 1st payment towards his freedom. Likely Primus Sike was the "middle man".

  1761 –
  Their second son, Cuff, is born. On Revolutionary War Pension applications dated 2 April 1818 Cuff says his age is 57. Application bears an original full signature.

  (1761) –
  VENTURE begins farming a plot of land he buys from Oliver Smith's in-laws next to Thomas Stanton's farm where Meg is still a slave.

  1763 – [summer]
  2ⁿᵈ payment £10 - total £40 16s - due £44 4s.

  1764 – [spring]
  3ʳᵈ payment £3 12s - "privilege" £1 4s - total £51 2s - due £40 12s.
  VENTURE is now 35

  1764 – [fall]
  4ᵗʰ payment £6 14s - "privilege" £13 6s. - total £51 2s due £33 18s.

1765 — [March-April]

5th payment £20 - total £71 2s or with "privilege" £85 10s. After five years of making payments to Oliver Smith Jr, largely with money earned from side jobs, VENTURE finally buys himself and regains his freedom.

VENTURE is now 36

1765 —

VENTURE sells his house and land in Stonington and moves to Long Island.

1769 —

VENTURE has saved enough money to redeem his entire family, even at an excessive price, which he expects Thomas Stanton to demand.

(1770) — [end of 1769 but likely first half of 1770]

VENTURE purchases his two sons, Solomon and Cuff, while on Ram Island (six Ram Islands existed in the Long Island basin, most likely was the Ram Island in Southampton). Stanton probably refused to sell Meg or Hannah just to spite VENTURE.

VENTURE is now 41

• **1770** — [December 1]

VENTURE buys a farm with 26 acres (from the in-laws of his former owner and now business associate Oliver Smith) on Stonington-point, next to Thomas Stanton's farm, for £60.

(1770-1771) — [but before 1772]

Goes whaling for Capt. Smith for 7 months. Likely in charge of a whale boat and overseeing Capt. Smith's interest.

(1770-1771) —

VENTURE acquires a farm on Long Island (probably on Ram Island, Southampton; Shinnecock land).

(1772) —

Eldest son, Solomon, goes whaling and dies at sea, age 16, beginning of 1773.

1772 — [late]

VENTURE purchases Meg's freedom for £40.

VENTURE is now 43

1772-1773 — [shortly after Meg]

VENTURE purchases two Negro men.

1773 —

A third son is born and named Solomon Jr.

• **1774** — [March 22]

VENTURE sells his land in Stonington for £100. Profit £40. He sells the farm to Thomas Stanton, recouping what he paid for it, plus the £40

TIME LINE

Stanton charged him for Meg.

1774 – [December]
Venture leaves Long Island for East Haddam, Connecticut. He works 5 weeks for Timothy Chapman and 6 weeks for Abel Bingham to pay for his first land purchase on Haddam Neck.

Venture is now 46

• **1775** – [March 3]
Venture buys 10 acres on Haddam Neck for £20.

1775 –
Venture purchases his oldest child Hannah, and shortly after, she marries Isaac.

Venture is now 46

(1776-1777) –
Venture buys six more acres on Haddam Neck, probably the "Bald Hill Lot" Venture said he purchased from Joseph Wells.

• **1777** – [March 14]
Venture buys 70 additional acres from Abel Bingham for £140 and builds his home.

1777 –
Daughter Hannah comes to live with Venture.

• **1777** – [August 18]
Venture and Stephen Knowlton buy 48 acres for £250.

• **1778** – [March 8]
Venture buys Knowlton's share.

• **1778** – [July 1]
Venture sells 12 acres to free blacks Whacket Freeman and Peter (Freeman?).

• **1778** – [October 26]
Venture purchases and frees Sawney Anderson of Glastonbury, but originally from Stonington. He was the fourth known Negro Venture purchased and freed. Gave him bill of sale/mortage October 26, 1778.

• **1782** –
Sawney repaid Venture and satisfied the mortgage.

• **1781-1783** –
Cuff enlists in the Continental Army on 4 December 1780, called up on 29 January 1781 for three years. Discharged December 1783.

1782 – Hires William Jacklin and Mingo. (With Cuff in the army, Venture needs help).

Venture is now 53

(1783) – Mingo tries to run away. Venture takes him to Justice of the

Peace Dyer Throop of East Haddam.

1783 –
Daughter Hannah dies of illness.

• **1785** – [March night of 12/13]
VENTURE is attacked by three men while sitting on Bald Hill. Justice of the Peace Ezra Brainerd found the three men guilty and ordered them to pay damages to VENTURE and a fine to the court .

(1786) –
Loss of clams and boat stolen on Long Island by James Webb.

(1790) –
Capt. Elisha Hart of Saybrook sues for loss of a barrel of molasses.

• **1795** – [January 9] Cuff is found guilty of taking firewood, fined and sentenced to be whipped.

1798 – [before the middle of October] VENTURE dictates his life story.

• **1798** – [October 20]
VENTURE sells Solomon 3 ½ acres of the farm for £ 17 16s before he mortgages the rest of the property. It contains a place where VENTURE, Solomon, and their families can live if necessary.

• **1798** – [November 3]
Edward Smith and four others certify the *Narrative*.

• **1798** – [November 24]
VENTURE mortgages his farm with Edward Smith for £ 200.

• **1798** – [December]
The *Narrative* is published/printed by *The Bee* of New London.
Six ads offering it for sale, probably written by Charles Holt, run in *The Bee*, starting December 28,1798.

• **1799** – [February 20]
The *Narrative* is offered for sale by the *Journal of the Times* in Stonington February 20 through May 14, 1799.

• **1802** April 12 – Solomon buys back the farm.

• **1804** May 16 – VENTURE sells his share of the Salmon River fishing rights and the part of the island they both own to William Ackley for one dollar.

• **1805** – [September 19]
VENTURE SMITH dies in his 77th year at Haddam Neck.

• **1809** – [December 17]
Marget Smith dies in her 79th year at Haddam Neck.

• **1812** –
Solomon serves in 2nd Reg't (Sanford's), Connecticut State Troops.

- **1822** – [January 13]
  Cuff dies and is buried in Westchester Cemetery.

- **1835** –
  A Descendant of VENTURE republishes the *Narrative*, leaving out
  VENTURE's criticism of his children.

- **1843** – [March 28]
  Solomon dies and is buried with his mother and father.

- **1889** – Third edition of the *Narrative*, revised and republished by H. M.
  Selden, Hamden, Conn., 1896; Printed by J. S. Stewart, Middletown Conn.,
  1897.

Marget "Meg" Smith's tombstone

The ongoing *Documenting VENTURE SMITH Project* continues to
update and revise the *Time Line*.

see: venture-smith.org

Please send comments, new information, or suggestions to:

info@VentureSmith.org

PAYMENTS

1760 –

> VENTURE is sold for the last time to Oliver Smith Jr., who has moved to Stonington Long Point from Groton. Smith agrees to let VENTURE purchase himself for £85, to be paid in installments. Oliver Smith moved into his newly built house in spring 1761.

> *VENTURE is now 31*

1760 –

> 1st payment £30 16s

> VENTURE makes 1st payment towards his freedom.

(1761) –

> VENTURE begins farming a plot of land he buys from Oliver Smith's in-laws next to Thomas Stanton's farm where Meg is still a slave.

1763 – [summer]
> 2nd payment £10

> total £40 16s   due £44 4s

1764 – [spring]
> 3rd payment £3 12s

> "privilege" £1 4s

> total £44 6s   due £40 12s

> *VENTURE is now 35*

1764 – [fall]
> 4th payment £6 14s

> "privilege" £13 6s.

> total £51 2s   due £33 18s

1765 – [March-April]
> 5th payment £20

> total £71 2s or with "privilege" £85 10s

After five years of making payments to Oliver Smith Jr, largely with money earned from side jobs, VENTURE finally buys himself.

> *VENTURE is now 36*

ENDNOTES

✦ ◦◁ ◁ ◦◈◦ ◈◦ ▷ ▷◦ ✦

Introduction (pp. 1–11)

1. In the 3ʳᵈ edition of *A Narrative of The Life and Adventures of Venture a Native of Africa, But Resident Above Sixty Years in the United States of America. Related By Himself.* New London: Printed in 1798. Reprinted in 1835 and Published by a Descendant of Venture. Revised and Republished with Traditions by H. M. Selden, Haddam, Conn., in 1896. Middletown, Conn.: J. S. Stewart, Printer and Bookbinder, 1897. Seldon was a local amateur historian whose work reflects the time, with a strong white privilege agenda, Seldon: "Tradition says Venture's amanuensis was Elisha Niles, of Chatham, who had been a school-teacher," but he quotes no documented source (something he does for almost every other story he presents). Furthermore there is no other reference to Niles being the scribe. Niles kept a personal daily diary (the typed transcription is over 1200 pages, at the Connecticut Historical Society), and in it he never mentions doing any work for VENTURE SMITH, a member of VENTURE's family, the printer Charles Holt, or even mentions VENTURE SMITH. Seldon probably did not have access to this diary. Also, stylistically, Niles' diary is completely different than the *Narrative*.

There is extensive scholarship on Holt, and like Niles, stylistically there is no relationship between Holt's writing style or subject matter that is similar to anything in the *Narrative*. We assume he acted as a contract printer and sold ads to fill his weekly newspaper.

2. VENTURE SMITH, *Preface* to *A Narrative of the Life and Adventures of Venture, a Native of Africa, But Resident above Sixty years in the United States of America. Related by Himself* (*The Bee*, New London, 1798), pages 3-4.

3. Olaudah Equiano, *The Interesting Narrative of the Life of Olaudah Equiano, or Gustavus Vassa, the African,* (London, 1789).

4. Many of the subscribers to the 1791 (pirated) New York edition of Equiano's Narrative were from Middletown and Wethersfield, Connecticut. Middletown: 88 (Isaac Riley, a young general store owner, bought 60 for resale), Wethersfield: 6, Westfield: 1, Wallingford: 2, Berlin: 1. Source Vincent Carretta and subscribers list.

5. The ad ran weekly from February 20, 1799 to May 14, 1799 except for

April 2 and 9. This ad does not have the promotional drama of the Holt ad and was probably written by VENTURE or one of his family.

6. *Narrative* page 32, Certificate dated November 3, 1798. Getting the confirmation of the five signers must have taken a few weeks. We can assume that VENTURE finished the draft of the *Narrative* by mid October so it could be circulated among the signers of the *Certificate*: Nathaniel Minor – Lexington Alarm, he went to Boston; Elijah Palmer – Capt. in the Revolution; Capt. Amos Palmer – Privateer in the Revolution; Acors Sheffield – Artillery Lt. in the Revolution.

7. Robert Forbes, "Representative Man: Venture Smith as African and American;" paper at American Historical Association; *From Enslavement to Freedom: The Significance of the Life of Venture Smith, Then and Now*, (Boston, 2011).

8. Beinecke Rare Book and Manuscript Library, Yale University.

9. Ages are sometimes given as "I was xx years old" or "I was in my xx year or age," which in the European tradition is one year later. VENTURE did not know the exact day and month of his birth, which is hardly surprising in a culture that did not keep such records. VENTURE decided on "New Years 1729" as the date for his birth. Earlier, when he runs away from his first owner, his dates are short by exactly three years. When the *Narrative* is broken into its two parts - the first part is the story of Africa which VENTURE had been telling for years, and the second part is the account of his life after he leaves the Mumfords - the dates can be aligned. Interestingly, the reconciliation of the dates in VENTURE's *Narrative* and those in the historical record ironed itself out with time: The dates align plus or minus six months. His own estimate of being 69 years old when he dictated his story in 1798 conforms closely with verified information.

10. In his appendix to the third edition in 1897, H. M. Sheldon wrote: "Several editions of the Life of Venture have been published successively by his family, and by them circulated throughout the county, ...," page 32.

11. Like VENTURE, Albert Gronniosaw came from the interior of West Africa near Lake Chad and took a similar route to the coast. He also sailed from the Gold Coast to Barbados, and then to New York. *A Narrative Of The Most Remarkable Particulars In The Life Of James Albert Ukawsaw Gronniosaw, An African Prince As Related by Himself*, (Bath, 1772).

12. People often order their tombstone years in advance, allowing them to work with the stone carver on its design. Then the "finished" stone only needed the age or date of death. Sometimes this led to the spacing of the date not fitting properly.

13. There are eight pages to each double sided printed sheet. VENTURE's

Narrative is made up of four printed sheets. Anything more than 32 pages required another sheet – 8 pages – and would have increased the cost to print by some 30 percent. So the booklet is either 24, 32, 40, etc. .

14. Likely Solomon saw it as both a possible money maker, but most importantly, a way of immortalizing his father's and preserving his legacy. Seeing his father's achievements in life similar to Benjamin Franklins to whom he compares his father preserving in the *Prologue*. In the end, this is an authentic African American literary work, which existed for years as a traditional oral story told by the principal and then turned into a printed autobiography. Commissioned, edited, and introduced by African Americans.

15. See endnote 6 above.

16. Susan Imbarrato, *A Brief List of Seventeen-and Eighteenth-century Early American Autobiographical Writings*, (email 17.08.17). Lists 16 autobiographical works besides VENTURE's.

17. Robert P. Forbes and Chandler B. Saint, *Venture's Narrative – the Making of the earliest know Entirely African American Literary Work*, paper presented at University of Cape Coast Symposium "Venture Smith Day in Africa", 19 September 2014, Cape Coast, Ghana.

The Early Years (pp. 13–48)

1. Guillaume Delisle Map of West Africa, issued by Phillippe Bauche, (Paris, 1742).

2. (see Endnotes *Final Years* #25).

3. Drescher, Forbes, Richardson, and Saint, *From Enslavement to Freedom: The Significance of the Life of Venture Smith, Then and Now*, American Historical Association, (Boston 2011). There are only a few 18th century accounts of birth in Africa – capture – march to the coast – and Middle Passage to the Americas that scholars believe are accurate. Interestingly, there are two that are autobiographies and both are stories of princes who take a similar long 1000 mile march to the Gold Coast and leave on a ship that sails from there to Barbados in the West Indies, and then to New England. (Delisle's second map of Africa published in 1722; and the map of West Africa published by Philippe Bauche, his son-in-law in 1742, color plate A-viii, after page 48).

4. See 1754 runaway ad page 195 - ".. *mark'd in the face, or scar'd with a knife in his own country*."

5. *Voyage du Chevalier des Marchais en Guiné, isles voisines, et à la Cayenne* (Paris, 1730).

6. Paul E. Lovejoy, *The African Background of Venture Smith* (paper for Documenting Venture Smith conference, Storrs, 2007).

7. Annamaboe was on the Gold Coast of West Africa, in present-day Ghana, known for its role as an embarkation point for slaves being taken to the West Indies and New England. The area was dotted with colonial fortresses and castles that became holding areas for slaves. Because they were built by a variety of colonial powers – the Dutch, French, Danes, and English – there were many spellings of the name in VENTURE's time, including Annamaboe, -ou, -oo, or Anamaboe, -ou, -oo, and Anomabo, -oe, or -u. The authors use the contemporary local spelling – "Anomabo" for the town, and historic spelling – "Annamaboe" for the fort. *The Royal African: or, Memoirs of the Young Prince of Annamaboe*, W. Reeve, G. Woodfall, and J. Barnes, (London, 1750), page 17.

8. David Eltis and Paul Lachance *A Note on the Voyage of Venture Smith and the Historical Record of Transatlantic Slave Trading*, (unpublished paper for AHA meeting, Boston, 2011), page 4.

9. The Young Prince, writing after Broteer had passed through Annamaboe, states that part of the fort still exists in the late 1740s. *The Royal African: or, Memoirs of the Young Prince of Annamaboe*, W. Reeve, G. Woodfall, and J. Barnes, (London, 1750), page 16.

10. Chandler B. Saint, *Confronting Slavery - Venture Smith to the Present*, Interpretation, Preservation, and Memory, (Connecticut Department of Environmental Protection, Hartford CT 2016).

11. The "Floating Factory" ship Argyle, anchored off the Annamaboe coast in the 1730s, was mastered by Captain George Hamilton and owned by a London syndicate led by Henry Lascelles, whose family made its fortune in Barbados land and sugar, and in the American slave and provisioning trades. Timothy A. Rooks, *The Social and Political Contexts Which Led to the Building of Harwood House* (Grossbritannien-Zentrum, Berlin, 2005), page. 41; Conrad Gill, *Merchants and Mariners of the 18th Century* (London, 1961), pages 90–95.

12. Timothy Fitch letters to Captain Peter Ginn, 8 November 1760 and September 4, 1761. Medford Historical Society, Medford, Massachusetts.

13. Anomabo was first a trading center for provisions – food and water to feed the a slaves on the ocean crossing, and then the locals began trading in slaves. It was more significant in the slave trade than the well-known and larger castles at Cape Coast, Elmina, or Accra. Anomabo had better access to the interior for foodstuffs and then slaves. It is estimated nearly 450,000 Africans left through Anomabo to take the Middle Passage, making it the 6th largest embarkation port in Africa. Its most active period was the 3rd quarter of the 18th century; in 1774 documented records show that at least 140 Africans were sold every week into slavery for the Middle Passage (that is more than 20

every day or nearly one an hour).

14. Jay Coughtry, *The Notorious Triangle: Rhode Island and the African Slave Trade, 1700–1807* (Temple University Press, 1981); slave voyages database, http://slavevoyages.org/tast/database/search.faces?yearFrom=1514&yearTo= 1866&shipname=Charming+Susanna

15. There was another slave named "Venture" owned by a sea Captain in Philadelphia; see ad by Capt. Charles Walsh, for runaway on 21 October, 1742; in Pennsylvania Gazette 11 November 1742.

16. *A Narrative Of The Most Remarkable Particulars In The Life Of James Albert Ukawsaw Gronniosaw, An African Prince As Related by Himself,* (Bath, 1772), page 9.

17. Ira Berlin, *Many Thousands Gone – The First Two Centuries of Slavery in North America* (Harvard University Press, 1998), pages 93–95.

18. A ship's captain and officers were given a "privilege" by the owner: They were allowed to buy a specific slave on their own account, and that slave was then "transported for free." Cost was figured at 5 to 7 pounds per slave for the passage. Later, to ensure the best condition of the cargo the privilege was for one or two unnamed slaves – the officer got the average sale price for his privilege. Clearly, Robinson was being treated exceptionally – probably because he was related to one of the owners of the voyage. VENTURE may have been what they called a "super cargo".

19. http://slavevoyages.org/tast/database/search.faces?yearFrom=1514 &yearTo=1866&shipname=Charming+Susanna

20. There were two triangular trades; leaving England to West Africa for slaves, to West Indies to sell slaves and buy sugar, and back to England; leaving New England with rum to West Africa, to West Indies to sell slaves and buy sugar and molasses to take back to New England.

21. A single-masted sloop, with a fore-and-aft rig, was the workhorse of the American slave and whaling trades. The ships, averaging 35 to 60 tons unloaded, were retrofitted for whatever job was required. Oddly, very few paintings or drawings of 18th-century American sloops can be found in New England historical archives. William B. Weeden, *The Early African Slave-trade in New England,* American Antiquarian Society, (October 1887), page 115.

22. Inventory of goods consigned to Captain George D. Sweet aboard the Brig Othello, owned by Samuel and William Vernon of Newport, Rhode Island, departing Rhode Island to the Coast of Africa September 5, 1774; 16 hogsheads best Mountain Tobacco, 3 hogsheads N.E. Tobacco, 3 barrels of Sugar, 2 barrels of Coffee,2 barrels of Tarr, 2 barrels of Turpentine, 30 barrels of Flower, 20 kegs White bread, 100 Quasten Cach Powder, 2 hogsheads and 4 bags of Pease, 3

hogsheads & 6 Tierce of Bread, 2 1/2 Cord Wood, 300 & 1/2 of Hoops, 400 feet of boards, box of medicine, box of Candy, 3 1/2 Gal oil, 1 cask Vinegar, 2 Iron bound gang casks, 6 hogsheads for Water, 1 pr Steelyards, 1 bolt Tichingburgh. New-York Historical Society, nyhs_sc_b-02_f-09_012-002.

23. *History of New London County, Connecticut, With Biographical Sketches of Many of its Pioneers and Prominent Men,* (J. W. Lewis, philadelphia 1882).

24. New England rum was prized in Africa over West Indian rum, which was weaker. Off the West African coast New England ships could trade rum with English, Dutch, or French ships for fabrics, iron, and other goods they would use to trade for slaves.

25. Gary B. Nash, *Forging Freedom: The Formation of Philadelphia's Black Community 1720-1840* (Harvard University Press, 1988); and Jean R. Soderlund, *Black Importation and Migration to Southeastern Pennsylvania, 1681-1810.* Proceedings of the American Philosophical Society, vol. 138; No. 2, Symposium on the Demographic Society History of the Philadelphia Region, 1600-1860, (June 1989).

26. Barry Unsworth, *Sacred Hunger* (Doubleday, 1992).

27. William B . Weeden, *The Early African Slave-trade in New England,* American Antiquarian Society, (October 1887), page 115.

28. David Eltis and Paul Lachance A *Note on the Voyage of Venture Smith and the Historical Record of Transatlantic Slave Trading,* page 6.

29. Barbara A. Barnes, *Venture Smith's Family*, (unpublished paper for graduate degree Wesleyan University), (Middletown, March 1996).

30. Analysis by Seymour Drescher.

31. Olaudah Equiano, *The Interesting Narrative of the Life of Olaudah Equiano, or Gustavus Vassa, the African.*

32. http://slavevoyages.org/tast/assessment/estimates.faces?yearFrom=1501&yearTo=1866&disembarkation=302

33. http://slavevoyages.org/tast/assessment/estimates.faces?yearFrom=1501&yearTo=1866&disembarkation=302; Berlin, *Many Thousands Gone — The First Two Centuries of Slavery in North America*, pages 106-108.

34. Robinson died around 1741, and his cousin Thomas, who was first mate aboard the Charming Susanna on VENTURE's voyage, died about 1755, both at sea.

35. David Eltis and Paul Lachance A *Note on the Voyage of Venture Smith and the Historical Record of Transatlantic Slave Trading,* page 5.

36. http://slavevoyages.org/tast/database/search.faces?yearFrom=1514&yearTo=1866&crewdiedFrom=&crewdiedTo=

37. Co 28/25 in the National Archives, London, England.

38. Linda L. Sturtz, *Within Her Power: Propertied Women in Colonial Virginia* (New York, 2002), pages 160-162.

39. Discussion at the University of Cape Coast, Ghana, led by Dr. Kwadwo Opoku-Agyemang, 27 October 2013.

40. Co 28/25 in the National Archives, London, England.

41. Barbados was a crown jewel of the British empire in the 18th Century and a primary destination for African slaves for several reasons: First, it was the closest Caribbean island to Africa, so it was the first stop; secondly it was an ideal site for growing sugar – with its consistently hot climate with well-drained soil and plentiful rainfall – and slaves were the engines of that industry. It also was the most impregnable of the islands because of wind and tidal patterns, thwarting outside invasion. But because of the brutal conditions and oppression, it was also the scene of a major slave rebellion in 1816.

42. http://slavevoyages.org/tast/assessment/estimates.faces?yearFrom=1501&yearTo=1866&disembarkation=302; Gregory E. O'Malley, *Beyond The Middle Passage: Slave Migration from the Caribbean to North America, 1619–1807*, 3rd Series Vol LXVI, (Williamsburg, January 2009).

43. Berlin, *Many Thousands Gone – The First Two Centuries of Slavery in North America*; and Coughtry, *The Notorious Triangle: Rhode Island and the African Slave Trade*.

44. *Slavery in America* (Grolier Electronic Publishing, 1995).

45. Joshua Hempstead inventory from Winthrop lease to George Mumford dated January 8, 1741/42, and extended on April 29, 1746. Lease in the collection of The Henry L. Ferguson Museum, Fishers Island, New York.

46. Transcript of the Winthrop lease to George Mumford, The Henry L. Ferguson Museum, Fishers Island, New York, color plate C-vi & vii, after page 200.

Lease Transcription by Sarah Malinowski:

This Indenture of Lease made the Eighth Day of January one Thousand Seven Hundred and Forty one Two, and in the Fifteenth year of the Reign of our Sovereign Lord George the 2nd of Great Brittain Ye King – Between Madm Anne Winthrop of New London in the Colony of Connecticut in New England, as she is Agent or Attorney for her Husband John Winthrop Esqr of New London Afor Sd (now Resident In Great Brittain) on the one part: and George Mumford late of South Kingston in the County of Kings County now of Fishers Island in the Province of New York And Colony of Rhode Island Ye In New England,^ yeoman, on the other part: Wittnesseth that ye Said Anne Winthrop. As She is Attorney as afore Sd. for & under ye rents, Covenants, articles, Considerations, & Reservations In these presents Here after Mentioned

& Expressed, hath Demis'd granted, Lett & to farm Letten, & by these presents
Do demise, Lett & to farm Lett, unto the Said George Mumford his Executors
& Administrs: all that Island Commonly Called & known By ye Name of
fishers Island in ye province of New York in America, together with ye Little
Islands or Hamocks there to Belonging with all ye Houses, Buildings, Edifices,
Barns, Stables, workhouses, fences of wood or Stone, & all Meadow Land
fresh or Salt, with ye Coaves, Creeks, & ponds, & all privilidges & appurtinances
to them Belonging or any wise Appertaining, & also such Stock of Neat
Cattle, Sheep, Swine, & Horsekind & According to a Schedule there of Here
to Annexed; Reserveing, & Excepting out of the above Demis'd & Granted
premisses unto ye Sd John Winthrop His Heirs or Assigns Dureing the Term
of this present Lease, the Run, pastureing or Keeping of Three Horse Kind or
any part of them, or Neat Cattle in the room or Stead of any of them, if ye
Leasor See not Cause to put on & Keep There so many horse Kind; also
Reserveing to the Lessor all Wrecks of the Sea & Great fish whales or others
which May at any time Come on Shore on any part of the Said land Demis'd as
afore Sd, as also Liberty to Set up any Mills Dam's or waterworks, & Digg any
Earth Clay or Stone & Cutt wood or Timber on Any part of Said Land, also
the Privilidges, profits, rights, Comodities whatsoever of Hunting, fishing &
fowling &c, with free Egress & Regress to what is Reserved & Excepted, To
Have & to Hold the above Demised premisses with all the appurtenances
(Reserveing and Excepting as is here in Reserved & Excepted) unto the Said
George Mumford his executors and Administrators from the 25th day of
March, One Thousand Seven Hundred & forty two, Dureing the Term of
Four Years Fully to be completed and Ended, In Consideration where of the
Said George Mumford doth oblige himself his Heirs &c by these presents to
pay or cause to be paid unto the said John Winthrop his certain attorney Heirs
Executrs & Administrs: Nine Hundred and Fifty Pounds, [Per] annum in
Currant Money, or true Bills of Creditt of ye Colony of Connecticut, or of any
of ye Neighbouring Governments that are Currant & passable At ye Mansion
house of the Said John Winthrop in New London or to his or their order
Elsewhere, ye afore Sd Rents in Currant Money to be paid: in the Mannor
following Viz [] Nine Hundred & Fifty Pounds, to be paid the twenty fifth day
of March one thousand seven hundred & forty three and Nine Hundred &
Fifty Pounds on the twenty fifth day of March then nest ensuing, and the same
Sum from Year to Year in the foregoing manner, until this lease be fully compleat
& ended, or if the Lessor shall have occasion, the one half of each of the
abovemention'd Sums, of Nine Hundred & Fifty Pounds to be paid Six Months
att least, before they are become due in the manner aforesaid; Also four Good

fatt Lambs to be Delivered at the house afore Sd, as the Lessor may have occation Annually, & the Said George Mumford for himself his heirs, Executors & Administrs Doth Covenant, & Promise to & with the Said Anne Winthrop as She is attorney as afore Sd that he will not Cutt or Suffer to be Cutt. Strip peal or destroy, any Vines, pines, Spruce, Cedar, Walnut, Chestnutt, Burch, Beach, Maple, Sassafrass, Ash, Elm, or any Cherry trees Tame or wild, and also preserve all ye fruit trees that now are or Shall be growing upon the premises, or any part there of, and that he will Not Suffer to be Cutt down or Lop't any Trees for firewood or any other Use excepting for ye Use of the Island, that is to Say for firewood & Such Nessessary Buildings, fences, & Utensils of ye Husbandry as shall be absolutely Necessary, and Not to Cutt any trees for fire wood or any other Use in the North Hill Pature Except Decay'd trees, and ye Sd George Mumford for himself his heirs Executrs & Administrs Doth Covenant & promise that the principal Stock at no time be putt or Sold off, or Embezell'd Contrary to ye true Intent & meaning of this Lease, but that there Shall be Kept near ye Same Stock on Said Land Demised both for number & value, and the Said George Mumford for himself his heirs Executors & Administrs doth further Covenant & promise to & with the Said Lessor his heirs Executors Administrs & assigns that at the expiration of this Lease as here in Mentioned, or other Determination here of to Surrender & Deliver up peaceably & Quietly to the Said John Winthrop his heirs Executors Administ— or Assigns all the Above Granted Lands Stock and premises, with all the Houses Edifices, buldings, and fences there on, In as good and Tenantable Repair as they now are or Shall hereafter be made, together with ye Like Stock of Neat Cattle, Sheep, Swine, Horses etc: Murrain, fire, & National Enemies Excepted   Provided also that if it should so Happen that ye yearly rent in Manner as afore Sd be behind & unpaid in ye whole or in part By the Space of twenty days Next after ye Same ought to be paid, that then and from thence-forth it Shall and may be Lawfull for the Said John Winthrop his heirs Executrs Administrs or assigns into ye Said Demised premises wholly to reEnter & the Said George Mumford his heirs Executors & Administrs to Expell Expell amove & Cast out and the Same to haave again Retain & Repossess as in their first & former Estate, this Indenture or anything herein Contained to the Contrary there of in any wise notwithstanding, & further the Lessor doth reserve the Liberty of one Chamber in the Best house for his own Use only, also ten Acres of Land on the North hill with Liberty of Setting up Fences warehouses Stables & out houses with free Egress & Regress to & from ye premises or any part thereof & the Said John Winthrop his heirs Executor Administrs or assigns Shall have Liberty to Come upon the demis'd Lands &

premises to Live there and to make Preparation for Improvement against another year two months before the Expiration of this Lease, and it is further agreed that no Swine is to run at Large on ye said premises, but are to be Kept in suitable Pastures or Inclosures where they may do the Least Dammage and are all to be Ring'd, to prevent their rooting & Spoinling the ground, and that the Said George Mumford Shall at no time break up Any of the Meadow or Mowing Land but what hath been Usual & Accostomary or Such an Equivolent And to lay down what is now or Shall be hereafter broken up, in good order and not to Leave the Same in Indian Hills and ye Said George Mumford his Executrs or Administratrs Shall at no time make over this Lease or any part thereof to any person or persons, without the approbation & free Consent of the Lessor and also all ye Deer, Patridges, peacocks, Quails, rabbits or any other Sort of wild Creatures, with Their Increase are to run at Liberty; & Remain there for the Use of the Lessor, & that the Lessee Shall Have Liberty to Continue on ye premises to Fodder and Look after the Creatures until the first day of May next after the Expiration of this Lease; in Wittness where of the parties to these presents above Written have Interchangeablely Set to their hands and Seals the Day & year first above Written

NB Interlin'd in the first side between 4th & 5th line this word /late/ between 5th & 6th line the first side these words /now of Fishers Island in the Province of New York/ above first line on this side these words ?first &? All were wrote before Signing & Sealing
George Mumford Signed,
Sealed, Delivered In Presence of J: Hempsted G: Saltonstall

April the 29th 1746 It is Covenanted and agreed by the Lessor & Lessee that this Lease Shall be & it hereby is Lengthned out one year after the Expiration of the Same & to Stand in full force in Every part thereof Excepting in the Sum pay= =able for the Rent. & the Sum to be paid for Rent this Current year in the Same Mannor as Expresed in the Lease is Two Hundred & Seventy five Pounds in Currant money of New York or Bills of Credit on this Colony or any of the Neighboring Gover =ments that are good & passable Equivolent to the aforsd N.York Currancy. as witness our hands the Day abovesd.
Wittness. George Mumford
Basill Winthrop
Margarette Miller

Schedule of Stock on Fishers Island
Refer'd to in this Lease
.4. four well Grown oxen one pair Eight year old ye other Seven

.42. fourty two Cows
.2. Two five year old Stears
.4. four four Ditto
.1. one Three 3yr old Stear
.1. one Three year old Bull
.1. one Three year old Heifer
.7. Seven two year old Stears
.7. Seven two year old Heifers
.12. Twelve yearlings
.81. These all Neat cattle
8 Breeding Mares
20 Swine one year old
1350 Thirteen Hundred & fifty Sheep with their fleaces and their Lambs

47. Mary E. Perkins, *Chronicles of a Connecticut Farm* (Norwich, 1900), page 74.

48. Ibid., page 72.

49. The merchants Thomas and David Mumford of Groton, Connecticut, consigned goods to Capt. Dudley Saltonstall, who shipped them on the sloop *Lyon* sailing from New London the week before 12 April 1771 to Guadeloupe, West Indies, and returned to New London in May. The list of goods shown on page 32 is Saltonstall's accounting for the Mumfords, showing what was sold, to whom and at what price. The currency is in old tenor pounds. Capt. Saltonstall charged the Mumfords a five percent commission for transporting and selling the cargo. This list shows the wide variety and quantity of goods carried on a small sloop to the Caribbean. List of goods (in the order presented): 21 horses, 100 barrels of flour, 49,413 shingles, 1 tierce bread, 12 barrels flour, 2 barrels flour, 2 barrels flour, 2 hogsheads fish, 14 bushels oats, 5 barrels flour, 2 barrels flour, 26 barrels flour, 14 bushels oats & a new hogshead, 1 tierce bread, 2,000 white oak staves, 2 empty hogsheads-left last voyage, 6631 shingles, 4 empty hogsheads, 1 empty hogshead; for transporting and selling the goods, Capt. Saltonstall received a commission of 1,469 pounds (illustration on page 42).

50. George Mumford's probate will lists 14 slaves, besides Venture's family.

51. Berlin, *Many Thousands Gone – The First Two Centuries of Slavery in North America*, page 8.

52. Winthrop Saltonstall, Quick Claim title, 15 July 1772, New London, Connecticut. Sale of property to Dudley Saltonstall, which includes three slaves - Will, Flora, and Neptune. Illustration on page 204.

53. Robert P. Forbes, Naushon reference.

54. Lerone Bennett Jr., *Before the Mayflower: A History of Black America* (Johnson, 1969).

The Crucible Years (pp. 49–72)

1. The Virginia 1723 slave law: "No negro, mulatto, or Indian slaves, shall be set free, upon any pretense whatsoever, except for some meritorious services, to be adjudged and allowed by the governor and council, for the time being." Also the Smithtown, Long Island selectmens' act.

2. http://www.history.org/Foundation/journal/Winter05-06/slavery.cfm.

3. Here is a likely case of the scribe getting a word wrong. VENTURE says Massepe River (or another spelling of the river, place Matsepe, or the people Massapeag – Masepeage, Massapequa, Masey, or other variations). They could not check it since it appears on no maps. Whatever was said, the type setter, corrected to the name he knew – The *"Mississippi River"*, a name most people cannot spell, and we end up with a story that makes no sense. The Massepe River ended in what is today Massapequa, 85 miles west of Montauk point on the south shore of long Island. Emails from John Strong and Carl Masthay 2 September 2014.

4. or *The New-York weekly post-boy* (paper was read in New Jersey,) Mumford believed Heddy was headed home to Newark. See illustration page 195.

5. The boat – probably a schooner with a canoe – was the most valuable item for Mumford.

6. The Stanton farms were on Stonington-point, not to be confused with Stonington Long Point where the main village is located today. Long Point was developed in the late 1750s.

7. *The Joshua Hempstead Diary, 1711–1758* (1901 edition, The New London County Historical Society), page 687.

8. On the *Narrative* Certificate, page 32, James Mumford is listed as the former owner, some time before December 1754, George had transferred ownership of VENTURE and Meg.

9. In 1668 at Winthrop's request, Governor Nichols of New York made Fishers Island a "Manor" and an entailed property, and the head of the Winthrop family was recognized as "Lord of the Manor" by the Crown. The Winthrops owned it for seven generations until 1863.

10. Leslie V. Brock Center for the Study of Colonial Currency, University of Virginia.

11. At this point Meg was probably pregnant with Solomon I, and James Mumford may be selling to eliminate the risk of death in child birth.

12. Robert P. Forbes with credit to William Freehling: "In West Africa, the Fante and Akan peoples give their children a common name that is the day of the week on which they were born. Kofi (Cuff, Cuffee) means Friday. Kwame is Saturday, etc.," conversations in 2007.

13. Mark A. Yanochik, Bradley T. Ewing, and Mark Thornton, *A New Perspective on Antebellum Slavery: Public Policy and Slave Prices* (Spring, Netherlands, 2001).

14. Alice Hanson Jones, *Wealth of a Nation to Be: The American Colonies on the Eve of the Revolution* (Columbia University Press, 1980).

15. Robet B. Forbes' email. Barbara J. Beeching, *African Americans and Native Americans in Hartford 1636-1800*: Antecedents of Hartford's Nineteenth Century Black Community, Trinity College, (Hartford, 11-29-1993), pages 26, 31, 34 and 49.

16. Ibid.. "Edwards, Daniel, Esq., owner of Dick, Jethro, and Mima, Negro children who were baptized 12 Oct. 1760, and who Edwards publicly engaged to bring up in the knowledge of the Christian religion" (First Church 222). Edwards was also owner of Betty who owned the covenant 26 Oct. 1760 and was baptized the same day (First Church 34, 223).

17. Daniel Edwards Probate Inventories, Hartford Probate District, 1776 No. 1816, Connecticut State Library, Hartford, pages 2-3.

18. http://www.history.org/Foundation/journal/Winter05-06/slavery.cfm; In New York with his size VENTURE would have stood out and likely been quickly captured.

19. Jill Lepore, *New York Burning, Liberty, Slavery, and Conspiracy in Eighteenth-Century Manhattan* (Random House, 2005).

20. Cameron B. Blevins, *Owned by Negro Venture: Real Estate Transactions in the Life of Venture Smith*, research for the Documenting VENTURE SMITH Project (Torrington, CT 2007).

21. Philip J. Schwartz, *Slave Laws in Virginia* (University of Georgia Press, 1996).

22. Jackson Turner Main, *Society and Economy in Colonial Connecticut* (Princeton University Press, 1983).

23. Farrow, Lang, and Frank, *Complicity*.

24. Mary's brother Edmond had died in 1758, he was in the process of developing Long Point and organizing a trading empire for the family. Thus, Oliver became the Denison Family point person in Stonington/West Indies.

25. Grace Denison Wheeler *Old Homes in Stonington*, (Salem, MA, 1903).

26. Richard Smith in a letter to South Kingston Monthly Meeting in 1757.

27. An unskilled laborer earned from 1.50 to 2.50 pounds per month. The

average 18th century person would have had to work full time for 3 to 5 years and save every penny (spending nothing on food or living) to amass what VENTURE (an extremely fast and productive worker) saved working part time in just five years. These numbers produce similar results for the four years VENTURE worked on Long Island, after he was free, and had amassed enough money to liberate his family.

The Transitional Years (pp. 73-93)

1. Sugar Act of 1764.

2. Berlin, Many *Thousands Gone – The First Two Centuries of Slavery in North America*, pages 190–192.

3. Richard Wheeler, *History of the First Congregational Church, Stonington, Connecticut, A-C,* (Norwich, 1875); Sikes baptism, "bapt. 19 May 1742 by Rev. Eellst."

4. Sikes and VENTURE appear to have had a business transaction involving land that VENTURE farmed on Stonington-point next to Thomas Stanton's farm; see *Andrew Stanton vs. Primas Sikes* case in the New London County, County Court, June 1767 term, file #536, Box 2, Folder 45, State Archives, Connecticut State Library.

5. Paul E. Lovejoy referring to *Slavery in the 19th Century Kano* (Department of History dissertation, unpublished, Ahmadu Bello University, 1975) referring to the Islamic Caliphate of Sokoto, in what is now northern Nigeria.

6. Douglas Harper, *Slavery in the North* (Lancaster, PA, 2003). www.slavenorth.com/connecticut.htm

7. *Making Freedom: The Life of Venture Smith – In His Own Voice*, panel #10. (Hartford, 2015)

8. Berlin, *Many Thousands Gone – The First Two Centuries of Slavery in North America*, page 239.

9. Patrica and Edward Shillingbury, *The Disposition of Slaves on the East End of Long Island From 1680 to 1796* (Shelter Island Historical Society, 2003).

10. Today the reservation is 800 acres, but the Shinnecocks have taken legal action to get back over 3,000 acres lost in a possibly fraudulent deed in 1859.

11. Richard Steckel, *The Global History of Health* (Ohio State University, 2004); and John Komlos and Francesco Cinnirella, *European Heights in the Early 18th Century* (University of Munich, 2005).

12. W. J. Rorabaugh, *The Alcoholic Republic: An American Tradition* (Oxford University Press, 1981).

13. Stonington Connecticut Land Records.

14. Brock Center, University of Virginia.

15. In 1765 Paul Revere sold a pair of silver shoe buckles for over 5 pounds. For Solomon, the buckles would represent more than three months' wages.

16. In 1812, when Solomon enlisted in the State Militia for the War of 1812, he gave his birth as 1777. It was actually in 1773. The one explanation is that he needed to be under 35 to enlist. He was in fact 39 at the time.

17. Charles J. Hoadly, *The Public Records of the Colony of Connecticut*, vol. 14, (Press of The Case, Lockwood & Brainard Company, Hartford, 1887). page 329.https://archive.org/stream/publicrecordsofco14conn#page/329/mode/1up

The Final Years (95–123)

1. *Narrative* pages 30-31. Perkins, *Chronicles of a Connecticut Farm*. (Norwich, 1900) p. 74. VENTURE seemed to be surrounded all his life by large men, like himself. The Mumfords for example, were so tall that others joked that six of them constituted "thirty-six feet of Mumfords."

2. VENTURE SMITH, *A Narrative of the Life and Adventures of Venture, a Native of Africa, But resident above Sixty years in the United States of America. Related by Himself*, Revised and Republished with Traditions by H. M. Selden (J. S. Stewart, Middletown, 1897), pages 32-36.

3. Arthur Zilversmit, *The First Emancipation: The Abolition of Slavery in the North* (University of Chicago Press, 1967), page 80.

4. Benjamin Quarles, *The Negro in the American Revolution* (Chapel Hill Books, 1961).

5. *The American Revolution*, Microsoft Encarta 98 Encyclopedia (Microsoft Corporation).

6. Pierce Rafferty, Director, Henry L. Ferguson Museum, Fishers Island New York, e-mails.

7. Perkins, *Chronicles of a Connecticut Farm*. (Norwich, 1900).

8. John C. Fitzpatrick, ed., *The Writings of George Washington from the Original Manuscript Sources 1745-1799* (Government Printing Office 1931–1944); reprint, (Greenwood Press, 1970).

9. Around one third of the residents of Southold, originally a part of Connecticut in the 17th century, were actually Connecticut families who returned to their relatives in Connecticut.

10. Six whale boats and sloop-of-war *Samson, History of Middlesex County, Connecticut*, (J. B. Beers & Co, New York 1884), pages 401-404

11. William L. Warren, "Prefabrication in Colonial Connecticut," *Connecticut Historical Society Bulletin 25, no. 2* (April 1960), pages 36-48.

12. Robert P. Forbes, David Richardson and Chandler B. Saint, text from Panel #10, in the exhibit *Making Freedom: The Life of Venture Smith – In his own Voice*, Marcus Garvey Library, London, UK, 2012.

13. George Brainerd(1845-1887) was a civil engineer in Brooklyn, NY; an amateur photographer and amateur natural historian. Brainerd was born on Haddam Neck, Connecticut, but moved to Brooklyn as a young child. He produced a total of 2,500 photographs before his early death at age 42 in 1887. The majority of these were images of Brooklyn, a vast documentation of the urban landscape. See: Wikipedia andhttp://www.brooklynmuseum.org/opencolletion/artists/7849/George_Bradford_Brainerd – *Down the Cove from Above, Salmon River, Connecticut*; collodion silver glass wet plate negative, Brooklyn Museum/Brooklyn Public Library, Brooklyn Collection, 1996.164.2-680. *Point of Meadow, East Haddam, Connecticut*, 1996.164.2-412

14. Roger Davis and Wanda Neal-Davis, *Chronology: A Historical Review, Major Events in Black History: 1492 through 1953*.

15. John Hope Franklin, *From Slavery to Freedom: A History of Negro Americans* (Knopf, 1947).

16. *Gale Encyclopedia of US History*: Rhode Island – "On 29 August 1778, the Continental Army and its new allies, the French, fought the British army in the Battle of Rhode Island. The battle was inconclusive, although the Black Regiment inflicted heavy casualties on the enemy's Hessians. On 25 October 1779, the British left Newport and moved to the southern colonies where the British army was suffering almost unendurable casualties in battles with the Army of the South, led by General Nathanael Greene, a Rhode Islander who had run an iron foundry in Warwick. Meanwhile, in 1778, Rhode Island ratified the Articles of Confederation."

17, White, David O., *Connecticut's Black Soldiers 1775-1783* (Pequot Press, 1973), page 35.

18. Abigail Adams to John Adams, September 22, 1774, from *Adams Family Papers* (Massachusetts Historical Society).

19. Brister Baker discharge certificate, Yale Sterling Library

20. Jushua Austin, petition to the State Legislature

21. Post war economic crisis - http://www.ushistory.org/us/14d.asp

22. Brainerd, Ezra, *1783 ledger*, page 17, Court ruling 9 January 1795, collection of Haddam Neck Congregational Church, archived at the Haddam Historical Society.

23. Forbes, *Biblical References in the Narrative of Venture Smith* (2007), presented at the *Documenting Venture Smith Conference*, October, 2007, Haddam CT.

24. Brainerd, Ezra, *1783 ledger*, page 10, Court ruling 14 March 1785.

25. For his first 60 years, VENTURE had not needed to know exactly when he was born, but to be buried as a Connecticut gentleman, his tombstone would require either his date of birth or his age at death. After careful calululations, VENTURE decided on January 1, 1729 for his birth date.

26. Selden, *A Narrative of The Life and Adventures of Venture a Native of Africa, But Resident Above Sixty Years in the United States of America. Related By Himself,* 3rd edition, page 36.

27. James A. Slater, *The Colonial Burying Grounds of Eastern Connecticut and the Men who Made Them,* (Archon Books, 1987), pages 69-70.

28. Page 122, tombstone of Domine Dyre 1740, and tombstone carved by John Stevens Jr., for Violet Hammond, wife of Cape Coast James, died 1772. Page 123, tomstone of Susaannah Scott, 1779.

Dinah 1762   Phyllis Banister 1773

29. Newport Cemetery African American tombstones surviving today, earliest is 1728 and there are well over 100 that the face is visible on.

30. Tombstone for Pompey Lynden, 1765 carved by Zingo aka Pompe Stevens, signed P. S., earliest know African American stone carver.

Conclusion (pp. 125-136)

1. *"Resident"* - VENTURE is stating his Americanism by using this term, often found in Deeds and Contracts – the language of business. This is how he is identified in his first property deed on Haddam Neck.

2. The appellation 'Citizen' became popular among American supporters of the French Revolution in the late 1790s, but it had little currency in Federalist rural Connecticut.

3. Archbishop Desmond Tutu. *Unfinished Business* Conference, WISE, University of Hull, 2007.

4. Ezra Brainerd, *Account Book 1786-1805*, index and pages 26-97, CHS.

Epilogue (pp. 137–148)

1. State of Connecticut, Department of Energy & Environmental Protection, Barn Island Wildlife Management Area.

2. Tatiano Kotlyarenko, *Trafficking in Human Beings and Terrorism: What are the Links?*, and Superintendent Ken Pennington, *Slavery, Radicalisation, Terrorism*; The Wilberforce World Freedom Summit, *Eradicating Contemporary Slavery*, Hull, UK, 29 September 2017.

3. https://www.c-span.org/video/?329487-1/venture-smith

4. State of Connecticut, Department of Energy & Environmental Protection, Barn Island Wildlife Management Area.

5. David Eltis and Paul Lachance *A Note on the Voyage of Venture Smith and the Historical Record of Transatlantic Slave Trading*, page 1.

Appendix (pp. 149–213)

1. Awnsham and Churchill, *A collection of voyages and travels, some now first printed from original manuscripts, others now first published in English ... vol. 5*, published by J. Walthoe, London, 1732: a. Early 18th-century map of the Gold Coast of Guinea, where VENTURE was held and sold as a slave to an American ship's officer; b. European owned castles and forts on Guinea's Gold Coast (region that is now Ghana) where African captives were held and sold to foreign slave ship captains for the triangular trade. These drawings, along with *Negro's Cannoes, carrying Slaves, on Board of Ships* (page 27) were done during VENTURE's time in West Africa by artists who actually visited the area.

2. The ad ran in *The New-York gazette, or, The New-York weekly post-boy* on April 1, 1754 and on April 8, 1754. Runaway ads were common in this paper. Two appeared on April 1 and three on April 8 for runaways either from New Jersey or headed there. Clearly, George Mumford considered Heday to be the ringleader and assumed he was trying to go home to New Jersey.

SUBSCRIBERS

✦ ✦ ✦ ◈ ✦ ◈ ✦ ✦ ✦

In the 18th century, books were sold by subscription with the patrons' and subscribers' names listed in the book. The following is the subscription list for the cloth-bound library edition.

A

Monica Adorno: Connecticut
Ruth & Alphonse Avitabile: Bethlehem, Connecticut
Joan & Stephen Altschuler: Torrington, Connecticut
Chief Amonu XI: Anomabo, Ghana
And Albert Foundation: Woodmansey, United Kingdom

ANONYMOUS

Seville, Spain
Mystic, Connecticut
Woodbury, Connecticut

B

Nana Baffoe IV: Accra, Ghana
Jean & William Barber: Torrington, Connecticut
E.B. Bartels: Fishers Island, New York
James G. Basker: New York, New York
Nana Okodom Bassaw VI: Cape Coast, Ghana
Kevin Belmonte: York, Maine
Ira Berlin: Washington, DC
Clifton D. Berry: St. Louis, Missouri
Andrew Bird: Shaftesbury, United Kingdom
Jody Blankenship: Hartford, Connecticut
Bobbie & Jeff Borne: Wallingford, Connecticut
Corinne Henry Brady: Cranston, Rhode Island
Silas Bronson Library, Friends of the Library: Waterbury, Connecticut
Marana L. Brooks: Litchfield, Connecticut
Lonnie Bunch: Washington, DC
Marguerite Burke: St. Thomas, US Virgin Islands
Nancy Byrne: Chester, Connecticut

C

Wendy Taylor & David Callegari: Torrington, Connecticut

Patricia & Vincent Carretta: Springfield, Virginia
Joanne Chapin: New York, New York
Anthony M. Cohen: Brookeville, Maryland
Cheryl Christensen: Canterbury, Connecticut
Connecticut State Library: Hartford, Connecticut
Joseph D. Courtney: Lebanon, Connecticut

D

Beatrice P. Dahlen: Portland, Maine
Otto L. Dahlen: Portland, Maine
Liesselotte E. Dahlen: Portland, Maine
Davenport-Dunbar Residence Library: Hamden, Connecticut
Audrey Davis: Alexandria, Virginia
Rosa L. DeLauro: New Haven, Connecticut
Dòwòti Désir: Fishkill, New York
Kathleen Devaney: Simsbury, Connecticut
Adriana DiCecco: Boxford, Massachusetts
Dorothea & Mario DiCecco: Litchfield, Connecticut
Mary & Bruno DiCecco: Westerly, Rhode Island
Katherine Dimanescu: Concord, Massachusett
Heather Dorosh: Litchfield, Connecticut

E

Elizabeth H. Esty: Cheshire, Connecticut
Nicholas J. Evans: Hull, United Kingdom
Tamara Enhuber: Saarbrücken, Germany

F

Russell & Christa Farnen: Jupiter, Florida
Alissa & Jon Fasman: Singapore, Indonesia
Henry L. Ferguson Museum: Fishers Island, New York
Patti Flynn-Harris: Chesire, Connecticut
Robert P. Forbes: New Haven, Connecticut
Mathew Foggy, Jr.: St. Louis, Missouri
Forman School: Litchfield, Connecticut
Naja Furrer: Zurich, Switzerland

G

Mary Glew: Kingston upon Hull, United Kingdom
Roger Gonzales: Warren, Connecticut
Marshall Goodman: Midlothian, Virginia
Karen Loiselle Goodwin: Fishers Island, New York
Steven Gray: Accra, Ghana

H

Haddam Historical society: Haddam, Connecticut
Hartford History Center, Hartford Public Library: Hartford,
  Connecticut
Amber Henry: East Falmouth, Massachusetts
Floyd Henry: Oak Bluffs, Massachusetts
Jazz Henry: East Falmouth, Massachusetts
Liesselotte W. Henry: Worcester, Massachusetts
Mandred Henry: East Falmouth, Massachusetts
Laura A. Holmes: Miami Beach, Florida
Joan L. Hunt: Wethersfield, Connecticut

J
R. L. Jackson: Roxbury Crossing, Massachusetts
David Johnson: Winsted, Connecticut
Doris Johnson: Windsor, Connecticut

K
Rosalie M. Karefa-Smart: Bethlehem, Connecticut
Elbrun & Peter Kimmelman: New York, New York
Margaret & Irwin Klein: Litchfield, Connecticut
Kazimiera Kozlowski: Lebanon, Connecticut
Stefanie & Michael Krimsky: Cheverly, Maryland
Sue Ann Krimsky: Southbury, Connecticut

L
Jennifer C. Lamb: Hamden, Connecticut
Marta Languell: Torrington, Connecticut
Brigitta Laube: Mesikon, Switzerland
Thorpe Leeson: Newport, Rhode Island
Philip & Christine Lodewick: Ridgefield, Connecticut

M
Nana Mbroba-Dabo I: Anomabo, Ghana
Lisa McCormick: South Glastonbury, Connecticut
Loretta McCray: St. Thomas, US Virgin Islands
Frank McKay: Accra, Ghana
Lisa Mensah: Chevy Chase, Maryland
Edmond Moukala: Paris, France
John Motley: Hartford, Connecticut
Edward Murphy: Litchfield, Connecticut
Anganzo Mwando: Torrington, Connecticut

N
Marilyn Nelson: East Haddam, Connecticut

Frank L. McGuire Library of the New London Maritime
    Society: New London, Connecticut
Gail Nordmoe: Groton, Connecticut

O

Karen Okra: Hull, United Kingdom
William O'Malley: Norwood, New Jersey
Amii Omara-Otunnu: Storrs, Connecticut
Kwadwo Opoku-Agyemang: Cape Coast, Ghana
M. R. Ostlund: Stonington, Connecticut

P

Edith Pestana: Hartford, Connecticut
Angelina H. Perron: Milford, New Hampshire
Christian L. Perron: Merrimack, New Hampshire
Evan W. Perron: Milford, New Hampshire
Hanna F. Perron: Milford, New Hampshire
Sarah Hale Porter: Fishers Island, New York

Q

Hugh Quarshie: London, United Kingdom

R

Pierce Rafferty: Fishers Island, New York
Susan W. Read: Litchfield, Connecticut
David Richardson: Beverley, United Kingdom
Laurie and John Richardson: Reading, Connecticut
Jennifer Rycenga: Berkeley, California
Peter Rudolph: Haverford, Pennsylvania

S

Carla Orleans-Saint: Seville, Spain
Timothy Saint: New York, New York
Gina Sartirana: Colebrook, Connecticut
Cheryl A. Savo: Hamden, Connecticut
Michael Schaffer: New Haven, Connecticut
Susan P. Schoelwer: Washington, DC
Liz Sevcenko: New York, New York
Robert Shenk: Mt Vernon, Virginia
Robert Silverthorne: Washington, DC
Irene Skolnick: New York, New York
George A. Sprecace: New London, Connecticut
Carey Sokolowski: Waterbury, Connecticut
Steve P Solley: Washington, Connecticut
Nancy A Somodevilla: Dallas, Texas

James Spady: Aliso Viejo, California
Nina M. Stein: Waterbury, Connecticut
Charles P. Stetson: New York, New York
James B. Stewart: St. Paul, Minnesota
Anne Stillman: Bridgewater, Connecticut
Keith & Theresa Stokes: Newport, Rhode Island
Gaynell Stone: Wading River, New York
Stonington Historical Society: Stonington, Connecticut
Southampton Historical Museums and Research Center:
    Southampton, New York
Johanna Odonkor Svanikier: Accra, Ghana

T

Suzanna Tamminen: Durham, Connecticut
The Gunnery School Library: Washington, Connecticut
Peter H. Tillou: Litchfield, Connecticut
Robert S. Tilton: Garden City, New York
Torrington Historical Society: Torrington, Connecticut
Torrington Library: Torrington, Connecticut
Thomas Turton: Stonington, Connecticut

W

David P. Warmsley: Rocky Hill, Connecticut
Florence P. Warmsley: Middletown, Connecticut
Fred W. Smith National Library for the Study of George Washington:
    Mt Vernon, Virginia
Vicki S. Welch: Ashford, Connecticut
Colonial Williamsburg Foundation, John D. Rockefeller, Jr.
    Library: Williamsburg, Virginia
Donald Williams: Brooklyn, Connecticut
Wisconsin Historical Society Library: Madison, Wisconsin
Wilberforce Institute for the study of Slavery and
    Emancipation, University of Hull: Kingston-upon-Hull,
    United Kingdom
Joanne and Cornell Wright: Stratford, Connecticut

Y

Donald Yacovone: Medford, Massachusetts

FURTHER READING

Books:

Bailyn, Bernard. *The Ideological Origins of the American Revolution*. Harvard University Press, 1967.

Ball, Edward. *Slaves in the Family*. Ballantine Books, 1998.

Bell, Herbert C. "The West India Trade before the American Revolution," *American Historical Review 22*, (January 1917): 272-87. Dinsmore Documentation, *Classics of American Colonial History*. www.dinsdoc.com/bell-1.htm

Berlin, Ira. *Many Thousands Gone – The First Two Centuries of Slavery in North America*. Harvard University Press, 1998.

Blumrosen, Alfred W. and Ruth G. Blumrosen. *Slave Nation: How Slavery United the Colonies and Sparked the American Revolution*. Sources Books, 2005.

Carretta, Vincent. *Equiano the African*. University of Georgia Press, 2005.

Carretta, Vincent. *Phillis Wheatly: Biography of a Genius in Bondage*. University of Georgia Press, 2011.

Coughtry, Jay. *Notorious Triangle, Rhode Island and the African Slave Trade, 1700-1807*. Temple University Press, 1981.

Davis, David Brion. *Inhuman Bondage: The Rise and Fall of Slavery in the New World*. Oxford University Press, 2006.

Eltis, David and Richardson, David. *Atlas of the Transatlantic Slave Trade*. Yale University Press, 2010.

Engerman, Stanley L. and Robert E. Gallman, eds. *The Cambridge Economic History of the United States*. Vol. 1, The Colonial Era. Cambridge University Press, 1996.

Fogel, Robert and Stanley Engerman. *Time on the Cross: The Economics of American Negro Slavery*. Reissue edition: W. W. Norton, 1995.

Frey, Sylvia R. *Water from the Rock: Black Resistance in the Revolutionary Age*. Princeton University Press, 1991.

Gates, Henry Louis Jr., *Finding Oprah's Roots: Finding Your Own*. Skyhorse Publishing, 2017.

Greven, Jr., Philip J. *Four Generations: Population, Land, and Family in Colonial Andover, Massachusetts*. Cornell University Press, 1970.

Harms, *The Diligent: A Voyage Through the Worlds of the Slave Trade*. Basic Books, 2001.

Hedges, James B. *The Browns of Providence Plantations: The Colonial Years* Brown University Press, 1968.

Horton, James Oliver and Lois E. Horton. *In Hope of Liberty*. Oxford University Press, 1997.

Horton, James Oliver and Lois E. Horton. *Slavery and the Making of America*.

Oxford University Press, 2004.

Main, Jackson Turner. *Society and Economy in Colonial Connecticut.* Princeton University Press, 1985.

McCusker, John J. and Russell R. Menard. *The Economy of British America, 1607–1789.* University of North Carolina Press, 1984.

Melish, Joanne Pope. *Disowning Slavery: Gradual Emancipation and "Race" in New England, 1780–1860.* Cornell University Press, 1998.

Nelson, Marilyn. *Freedom Business.* Front Street Books, 2008.

North, Douglas C. *Economic Growth of the United States, 1790 to 1860.* W. W. Norton Press, 1961.

Piersen, William D. *Black Yankees: The Development of an Afro-American Subculture in Eighteenth-Century New England.* University of Massachusetts Press, 1988.

Poulson, Barry W. *Economic History of the United States.* Macmillan, June 1981.

Sparks, Randy J. *Where the Negroes Are Masters.* Harvard University Press, 2014.

Steiner, Bernard C. *History of Slavery in Connecticut.* Johns Hopkins University Press, 1893. Dinsmore Documentation, *Classics of American Colonial History, Period I: 1636–1774.* www.dinsdoc.com/steiner-2-0a.htm

Stewart, James Brewer. *Holy Warriors: The Abolitionists and American Slavery.* Revised edition: Hill and Wang, 1996.

Stewart, James Brewer, Editor. *Venture Smith and the Business of Slavery and Freedom*, University of Massachusetts Press 2010.

Walton, Gary M. and James F. Shepherd. *The Economic Rise of Early America.* Cambridge University Press, 1979.

WEB SITES:

Africans in America (PBS). www.pbs.org/wgbh/aia/home.html

BBC: *Abolition.* www.bbc.co.uk/history/british/abolition/

Digital History: *Learn About Slavery.* www.digitalhistory.uh.edu/modules/slavery/index.cfm

Handler, Jerome S. and Michael L. Tuite Jr. *The Atlantic Slave Trade and Slave Life in the Americas: A Visual Record.* www.hitchcock.itc.virginia.edu/ Slavery/index.php

Schomburg Center for Research in Black Culture. www.schomburgcenter.org

Rhode Island's Slave History. *The Unrighteous Traffic.* www.projo.com/extra/2006/slavery

The Trans-Atlantic Slave Trade Database. www.slavevoyages.org

ACKNOWLEDGEMENTS

✢ ◄ ◄ ◄ ◉ ✢ ◉ ► ► ► ✢

This book would have simply and profoundly fallen short of its intentions had it not been for a collaboration of friends and associates, who have been as committed as I am to finding the truth. George was with me for most of this voyage and has my fondest thoughts.

Among these individuals, I want to single out Robert Pierce Forbes in particular, who has researched, written and lectured extensively on VENTURE SMITH. For years, he was the "voice in the wilderness," trying to get VENTURE SMITH's story told and his farms and home sites saved for posterity.

In keeping me on true course, I especially would like to thank David Richardson, the *Beecher House Center's* partner at faraway but always accessible *Wilberforce Institute for the study of Slavery and Emancipation* at the University of Hull in the UK; *Beecher House Center* chairman and slave scholar James B. Stewart, emeritus of Macalester College; Dr. Kwadwo Opoku-Agyemang our African partner at the University of Cape Coast, Ghana; Robert L. Hall, emeritus of Northeastern University for interpreting VENTURE; and Vincent Carretta, emeritus of the University of Maryland.

I am grateful to the following emeritus professors at the University of Connecticut, Robert Tilton and former Connecticut State archeologist Nicholas Bellantoni. I would also like to thank former poet laureate of Connecticut Marilyn Nelson for her inspiration throughout the *Documenting VENTURE SMITH Project*.

For taking the lead in bringing this story deeper into the public domain and being champions of equal rights, I thank Congresswoman Rosa L. DeLauro, Jennifer Lamb, Lonnie G. Bunch, and Henry Louis Gates Jr..

My gratitude also goes to Connecticut State Librarian Kendall Wiggin and his associate Jane Beaudoin who made possible the exhibition in 2011 and the program at the State Capital in Hartford in February 2013.

Special gratitude for their support and encouragement throughout this project is due to the descendants of VENTURE and Meg, notably, Florence P. Warmsley, Floyd, Corinne, Angi, and Susi Henry and the late Coralynne H. Jackson, her brother Mandred T. Henry, and Frank W. Warmsley, Sr., who were instrumental in launching the *Project*.

My deep thanks go to my wise (and very patient) editor at Wesleyan University Press, Suzanna Tamminen, who shares my vision and understood the importance of telling the story of VENTURE's struggle for freedom.

I reserve a special place for good friend Dorothea V. DiCecco who spent countless hours reviewing and proofreading the text, not to mention her constant and cheerful affirmation that this was a worthwhile project.

Along roads like this, there are always friends with a useful idea or suggestion, even if it's only one among dozens proffered. For those occasional but shining gems, would like to thank (the late) Mike Citron, Tom Crider, Kate Dimancescu, Kathleen Devaney, Seymour Drescher, David Eltis, Nadja Furrer, Alissa Fasman, Doris Johnson, Kazimiera Kozlowski, Michael Krimsky, Gail Kruppa, Brigitta Laube, Mieke Maas, Elizabeth Hart Malloy, Grace E. Malloy, Mark McEachern, David Murdan, Laurie and Ted Murphy, Kwadwo Opoku-Agyemang, Edith Pestana, Christine Pittsley, Laurie and John Richardson, Jorge Romero, Peter Stever Rudolph, Steve Solley, Theresa and Keith Stokes, Louisa Watrous, Vicki Welsh, and Julie Winkel.

Thanks go also, in spirit, to my late friend Pete Seeger for his lifelong support of this and other projects aimed at telling America's Freedom Story.

George, before his death had, fondly thanked his wife, Paula Gibson Krimsky, for her knowledge of history, her patience, and her good humor when all three were needed.

Finally, a very special thanks to my friend Peter Tillou, who never gave up championing our cause and whose generosity provided the lifeblood for this project.

CREDITS

✤·✦·✦·◈·❖·◈·✦·✦·✤

Alexandra Eames: A-vi-vii, 83; Beinecke Rare Book and Manuscript Library, Yale University: 8, 27, 45, B i,130, 150, 151, 152, C viii. 190-191, 192-193, 194; Beecher House Center: A ii, A vii, B iv, B vii, 81, 129; Cameron Blevins; 101, 103, 201; Chandler B. Saint 12, 14, 21, 22, 23, 24, A ii, A iii, A iv, A viii, 53, 56, 66, 69, 70, B ii, B v, B viii, 74, 104, 109, 113, 120, 121, 122, 135, 139, 212; Courtesy of the Brainerd Memorial Library:104; Courtesy of the Brooklyn Museum/ Brooklyn Public Library, Brooklyn Collection: 105, 116, 139; Courtesy of the www.colonialcemetery.com: 122, 123, 230; Courtesy of the Connecticut Historical Society, Harford, Connecticut: xvi, 3, 80 91, 101, 130, 139, 153-182; Courtesy of the Connecticut State Library: 196-199, 202, 203, C iii; Courtesy of the Haddam Neck Congregational Church: Ci, Civ, Cv; Courtesy of the Franklin Collection, Sterling Memorial Library Yale University: 88; Courtesy of the Haddam Historical Society: 94, 185; Courtesy of The Library Company of Philadelphia: 51, 195; Courtesy of the Massachusetts Historical Society: 112; Courtesy of Mystic Seaport, G. W. Blunt Library, Mystic, CT: 23; Courtesy of the New London County Historical Society, CT: iii, 3, 10, 42, 99; Courtesy of the Silas Bronson Library, Waterbury, CT: 57; Courtesy of the Sterling Memorial Library Yale University: C ii; Courtesy of the Yale Center for British Art: 30; Courtesy of the Yale University Art Gallery 120; Courtesy of the Yale University Libraries: 2, 21, 29, 46, 186; Dorothea V. DiCecco: 5, B ii, B iii, B vi; Emmanuel Saboro:B v, 145; George A. Krimsky: 115, C iii; H.A. Crosby Forbes: 33, 90; Haddam, Connecticut, Land Records: 106, 200; *The Hartford Courant*: 142; James Brewer Stewart Collection: 45, 204; Jennifer C. Lamb: A iv; Thorpe Leeson: 96, 187, 188, 189; Phillippe Semanaz: 14, A vi; John J. Spaulding: 140; Library of Congress: 25, 35, 51, 98, 100, 112; National Archives: 126; Nicholas Evans: 1B v; Paul Murphy, BBC Look North: 141; The Henry L. Ferguson Museum: C vi, C vii; The National Archives, London, UK: Ai; USGEO: 75, 84; U. S. national Library of Medicine: 11; Yale University Art Gallery 120.

Front Cover: Image of art work, *Diaspora Colors* by Chandler B. Saint
Inside covers: Front , *Americas* by J. B. Homann (Homann's Heirs), Nuremberg, 1746; rear *Documenting Venture Smith Project* map, *Venture Smith in America 1739-1805*, derived from Thomas Jefferys' *A Map of the Most Inhabited Part of New England*, 1755 edition; Library of Congress.

Photograph of Chandler B. Saint; by Dorothea V. DiCecco

DEDICATIONS

✦·◦·◦·◦⟨◎⟩◦⟨◎⟩◦·◦·◦·◦·✦

Peter Tillou

Peter Tillou is a truly remarkable man whose wisdom, encouragement and generosity make the publication of this book possible.

The world knows Peter as a cosmopolitan gentleman, a gifted practitioner of historical conservation, and as one of the world's preeminent collectors of rare antiquities.

The *Beecher House Center for the Study of Equal Rights* also knows him as a quietly fierce advocate of racial equality. For Peter, learning from the past is essential for the advancement of social justice – which explains his unstinting support for the *Documenting Venture Smith Project* and for the development of this book. For this, the *Project* expresses our deep gratitude and appreciation.

Chandler B. Saint

— admirers of Venture Smith
and fighters for freedom and equality

✢ ⊰ ⊰ ⊰ ◈ ⬥ ◈ ⊱ ⊱ ⊱ ✢

I dedicated this book to the three people who inspired, pushed, and taught me how to do it. Although they were not alive to help in the final writing, their guidance and ideas were constantly in my thoughts as I solved each problem.

Rachel Freeman Saint ~ 1906-2007

A founder of the *Beecher House Society*, her ninety-eighth year saw her editing scholarly writing on Venture Smith, managing the Society's annual dinner and conversing affably with Pete Seeger.

Peter Seeger ~ 1919-2014

The world celebrates Pete Seeger's musical genius and democratic vision, the same rich gifts he contributed as an ardent supporter and Patron of the *Beecher House Society* and the *Documenting* Venture Smith *Project.*

George A. Krimsky ~ 1942-2017

See pages vi and 255.

Chandler B. Saint

INDEX

✦•‹•‹‹◈✦◈›•›•✦

INDEX

INDEX

Chandler B. Saint

Is a historian and preservationist who has devoted his recent years to documenting the life and times of VENTURE SMITH and saving his farmstead. While a studio art major at Wesleyan University in the 1960s, he met Dr. Martin Luther King, Jr., Malcolm X, and James L. Farmer. He later served with Pete Seeger and others in the emerging New England side of the civil rights movement. Greatly influenced by these giants, civil and equal rights have been central to Saint's life. For the last 40 years he has worked at restoring and preserving Early American buildings and artifacts. He has also served as a consultant in art fraud and authenticity to the U.S. Justice Department and other law enforcement agencies in the United States and Europe.

With a Connecticut family legacy dating back more than 300 years, Saint has devoted his life to preserving sites which teach America's story. In 1997, he led the effort to save from the wrecking ball the birthplace of Harriet Beecher Stowe and her brother Henry Ward Beecher in Litchfield, Connecticut. As founder and president of the *Beecher House Center for the Study of Equal Rights*, he has initiated such projects as the reenactment of the historic Lane Debates of 1834 (the first major debates held on abolition), and the *Documenting VENTURE SMITH Project* (now in its 13th year), which has attracted international attention and cooperation from scholars in Britain, Canada, Africa, and the United States.

Robert Pierce Forbes

Is a historian of the early United States, specializing in the impact of slavery on the development of American institutions. He served as the founding associate director of the *Gilder Lehrman Center for the Study of Slavery, Resistance, and Abolition* at Yale, and is the author of *The Missouri Compromise and its Aftermath: Slavery and the Meaning of America*. He is currently completing an annotated edition of Thomas Jefferson's *Notes on the State of Virginia*, for which he has received fellowships from the National Endowment for the Humanities, the International Center for Jefferson Studies, and the John Carter Brown Library.

David Richardson

Is a Professor of Economic History at the University of Hull (UK) and founder and former Director (2004-2012) of the *Wilberforce Institute for the study of Slavery and Emancipation* (WISE) at the University of Hull. He has held visiting fellowships at the DuBois Institute (Harvard University) and the *Gilder Lehrman Center for the Study of Slavery, Resistance, and Abolition* at

Yale. He gave the annual David Brion Davis lectures at Yale in 2007. He is co-editor of the slave voyages database (Emory University) and has been advisor to the Slave Route project (UNESCO, Paris). His more than 100 publications include (with David Eltis (Emory) the multi-award winning *Atlas of the Transatlantic Slave Trade* (Yale University Press, 2010). He is currently co-editing volumes 2 and 4 of the Cambridge World History of Slavery and writing a book on the British slave trade and its abolition (Yale Univeristy Press).

George A. Krimsky

Was an author and journalist who spent much of his career abroad and had recently returned to community journalism in his home state of Connecticut. An unabashed believer in "the invincibility of ink on paper," he noted that the story of Venture Smith would never have come to light if a newspaper had not printed the former slave's narrative more than 200 years ago.

In a 16-year career with the Associated Press, Mr. Krimsky reported from Moscow before being expelled from the Soviet Union for his coverage of the dissident movement. Assigned to the Middle East, he was nominated for a Pulitzer Prize for reporting on the Lebanese civil war. He later served as World News Editor for the international news agency. In 1985, he cofounded a non-profit organization to train and assist journalists from developing nations. The International Center for Journalists in Washington, D.C., remains today the preeminent institution working with the worldwide news media.

He worked in more than 40 countries, including a two-year tour in Central Asia to help journalists who were raised under Communism develop an independent press system.

After returning to newspaper work in Connecticut, he was awarded in 2009 the Yankee Quill award for his contributions to New England journalism. He was also co-author (with John Maxwell Hamilton) of a 1995 book on the U.S. newspaper industry, entitled *Hold the Press*.

Authors

Book design and composition by Chandler B. Saint, using ITCFounder's Caslon Thirty type (designed by Justin Howes).
Cover design Peter Stever Rudolph and Chandler B. Saint
Printed in the United States of America by Thompson-Shore on 70# Huron Matte paper and 70# Huron Gloss paper.